WHOSE GOVERNMENT IS IT?

The renewal of state–citizen cooperation

Edited by Henry Tam

BRISTOL
UNIVERSITY
PRESS

First published in Great Britain in 2019 by

Bristol University Press
1-9 Old Park Hill
Bristol
BS2 8BB
UK
t: +44 (0)117 954 5940
www.bristoluniversitypress.co.uk

North America office:
c/o The University of Chicago Press
1427 East 60th Street
Chicago, IL 60637, USA
t: +1 773 702 7700
f: +1 773-702-9756
sales@press.uchicago.edu
www.press.uchicago.edu

© Bristol University Press 2019

British Library Cataloguing in Publication Data
A catalogue record for this book is available from the British Library

Library of Congress Cataloging-in-Publication Data
A catalog record for this book has been requested

ISBN 978-1-5292-0093-5 paperback
ISBN 978-1-5292-0098-0 hardcover
ISBN 978-1-5292-0095-9 ePub
ISBN 978-1-5292-0096-6 Mobi
ISBN 978-1-5292-0094-2 ePdf

The right of Henry Tam to be identified as editor of this work has been asserted by him in accordance with the Copyright, Designs and Patents Act 1988.

Cover design by blu inc, Bristol
Front cover image: iStock
Printed and bound in Great Britain by CMP, Poole
Bristol University Press uses environmentally responsible print partners

Contents

List of Figures and Tables

Figures

Tables

Notes on Contributors

Marian Barnes is Emeritus Professor of Social Policy at the University of Brighton.

Hazel Blears – the Right Honourable Hazel Blears – is a director of the Coop Group and formerly Secretary of State for the Department of Communities & Local Government.

David Blunkett – Lord Blunkett of Brightside and Hillsborough – is Professor of Politics in Practice at the University of Sheffield and formerly Home Secretary; Secretary of State for Education & Employment; and Secretary of State for Work & Pensions. He is a Fellow at the Academy of Social Sciences.

Simon Burall is the Programme Director of Sciencewise and Senior Associate at Involve.

Pat Conaty is a Fellow of the New Economics Foundation and a Research Associate of Cooperatives UK.

Anna Coote is Principal Fellow of the New Economics Foundation and formerly Head of Engaging Patients and the Public at the Healthcare Commission, and Head of Health Policy at the King's Fund.

Matt Flinders is Professor of Politics and Director of the Crick Centre for the Public Understanding of Politics at the University of Sheffield.

Marjorie Mayo is Emeritus Professor at Goldsmiths, University of London.

Zoraida Mendiwelso-Bendek is Senior Research Fellow in Citizenship at the University of Lincoln.

Carol Packham is the Former Director of the Community Audit and Evaluation Centre at Manchester Metropolitan University.

Nick Pearce is Professor of Public Policy and Director of the Institute for Policy Research, University of Bath. He was formerly Head of the No. 10 Policy Unit and Director of the IPPR think-tank.

Barry Quirk is the Chief Executive at the Royal Borough of Kensington & Chelsea. He was initially brought in by the Government and the Local Government Association following the Grenfell fire tragedy in June 2017. Before that he was Chief Executive at the London Borough of Lewisham for over 20 years. He chaired the landmark 'Quirk Review' of asset transfers to communities.

Jane Roberts – Dame Jane Roberts – is Research Fellow in Public Leadership at the Open University Business School and Chair of the New Local Government Network. She was formerly Leader of London Borough of Camden and Chair of the Councillors Commission set up by the Department of Communities and Local Government.

James Sloam is Reader in Politics and International Relations, Royal Holloway, University of London.

Graham Smith is Professor of Politics and Director of the Centre for the Study of Democracy at the University of Westminster and Chair of the Foundation for Democracy and Sustainable Development.

Henry Tam is Director of Question the Powerful and formerly Director of the Forum for Youth Participation and Democracy at the University of Cambridge and Head of Civil Renewal at the UK Home Office.

Marilyn Taylor is Visiting Professor at Birkbeck, University of London and Visiting Research Fellow at the Institute for Voluntary Action Research. She was formerly Emeritus Professor of Urban Governance and Regeneration at the University of the West of England.

James Weinberg is a Postdoctoral Researcher on the Q-Step program at the University of Sheffield and an Associate Fellow of the Sir Bernard Crick Centre. He is Lead Fellow for citizenship on the All-Party Parliamentary Group for Democratic Participation and currently a convenor of both the Political Psychology, and Young People & Politics specialist groups at the UK Political Studies Association.

Preface

When the UK Government launched the 'Together We Can' programme in 2003, it was the first programme of its kind to review findings on citizen empowerment initiatives from around the world, and systematically promote their application to policy and project development across the country. Being in charge of the programme enabled me to examine closely what worked well and what did not in improving collaboration between citizens and state bodies at the national and local levels. It also meant that I would come to know many of the foremost academics and policy makers in this vital field.

Alas, despite the programme's impact on increasing the use and benefits of diverse forms of democratic engagement, a change of government brought the programme to an end in 2010. Since then, while the lessons from 'Together We Can' and other empowerment research have largely gone unheeded, the gap between state and citizens has inexorably widened.

There is now a palpable sense that political alienation has hit crisis point. In the UK, the US, and many other democracies, the civic rift is undermining the rule of law, and ruthlessly exploited by extremist politicians. Instead of allowing this to continue, those of us with the relevant knowledge and experience must do our part to highlight what should be done to reconnect the public with public institutions.

Following an event I convened at the University of Cambridge on cooperative problem solving in the public realm, I was heartened by the interest and support expressed for developing an up-to-date guide to the challenges posed by democratic disengagement, and how they could be most effectively tackled. In putting together *Whose Government Is It? The renewal of state-citizen cooperation*, I have been able to call on leading experts and practitioners who have, between them, reviewed, scrutinised and experimented with just about every type of deliberative and participatory decision making.

You will see from the notes on our contributors their impressive credentials. I would like to take this opportunity to thank them, both for finding time to write their respective chapters, and for their longstanding commitment to exploring different approaches to getting governments and citizens to work together in defining and pursuing the public good. Because of them, we know far more about why and how governments should change the way they involve citizens as real partners in shaping public outcomes.

I would also like to thank the team at Bristol University Press – Alison Shaw, Stephen Wenham, Jamie Askew, Kathryn King, Laura Cope and Ruth Wallace – who as ever have been most supportive at every stage of the process in getting this book to you, the reader.

Most of all, I want to thank Celia for her steadfast encouragement whenever I ponder embarking on another book. Without it, I might be pondering still.

Introduction

Government With The People

Henry Tam

The civic ideal of self-governance proclaims that none but the citizens should rule over themselves. In theory, this sets the ultimate goal for democracy. In practice, it raises the perennial question of how much any government can realistically leave the people to decide for themselves.

It is simply not possible for governments with jurisdiction over millions of people to bring them together to discuss every issue that needs to be dealt with and reach an informed agreement about what is to be done. This could mean that an increasing number of decisions are made by just a few without much involvement of the vast majority of the people, who become ever more doubtful if their views count for anything at all. On the other hand, more decisions could be passed to the people at the risk of choices being made without due consideration of the facts or arguments, and public policies are left to shift as a result of whims, ignorance and manipulation.

One response to this conundrum is to reduce the scope of the state. If a government has fewer responsibilities, then it should be relatively easier for it to keep in touch with citizens about how it will exercise those responsibilities. Accordingly, to get to a more 'focused', 'streamlined' or 'minimalist' state, a wide range of public actions are to be abandoned, while any needs previously addressed by them will be left to the market or communities to deal with. Since the 1980s, in the UK, the US and many other countries, this became a favourite policy stance among those who want to shrink the state. Leaving aside the arguments about the impact of such changes (Drakeford, 2014; Hermann, 2015), unless citizens are involved in assessing and shaping the decisions over what options to adopt, such an approach would in itself constitute a large-scale exercise in removing citizens' control. Whatever the motives behind pushing ahead with it, it removes democratic accountability for all that is unilaterally taken out of the public domain without giving citizens any greater say over what remains (Tam, 2011; Maugham, 2015).

From the 1990s, what came to be known as New Public Management emerged as a model for developing a more responsive state (Ferlie et al, 1996; Lane, 2000). It applies private sector managerial practices to the development and delivery of public policies. It promotes the use of market research techniques to ascertain what people like and dislike; sets performance targets; incentivises managers and delivery agents to meet those targets; and allocates rewards and penalties on the basis of routine performance reviews. Unfortunately, this attempt to reorient public administration along the lines of private sector management is inherently flawed because it ignores the fact that the public realm by its very nature has to mediate between individual interests for the common good. Instead of asking individuals for their unreflected views, or setting targets based simply on aggregated preferences, the government should enable citizens to devise collective solutions to problems they cannot deal with on their own, and find optimal routes out of prisoners' dilemmas that would otherwise trap those only thinking about their own positions.

The inability of New Public Management approaches to provide a genuine bridge between state and citizens has been exposed by advocates of 'public service ethos' (Ranson and Stewart, 1994) and 'public value' (Moore, 2013; Bryson et al, 2015). These critics stress that the state exists to serve the public, and this can only happen if the priorities and activities of government institutions are guided by values that support the public good, not atomised private interests. The goals must accordingly be shaped by informed deliberations of the stakeholders and pursued in line with collectively defined procedures, so none is unfairly disadvantaged. Champions of 'public work' (Boyte, 2011) go even further and argue that citizens should develop their own activities to serve the public good beyond giving their views on what government institutions are up to.

In parallel with these critiques, there has been a growing interest in how state and citizens can be brought together to shape the public agenda. What should be taken on by the state, left to the market or communities, or done in collaboration; and what objectives should be set, how differences are to be reconciled, what should be consolidated or reformed – these all become questions that are to be answered through state-citizen cooperation. In the 1990s the National Commission on Civic Renewal was established in the US to study and publicise the value of active citizenship. In the 2000s, the UK Government took forward a civil renewal[1] programme under the name of 'Together We Can' to provide action learning support to activities at the local, regional and national level that helped citizens and state bodies work together in identifying and implementing solutions to public problems. An increasing number of academics began to track the development of new participatory practices (Fung, 2006; Smith, 2010), and the emergence of new collaborative movements (Sirianni and Friedland, 2001; White and Leighton, 2008).

Yet before there was sufficient momentum to secure any long-term commitment to the systematic strengthening of state-citizen cooperation, the banking crisis of 2008 led to a downturn that exacerbated the socioeconomic uncertainties facing the majority of people on both sides of the Atlantic. 'Conventional' government was no longer to be trusted, and the vacuum ended up being filled not by deliberative input from citizens, but by demagogues who are adept at attacking scapegoats – immigrants, refugees, benefit claimants, and any political groups or institutions that are supportive of them. 2016 was not only the year of 'post-truth', but also 'post-decency', with the sharp rise of hate crime following the Brexit vote and Trump's victory, and the disturbing mainstreaming of xenophobia.

With public services continuously reduced in the name of austerity, while facilitating tax cuts for the wealthiest, the sense of disempowerment inevitably spreads further. The hollow cry of 'take back control' reverberates as individuals struggle with stagnant wages, a broken social safety net, and their deteriorating quality of life. Against this background, it is tempting to accept that ideas about civic engagement and democratic participation will stay on the margins.

But it is precisely because the widening gulf between state and citizens has been such a boon to demagogic manipulation that it must be urgently bridged by effective forms of civic collaboration. State institutions, which exist to serve the public, are at risk of being usurped by a powerful few. It is vital for anyone who may influence the thinking of reform advocates and policy makers to have a clear grasp of why and how state-citizen cooperation should be radically renewed.

To this end, our book brings together theorists and practitioners who have been at the forefront of assessing and applying options for citizen empowerment and deliberative engagement. It has three main

---

[1] What is generally termed 'civic renewal' in the US and 'civil renewal' in the UK tends to refer to efforts or activities to promote citizens' interests, abilities and impact in relation to the shaping of public decisions and actions that affect them.

parts, covering, respectively, 'Why we need state-citizen cooperation'; 'What is required for effective engagement; and 'How to expand our civic capability'.

Why we need state–citizen cooperation

One of the biggest obstacles to the development of better state-citizen cooperation is undoubtedly the sceptical rejection of it as an ineffectual sideshow to how politics must in reality be conducted. From what has been termed a 'realist' perspective, some critics have argued that the very nature of government and human interactions would always render it highly unlikely for informed, rational deliberations to prevail in shaping public policies (Lee et al, 2015; Achen and Bartels, 2016). In his chapter on 'Realism and Democratic Renewal', Nick Pearce – one of the few politics professors who were also at one time Head of the Policy Unit at No 10 Downing Street – examines the extent to which attempts to secure more deliberative participation in politics may be hampered by the limited scope for rational discourse, especially when the public domain can so easily be saturated with claims that play on people's emotions, while facts get swept aside by false or misleading assertions.

But is the 'realist' rejection of state-citizen cooperation as overly idealistic itself based on an abstract conception of such cooperation that fails to pay enough attention to what really happens in actual engagement between government institutions and citizens? Academics who emphasise passions, conflicts, contesting mind-sets as barriers to rational consensus building may have overlooked how these factors can in practice be taken into account as integral elements of processes for reconciling contrasting views and exploring common objectives (Galston, 2010).

Pearce goes on to consider a range of approaches, from citizens' assemblies to decentred governance, to make the case for learning from how deliberative engagement works in real-life situations, with the participation of people along with their highly charged emotions, rather than dismissing them on the theoretical basis that they cannot deliver some 'perfect responsiveness' only ever promised by the proverbial straw man (Sabl, 2015).

In addition to securing improvements to public decision making, state-citizen cooperation is also essential for reversing the widespread sense of powerlessness among the public. In 'The Importance of Collective Control', Anna Coote draws on her extensive research work at the New Economics Foundation, as well as her practical experience with health policy and public engagement at the Healthcare Commission and the King's Fund, to examine the need for political efficacy.

She cites studies in systems change, social movements for health, and initiatives designed to reduce health inequalities by enhancing collective control at the community level, which show how public bodies, by ensuring people are given a meaningful say on an equal footing with other citizens, can make a significant difference in boosting people's mental and physical health, as well as extending their influence over public affairs.

Coote goes on to examine collective control and state-citizen cooperation in relation to 'the commons'. There is growing interest across the world in claiming and controlling resources that are essential for human survival and flourishing. The scope for 'commoning' offers a lens through which to explore the value of constructive collaboration as opposed to conflict, and how shared control by the state and citizens can be advanced.

As for how the exchange of ideas and formation of informed assessments can in practice be engendered, in his chapter, 'Deliberative Engagement with Complex Policies', Simon Burall explains the strategies and processes that can enable deliberative engagement to deal with even the most intricate and controversial issues. He points out that public participation can supplement representative democracy, and the involvement of citizens in policy discussions can help to counter the growing concerns over civic disengagement and political misdirection (Tam, 2018a).

In addition to approaches such as the Danish Board of Technology's Consensus Conferences in the 1970s, and the World Wide Views events in the 2010s, Burall introduces us to the UK's Sciencewise programme (of which he is the Director) that applies deliberative techniques to engage the public in a range of policies relating to science and technology innovation. Instead of public scepticism or misunderstanding, case studies such as the one relating to mitochondrial replacement show how well-structured involvement can help to shape the formulation of policies in what may have been highly contested areas, and lead to better informed engagement with public policy proposals.

Scaling up deliberative participation, however, poses a different challenge. There is often not enough executive or financial backing to extend its use or communicate its results to the wider population. To counter this, a culture change is necessary with those who currently have decision-making powers. In parallel with grasping the improvements

7

that can be made from thoughtful engagement of citizens, there should be a steady increase in the number of opportunities for participatory input, and support in the form of an Office for Public Debate for citizens to learn more about the issues they are asked to reflect on and discuss constructively with others.

In the final chapter of Part One, having dealt with the objections and reservations that academics and practitioners may have about giving more support to state–citizen cooperation, we turn our attention to the views of politicians. It is a fact that many who have got themselves elected come to believe that they have the mandate to make decisions on their own. Some even look askance at suggestions that the public should be involved more in the development of government policies because they think it would cause excessive delays, or become destabilising and counterproductive. To anyone who tries to put a different view, they would simply insist that no one can understand their perspective unless they have been through the electoral process and experienced the challenges of being in government.

Against this stance, in 'The Road to Empowerment' Hazel Blears and David Blunkett set out why the temptation to exclude the public from policy development should be resisted, and how the alternative of working with citizens should be pursued instead. Their arguments are backed by extensive political experience in contesting elections and taking on key roles in government. That experience convinced them that sharing decision-making powers with citizens is vital.

Blunkett and Blears have been leading figures in local government, and were Secretaries of State in charge of, respectively, the Home Office and the Department for Communities and Local Government. They initiated and oversaw the development of the government's Together We Can programme for civil renewal and community empowerment, which supported deliberative participation and co-production with communities through policy support, funding and research dissemination. Reflecting on what they have learnt as politicians, they go on to explain how state–citizen cooperation can more reliably help to identify what changes are needed, and engage the public in determining how those changes are to be brought in.

What is required for effective engagement

In Part Two, five leading experts reflect on different approaches that have been adopted in relation to areas they have closely examined. Each of them will help us differentiate those that are more likely to secure effective engagement and improve outcomes from those that at best will have very limited impact. In 'Lessons from Democratic Innovations', Graham Smith reviews the studies undertaken in the last decade on the changing relations between state and citizens (Ganuza and Baiocchi, 2012; Font et al, 2014; Nabatchi and Leighninger, 2015). Many new methods have been tested in different countries, but the success of one in certain areas does not mean it can be readily replicated, and the lack of impact of another in other parts should not automatically be taken as a sign of its inefficacy. The context of an experiment and the process design factors are critical in considering the benefits it can bring, and how they can be realised under different social and political conditions.

Smith goes on to provide a detailed examination of two prominent types of engagement practice: participatory budgeting (PB), and randomly selected mini-publics such as citizens' juries. Many state bodies utilising PB have not been able to realise its transformative potential because they have neglected to put the key components for its successful implementation in place. Similarly, with mini-publics such as citizens' juries and planning cells, it is only where the process design and requisite participation infrastructure are expertly handled that they have had significant impact on political decision making.

The challenge is to focus on acquiring the relevant expertise and experience so that the potential benefits from well-designed practices are fully realised. The extensive cuts to public services and the rise of 'populist' parties with extremist agendas have placed further burdens on citizen engagement. Getting it wrong might fuel even greater public disillusionment, but getting it right could just be key to rebuilding trust and cooperation between citizens and their state.

Since its emergence in the UK and the US in the 1960s, community development has been an important discipline in connecting governments' attempts to improve the lives of deprived communities with the views of the people living in those communities. In the subsequent decades, standards and methodologies have evolved to guide efforts to bridge the gap between public policy thinking and how people think the problems they face ought to be dealt with.

In 'The Potential of Community Development', Marilyn Taylor looks at the many ways it has been deployed, and why it works better in some cases than others when the relevant factors have been taken into account. This requires community activists to adapt their approaches to fit different settings, and government representatives to support community development with wider socioeconomic policies that can respond to the concerns articulated by energised communities.

Not giving communities a shared and informed platform to speak from will aggravate the disempowerment of ordinary people, and increase the likelihood of them being routinely misled about what collective actions should really be taken. Responsible public bodies should apply community development in line with expert advice so that citizens can work through conflicting options and take ownership of policy outcomes that flow from their own deliberations.

One of the key factors for enabling participatory events or ongoing community development to work is the presence of healthy community relations. In 'Community Action and Civic Dialogue', Barry Quirk explores the critical difference that can be made by civic relationship building. Democracy has its roots in community deliberations and action, but social and economic changes have pushed more and more people to view their experiences as isolated individuals. To counter these trends, people in diverse communities need to be empowered to come together to exchange ideas, share perspectives and consider what should be done for their common good.

Quirk reflects on local authorities' changing approaches to public service development and delivery, and compares those that have left people feeling marginalised with those that have managed to strengthen long-term trust and satisfaction through sustained efforts to cultivate informal communication with residents; discuss options without predetermined answers; involve those who would be affected in setting policy priorities; and, where appropriate, pass defined resources and specific public assets over to community groups to control.

He believes that the correct approach to empowering community action must embed civic dialogue at the heart of public engagement. Despite the managerialist mantra that champions platform economies and the benefits of standardisation, the design and delivery of public services can achieve much more through well-facilitated and sustained dialogues with communities, which are then more likely to play an active and dependable role in the stewardship of local resources and assets.

Another dimension that public leaders and officials need to recognise is that effective participation requires respect and understanding of diverse individuals. The differences between citizens can sometimes be too readily ignored and a monolithic engagement approach is rolled out. Marian Barnes, in her chapter on 'Old Age and Caring Democracy', examines this issue in relation to older people, who are not just different from younger members of society, but are themselves a highly diverse group. The ageing process affects people differently, and when that is combined with contrasting backgrounds and dispositions, it makes any generalised assumption about how best to engage older people highly suspect.

Austerity policies have also stoked negative perceptions in many quarters that older people are somehow to be blamed for the cuts in services and funding support for younger people, and that too much emphasis is placed on meeting the needs of the older population. Against ignorance and prejudice, government organisations will need to find ways to engage with older people to make sure their unique concerns and circumstances are not overlooked in policy development.

Barnes' chapter looks at how this can be done to improve service provision and public satisfaction by reviewing examples of older people's participation in a number of countries. As well as 'ageing activism' within seniors' forums and interest organisations, it considers participation in contexts not often regarded as 'political', such as within residential homes and in research projects. It will be seen from these examples that 'deliberating with care' with older people offers transformative potential not only in relation to specific services and policies that can benefit all citizens as we grow older, but also in counteracting damaging intergenerational conflict, enhance personal wellbeing and promote social justice.

At the other end of the age spectrum, while it is widely noted that 'everyday democracy' has increasingly been offering a helpful route to political engagement (Pattie et al, 2004), it is not one that is readily taken up by young people. As James Sloam shows in his chapter, 'Young People and Everyday Democracy', civic engagement with politicians and public officials is primarily undertaken by those who are middle-aged, college-educated and financially well-off. In the UK, where governments often regard the promotion of volunteering among young people to do good work in the community as a policy priority in support of 'civic engagement', the rate of actual civic engagement between young people and government representatives has continued to languish at the bottom when compared with the rest of Western Europe.

Sloam shows how arrangements that facilitate young people's participation in focused policy explorations can help to tackle the sense of exclusion, build trust in the political system and develop their confidence in being able to make a difference to issues that concern them. Furthermore, the experience of assessing the feasibility of rival options, the relevance of diverse proposals and the affordability of turning seemingly appealing ideas into deliverable schemes carries substantial developmental benefits in equipping young citizens with the know-how for shaping public policies.

To illustrate what may help or hinder in involving young people in cooperative decision making with state bodies, Sloam points to the role that can be played by institutions such as local councils, schools and universities (Flanagan and Levine, 2010), and concludes with a look at successes and failures in three case examples of attempts to engage younger citizens in everyday democracy.

How to expand our civic capability

In the final part of our book, we will consider how the long-term barriers to effective state-citizen cooperation are to be overcome with sustained expansion of our civic capability. Anyone who has worked on building bridges between government organisations and the public will be aware of the need to go beyond the development of engagement practices to address a range of competence issues on both sides. No participatory process can work well if those involved, from state bodies or the wider community, are unable to make use of what has been put in place.

One familiar barrier is the lack of understanding of government and policy-making arrangements. Without sufficient comprehension of basic terms or key practices, the way open deliberations should work, or how one can express oneself clearly and constructively – particularly when one is in disagreement with others – one could find oneself in a fish-out-of-water situation, not knowing how to be an effective participant.

In 'Improving Citizenship Education', James Weinberg and Matt Flinders of the Bernard Crick Centre for the Public Understanding of Politics look back on the publication of the Crick Report (Crick, 1998), which led to the introduction of citizenship education as a statutory feature of the national curriculum in England. They begin by setting out the potential value of citizenship education, and point out that the existing research and data on its impact globally indicate particular correlations with sociopolitical outcomes (Schulz et al, 2017).

However, the effectiveness of citizenship education depends on a number of critical factors. Using the UK as a case example, Weinberg and Flinders explore a number of obstacles that have hindered its full potential from being realised. At the level of education policy, they highlight both the implementation gap under New Labour and the vision shift under the subsequent Coalition Government that have virtually eradicated the radical potential of citizenship education. Other problems include the lack of effective teacher training and the prioritisation of competing policies such as Prevent, resulting in depleted interest and capacity to teach the subject well.

In order to realign citizenship education with the goal of inducting each new generation in society into their role as democratic citizens, a number of suggestions are put forward. These cover policy steers to move public discourse, especially in government circles, away from nationalistic introspection; changes to initial teacher training and CPD (continuing professional development) that will make citizenship an integral aspect of education in the same manner that, previously, the Coalition Government tried to enforce 'character development' through SMSC (spiritual, moral, social, cultural) education; and curriculum redesign that reconceptualises the horizons of sovereignty (and thus democratic citizenship) for young people.

Of course, it is not just those going through the school system that need to learn about state–citizen cooperation. Citizens who have attained political office also have a responsibility to develop their understanding of how they can help government bodies and the public work together in a more mutually supportive way. In 'Rethinking Civic Roles', Jane Roberts draws on her research work, and her experience as Leader of the London Borough of Camden and Chair of the New Local Government Network, to set out what elected representatives should do to raise their constituents' interest in and awareness of what it means to be partners in public policy development.

In addition to outreach work, elected representatives should also consider how to develop better relationships with the people they represent. With the perception that political power goes predominantly to those who are economically well-off, professionally qualified and/ or exhibiting the more traditional 'white male' characteristics, those in office ought to be more conscious about and adept at engaging with citizens in a manner that puts the latter at ease and gives them belief that there is a real intention to resolve problems together.

A further dimension Roberts bring out is that politicians at all levels of society can play a key part in making political roles more accessible to people. One approach is to support term limits so more vacancies come up regularly, and to introduce, in some cases, rotation as a mechanism for citizens to take turns in certain public positions so that they gain experience in what is involved in carrying out wider responsibilities. Another is for those who have stepped down from office to share their knowledge and experience with others in the community, with diverse backgrounds, so that there is an ongoing exchange of insights and ideas that will enrich public understanding of how to work with government representatives and improve public decisions.

Beyond the capability that should be inculcated specifically among students and civic leaders to help them and those they interact with play a positive part in state-citizen cooperation, all citizens should be able to access learning opportunities that will enhance their interest and skills in democratic participation. The shortage of such opportunities has meant that the majority of people have relatively little comprehension of why and how a system of government should be run to secure what would otherwise be lost to individuals acting alone with no enforceable rules and collectively funded arrangements.

How this civic learning gap can be tackled is addressed in the chapter on 'Promoting the "Take Part" Approach' by Marjorie Mayo, Zoraida Mendiwelso-Bendek and Carol Packham. The Take Part approach was originally developed through a series of government initiatives under the UK Government's Together We Can programme, to facilitate active learning for active citizenship, based on the values of social justice, equality and respect for diversity. Delivered through community-university partnerships, it helped to empower citizens and their communities to acquire the confidence and competence to set out their concerns, and encourage the relevant structures of governance to learn to listen and respond more effectively. Examples ranged from enabling diverse communities to learn together about shared public challenges in South Yorkshire; supporting citizen-led initiatives with mentoring and community radio programmes in Lincolnshire; to facilitating mutual learning among care providers, people with disabilities and policy makers in Exeter.

Take Part exemplifies many of the ideas of Paulo Freire (Freire, 1972), Orlando Fals-Borda (Fals Borda and Rahman, 1991) and other international pioneers of active learning for social transformation. It can be taken forward via a variety of delivery mechanisms, depending upon the needs and the interests of the communities in question, and the specific barriers to be overcome. The value of its deployment is illustrated with further examples such as the use of the approach in the US by universities and libraries in responding to the growth of far right politics; and its application in Colombia, where universities have been developing strategies for working with communities to support the peace process.

Contrary to the view that most people would not want to have anything to do with government organisations, research has consistently found that people want to be involved provided they can make a real difference. With the appropriate learning support and engagement process, few citizens would turn down the chance to have an informed and meaningful say about matters that affect them and their wider community. Indeed, in relation to issues where a substantial and sustained impact can be achieved, it is not surprising that many would be willing to play an even bigger part in shaping public outcomes.

In 'Developing Public-Cooperative Partnerships', Pat Conaty sets out how a variety of co-production initiatives have emerged by drawing on the ideas from associative democracy, cooperative management, the solidarity economy and the commons movement. For example, city government, trade unions and local communities in northern Italy have worked together to develop public cooperative partnerships to provide social care for the elderly, the disabled and marginalised groups. In the US, with the proactive support of Bernie Sanders when he was Mayor of Burlington in Vermont, community land trusts became more widely established and later flourished across the city and more widely in Vermont and other parts of the US. The Welsh Government empowered local communities to develop forms of democratic housing and pioneer new housing co-ops and community land trusts in a growing number of Welsh cities and towns.

Cities such as Ghent and Bologna are promoting new public-cooperative partnerships by drawing up contracts that are backed by local authority bylaws. These regulations formalise the development of commons and co-op solutions to secure the common good with local government support. Conaty concludes that these innovative approaches are not only opening up new ways for local people to devise solutions in partnership with state bodies, but they are also offering governments at all levels around the world important lessons in how public policy objectives can be greatly advanced by strategically cooperating with citizens and community groups in making the most of common resources to meet needs identified by the people themselves.

Conclusion

Some in government may be tempted to say about citizens: you can't live with them, you can't live without them. The truth is that any government that does not seriously engage citizens in developing a shared approach will rightly lose public trust and legitimacy. This is not just a theoretical problem for academics to solve. Evidence is proliferating around us that the disengagement between citizens and government institutions is causing ruptures in our governance, and that is being exploited by an unsavoury mix of those who want to amass power and wealth for themselves and those who seek to recruit fodder to help advance their extremist agenda.

It is quite possible that instead of looking to develop better cooperation with public agencies, disaffected people may resort to bypassing, pressuring, or even challenging the state. But how are legitimate acts of resistance to be distinguished from actions by groups which are driven by a sense of outrage fanned by the unscrupulous? How is civil disobedience triggered by threats to moral standards to be differentiated from attempts to evade the laws in response to some 'inner voice' or a simple disinclination to pay taxes? The notion of the common good, as opposed to individual interests, can only be ultimately defined and sustained by a cooperative relation between the people and their government.

While cynics are too rash in dismissing state-citizen cooperation as impossible, no one should be hasty in assuming that it can be easily achieved either. Economic insecurity, political misdirection, bureaucratic structures, biased media coverage, lack of experience in unpacking policy claims, all make it difficult for citizens to play an informed role in engaging with the deliberations of public bodies (Berger, 2011; Tam, 2018b).

However, as this introductory chapter has shown, the contributions to this book will provide in-depth arguments, pertinent examples and experienced guidance to help civic educators, community activists, policy advisors, political leaders and public officials to attain a better understanding of why and how state-citizen cooperation should be engendered. Our final chapter will bring together a set of recommendations on how to take its development forward. They will highlight the key factors to bear in mind and what actions should be prioritised. Ultimately, the most important catalyst for change depends on the extent to which those seeking or holding public office are prepared to learn to govern with the people.

References

Achen, C. H. and Bartels, L. M. (2016) *Democracy for Realist: why elections do not produce responsive government*, Princeton, NJ: Princeton University Press.

Berger, B. (2011) *Attention Deficit Democracy: the paradox of civic engagement*, Princeton, NJ: Princeton University Press.

Boyte, H. C. (2011) 'Constructive politics as public work: organizing the literature', *Political Theory* 39: 630-660.

Bryson, J. M., Crosby, B. C. and Bloomberg, L. (eds) (2015) *Public Value and Public Administration*, Washington, DC: Georgetown University Press.

Crick, B. (1998) *Education for Citizenship and the Teaching of Democracy in Schools*, London: Qualifications and Curriculum Authority.

Drakeford, M. (2014) *Social Policy and Privatisation*, London: Routledge.

Fals Borda, O. and Rahman, M. A. (1991) *Action and knowledge*, London: Intermediate Technology.

Ferlie, E., Ashburner, L., Fitzgerald, L. and Pettigrew, A. (1996) *The New Public Management in Action*, Oxford: Oxford University Press.

Flanagan, C. and Levine, P. (2010) 'Civic engagement and the transition to adulthood', *The Future of Children* 20 (1): 159–179.

Font, J., della Porta, D. and Sintomer, Y. (2014) *Participatory Democracy in Southern Europe: causes, characteristics and consequences*, New York: Rowman & Littlefield.

Freire, P. (1972) *Pedagogy of the oppressed*, Harmondsworth: Penguin.

Fung, A. (2006) *Empowered Participation: reinventing urban democracy*, Princeton, NJ: Princeton University Press.

Galston, W. (2010) 'Realism in political theory', *European Journal of Political Theory* 9 (4): 385–411.

Ganuza, E. and Baiocchi, G. (2012) 'The power of ambiguity: how participatory budgeting travels the globe', *Journal of Public Deliberation* 8 (2), Article 8. www.publicdeliberation.net/jpd/vol8/iss2/art8

Hermann, C. (ed) (2015) *Privatization of Public Services*, London: Routledge.

Lane, J.-E. (2000) *New Public Management: an introduction*, London: Routledge.

Lee, C. W., McQuarrie, M. and Walker, E. T. (2015) *Democratizing Inequalities: dilemmas of the new public participation*, New York: New York University Press.

Maugham, J. (2015) 'The government's not trying to balance the books, but to shrink the state', *The New Statesman*, 2 November.

Moore, M. H. (2013) *Recognizing Public Value*, Cambridge, MA: Harvard University Press.

Nabatchi, T. and Leighninger, M. (2015) *Public Participation for 21st Century Democracy*, Hoboken: John Wiley & Sons.

Pattie, C., Seyd, P. and Whiteley, P. (2004) *Citizenship in Britain: values, participation and democracy*, Cambridge: Cambridge University Press.

Ranson, S. and Stewart, J. (1994) *Managing for the Public Domain: enabling the learning society*, Basingstoke: Macmillan Press.

Sabl, A. (2015) 'The two cultures of democratic theory: responsiveness, democratic quality, and the empirical-normative divide', *Perspectives on Politics* 13 (2): 345–365.

Schulz, W., Ainley, J., Fraillon, J., Losito, B., Agrusti, G. and Friedman, T. (2017) *Becoming Citizens in a Changing World: The International Civic and Citizenship Education Study 2016*, Amsterdam: IEA.

Sirianni, C. and Friedland, L. (2001) *Civic Innovations in America: community empowerment, public policy and the movement for civic renewal*, Berkeley and Los Angeles: University of California Press.

Smith, G. (2010) *Democratic Innovations: designing institutions for citizen participation*, Cambridge: Cambridge University Press.

Tam, H. (2011) 'The big con: reframing the state–society debate', *PPR Journal* 18 (1): 30–40.

Tam, H. (2018a) *Time to Save Democracy: how to govern ourselves in the age of anti-politics*, Bristol: Policy Press.

Tam, H. (2018b) *What Should Citizens Believe? Exploring the issues of truth, reason & society*, Sheffield: Citizen Network.

White, S. and Leighton, D. (eds) (2008) *Building a Citizen Society: the emerging politics of republican democracy*, London: Lawrence & Wishart.

PART ONE

Why We Need State-Citizen Cooperation

2

Realism and Democratic Renewal

Nick Pearce

As the Berlin Wall came tumbling down in 1989, the American political theorist Francis Fukuyama famously declared that liberal democracy was 'the End of History'. It had defeated all of its twentieth century rivals, from fascism to communism, and had nothing left to fear except the blandness of the prosperous human life it guaranteed (Fukuyama, 1992).

Today, we are more likely to read about liberal democracy coming to an end. Western democracies are assailed on all sides: internally, from declining legitimacy, rising polarisation, illiberal populism and 'fake news'; externally, from the intrusion of foreign powers in elections to the allure of alternative, undemocratic models of government. Debate turns increasingly to how democracy might end, not whether it will survive (Runciman, 2018).

The recent election of Donald Trump, the swing towards 'illiberal democracy' in Eastern Europe, the rise of radical right-wing parties, and even the Brexit referendum result, are often considered symptomatic of a deeper democratic malaise (Streeck, 2017). This is that Western democracies have been steadily hollowed out in recent decades under the twin pressures of global capitalist economic development and neoliberal governance. Nation states – which remain, for the most part, the fundamental unit of democratic government – have ceded powers over fiscal and monetary policy, financial regulation and trade to independent bodies like central banks, or transnational institutions like the European Union and World Trade Organization. Western economies have been financialised, living off public and private debt and cheap money, while market principles have been extended into the institutions of the state. The scope for democratic choices over taxation, public spending and other critical areas of public policy has narrowed. Accumulated obligations to fund state pensions and maintain core public services like education have progressively limited the fiscal headroom available to politicians: austerity in the eurozone, the UK and elsewhere has simply tightened the screw. Democratic welfare capitalism is coming apart (Schäfer and Streeck, 2013).

In these circumstances, scholars have argued, political parties become progressively less responsive to their core voters. Instead of representing popular interests, they increasingly represent the state to the people (Mair, 2013). Simultaneously, inequalities in income and wealth have been translated into inequalities in political power: working class voters stay away from the polls, or register their discontent by shifting allegiance to the radical right, while policy making is dominated by the interests and ideas of the wealthy, who buy influence through campaign donations, ownership of media outlets and the funding of think-tanks and 'astroturf' lobbyists. The institutional firewalls of democracy, which were erected to protect politics from colonisation by economic power, have been breached. Contemporary Western polities, while displaying the outward form of democracies, are better understood as 'post-democracies' (Crouch, 2004).

Can liberal democracy resist this fate? Is it doomed to maintain the outward appearance of democratic government, while steadily shedding its substantive core? In this chapter, I will begin to answer this question by considering two kinds of 'realist' challenge to contemporary liberal democracies. The first is an empirical one and is exemplified by the recent landmark work of American political science, *Democracy for Realists* by Christopher Achen and Larry Bartels (2016). This sets out to dethrone both what it calls the 'folk theory' of democracy, that governments are responsive to the preferences of individual citizens expressed in free and fair elections, and another, more specialist account of democratic government, that citizens choose their leaders on the basis of 'retrospective' evaluation of their performance. Achen and Bartels argue that citizens are not rational, do not have clear preferences, and assess the performance of governments based on short-run evaluations, not sober retrospective assessments of their full terms in office. They vote as groups – religious, ethnic, occupational or otherwise – on the basis of inherited partisanship and social identities, rather than coherent ideology or thought-through policy positions. The result, they argue, is that 'from the viewpoint of governmental representativeness and accountability, election outcomes are essentially random choices among the available parties – musical chairs' (Achen and Bartels, 2016, p 312).

In parallel to this critique of representative democracy, scholars have also taken aim at the empirical claims of public deliberation and deliberative democracy. Inter alia, critics argue that the use of 'mini-publics', citizens' assemblies and other deliberative mechanisms are either marginal to mass democracy and inconsequential to its institutions and practices (Achen and Bartels, 2016); a dangerous distraction of citizens from the inequalities and dysfunctions that plague contemporary politics (Shapiro, 2017); or, worse, a 'strategic tool' deployed by an emerging 'deliberation industry' to massage citizen demands and neuter public hostility to austerity measures and corporate interests (Lee and Romano, 2013). If representative and direct democracy have their flaws, these critics argue, the solutions will not be found in extending deliberative democracy (Shapiro, 2017).

The second realist challenge to liberal democracy is normative. It comes from a diverse set of political theorists who, over the past quarter of a century or so, have assembled a range of realist critiques of post-Rawlsian liberal political philosophy. Their arguments cannot be neatly arrayed into a set of common positions and it is questionable whether anything like a 'realist school' exists (Miller, 2016). But a number of realist themes emerge from this body of work (Galston, 2010). A primary one is that political theory is not applied ethics or morality: it is not the job of political philosophers to develop ideal theories with which to measure or judge political institutions. The 'real world' of politics is a distinct and autonomous realm that must be studied on its own terms. Political actors have interests, emotions and passions, and practise crafts, that do not conform to the demands of rational and un-coerced communication or dispassionate and 'evidence-led' policy making.

More strongly, realists often assert that conflict and antagonism is irreducible in human affairs, and that the search for public consensus or universal agreement is illusory: politics emerges precisely to enable us to accept legitimate government and to disagree without continual recourse to violence. On this account, the first question for politics is whether it delivers order and stability (Williams, 2005). A 'hyperrealist' might go further and argue that politics is about power and not much else: principles or values do not come into it, and if they do, they are simply ideological cloaks behind which lurk naked interests (Miller, 2016).

Realism is not all pessimism, however. An 'agonist' view that conflict is irreducible can be channelled into a liberating realist politics of active citizenship. On this more radical realist account, democracy is at its most vital when we recognise that it overflows with emotion, intemperance and loud demands, and at its most important when we clash over 'public things', not the deracinated search for foundational consensus or procedural fairness (Honig, 1993; Honig and Stears, 2014).

In what follows, I will briefly outline and assess these twin realist challenges to liberal democracy. I will suggest some ways in which empirical and normative realism require us to rethink liberal democratic theory and practice, sketching out the elements of a democratic renewal which is realistically premised.

Democracy for realists

In *Democracy for Realists*, Achen and Bartels (2016) mount a relentless assault on the ideal of popular sovereignty, or what they term the 'folk theory of democracy'. This theory, embodied in Abraham Lincoln's famous refrain that democracy is government 'of the people, by the people, for the people', specifies that citizens elect political representatives to enact their policy preferences, and that the quality of democracy resides in the responsiveness of, or congruence between, public policy and citizens' preferences. The folk theory is demonstrably false, argue Achen and Bartels. Citizens give little time and thought to politics. They do not rationally evaluate political choices and express well-considered policy preferences at the ballot box. They vote on the basis of group loyalties and social identities: 'at election time, they are swayed by how they feel about the 'nature of the times', especially the current state of the economy, and by political loyalties typically acquired in childhood' (Achen and Bartels, 2016, p 1). A battery of historical cases, predominantly drawn from the twentieth century history of the USA, is adduced to provide empirical proof of this argument. Elections do not ensure ideological responsiveness to the popular will, 'leaving elected officials mostly free to pursue their own notions of the public good, or to respond to party and interest group preferences' (Achen and Bartels, 2016, p 14). To ground democracy in the rationality of monadic individual citizens, to whom elected representatives will be responsive in the offices of government, is therefore unrealistic and indefensible.

Achen and Bartels close off a number of potential routes out of this quandary. We might accept, as Joseph Schumpeter did, that citizens do not elect representatives to carry out the people's will, but still regard elections as the means by which citizens choose who is to govern them. Citizens can control their political leaders by using elections to make *retrospective* evaluations of their performance. Unfortunately, citizens do not meet this more limited test of democratic government either.

They typically hold politicians to account for acts that are beyond their control – droughts, floods and even shark attacks – but fail to evaluate the record of political leaders over a term of office, judging politicians instead myopically on whether their incomes have grown or fallen in the space of the few months before an election. Achen and Bartels (2016, p 16) draw a bleak conclusion from the study of retrospective voting: elections are 'mostly just erratic reflections of the current balance of partisan loyalties in a given political system' and, worse, in a two-party system, the choice between the candidates is 'essentially a coin toss'.

Achen and Bartels further deny that a switch to direct democracy – such as the use of primaries to select candidates, plebiscites, citizens' initiatives and participatory decision making – can overcome these problems with democratic theory. In their survey of the evidence, direct democratic mechanisms simply produce irrational or short-sighted decisions, like cutting the taxes that are needed to pay for vital public services. Popular opinion is easily manipulated by vested interests and direct democracy ends up denuding government of the leadership skills, long-sightedness in policy making, and careful assessment of trade-offs that it requires.

Achen and Bartels (2016, p 302) are equally dismissive of deliberative democracy, and attempts to use deliberative fora to improve citizens' knowledge, deepen their engagement with policy choices, and come to considered collective judgements. 'Most ordinary citizens', they argue, 'do not want politics to be more like a philosophy seminar.' Thus the 'practical impact of deliberative theory has been quite modest'. Human nature apparently imposes its constraints on democracy, even in the most reflective, respectful and purposeful settings.

A more fine-grained critique of the practical use of public deliberation emerges from the work of organisational sociologists and anthropologists. This strand of research delineates how public deliberation is initiated by elites and delivered by a 'public engagement industry' that sells citizen deliberation as a strategy for demobilising opposition, channelling discontent away from substantive socioeconomic change and legitimising inequality. Deliberation is typically used when social unrest has taken place or is likely to occur, and oriented to manufacturing consent for the 'tough choices' that flow from austerity (Lee and Romano, 2013). It shapes citizen preferences to align with the organisational goals of public authorities and corporations, such that 'the end result of all these little steps to empowerment is, unfortunately, not a long journey to social justice, but a tightening spiral of resignation from public life' (Lee, 2015, p 26).

These are powerful challenges to contemporary democratic theory. Yet in important respects, they are wide of the mark. To begin with, as Andrew Sabl (2015) has argued in a careful dissection of the argument, the 'folk theory' of democracy is not one that democratic theorists in fact hold. In particular, few if any theorists argue that democratic quality is to be measured by pure 'responsiveness' to citizen preferences. A well-functioning democracy will have clear institutional structures for reflection and deliberation upon citizen preferences, so that there are time lags between preference formation and policy making, and mechanisms to prevent government responding to fleeting shifts in public opinion. A liberal democracy will enshrine human or constitutional rights that cannot be subject to override by majoritarian decision, such as the right to freedom of speech. Citizen preferences – for example, for the death penalty in the United Kingdom – will be ignored or rejected when those rights are at stake. The judiciary will subject executive actions to judicial oversight and review, limiting policy responsiveness to ensure compatibility with the rule of law. Democratic institutions will structure deliberation – whether by citizens, legislators or the executive branch itself – into the formation and execution of public policy, thus moderating pure responsiveness. In each of these cases, we can see that judging democracy by responsiveness criterion alone is to hold democratic theory to a standard it does not itself defend (Sabl, 2015).

Of course it is a familiar complaint that citizens are too ignorant, irrational or uninterested to exercise their democratic rights or govern themselves effectively; those arguments can be traced back as far as Plato and were routinely adduced in opposition to extensions of the franchise in the nineteenth and twentieth centuries. The more distinctive charge levelled against democratic theory by Achen and Bartels is that people vote in groups, on the basis of social identities, not as individual citizens rationally weighing up their preferences. But is this critique really so fatal? Political scientists have long studied public opinion, political parties and democratic elections on the basis of the aggregation of individuals into social classes, ethnic minorities or faith groups. Religion and social class were the most important structural determinants of twentieth century politics in Western Europe, in particular. The waning of religious belief and the fracturing of industrial social class blocs, coupled with increased immigration, has produced a more complicated electoral geography in most advanced democracies, but class, ethnicity and occupation still provide the building blocks of political analysis (Beramendi et al, 2015; Oesch and Rennwald, 2018).

Moreover, there is considerable evidence that different occupational groups exhibit preferences for economic and social policy that demonstrate continuity over time and are not simply reducible to spasmodic episodes of will formation. Political parties respond to these preferences, not in a linear or contemporaneous fashion, but by developing strategies to align themselves with key electoral groups and engaging in processes of shaping citizens' ideological horizons in a two-way interaction of supply and demand (Beramendi et al, 2015). The breakdown of the two-party political systems of industrial class societies has accentuated processes of realignment, opening up new political space for 'niche' parties and forcing mainstream ones of the centre-left and centre-right to appeal to new occupational groups, such as the sociocultural professionals of the public sector, while fighting to retain their core class voters (Oesch and Rennwald, 2018). Each does so in the context of distinct institutional frameworks which have evolved over time, and which structure democratic politics. In the Anglophone countries, majoritarian electoral systems have co-evolved with liberal market economies and relatively limited welfare states; in Continental and Northern Europe, proportional electoral systems accompany the coordination of social class interests in the economy, alongside universal or social insurance welfare states (Iversen and Soskice, 2009). It is hard to reconcile the historical evolution and persistence over time of these fundamental political-economic institutions with the 'toss of a coin' and 'musical chairs' account of electoral politics offered by Achen and Bartels.

Indeed, a blind spot in their realist theory of democracy is that by focusing on close elections, swayed by apparently trivial events or myopic evaluations, they miss what is important but taken for granted and not up for grabs – enduring institutions or entitlements that command widespread public support, like state pensions or publicly funded schools. As Sabl (2017a, p 156) points out:

> the effect is to exaggerate the arbitrariness and variability of political decisions. By stressing instances in which democratic control is undermined when voting decisions are affected by random events, Achen and Bartels obscure the pervasive degree to which control might be enabled by non-decisions that are immune to such events (but tied to very clear preferences – that large swathes of policy change fairly little).

The force of Achen and Bartel's argument is apparent in their survey of the empirical evidence on policy formation, and the strength, particularly in US politics, of organised lobbying groups, special interests and professionalised cadres of political consultants and advisers. Any realistic theory of democracy must account for the role of these groups, the practices of political elites and the inequalities of power exercised in policy making. But it is important to denote the theoretical limits to what we might call realist groupthink. It is part of the 'facticity' of modernity that the constitutions and laws of liberal democracies are founded on individual citizens and their rights. Even if particular groups or communities are given protection in law or special rights for the preservation of cultural practices, for example, individual citizens remain the bearers of the rights and obligations of citizenship, at the ballot box, in the courts or in the welfare state. Moreover, individuals may be socially embedded, but in pluralist liberal societies they have multiple identities and can critically reflect on the norms, beliefs and political loyalties of the communities and groups to which they belong. For all these reasons, a corporatist recasting of democratic constitutions, giving representation to faith groups, estates or corporate legal entities, would be utterly anachronistic. Democratic theory will therefore unavoidably return to the individual citizen, even it is enriched by insights from the sociology of class power or group life.

Direct and deliberative democracy, and their limits

Are Achen and Bartels nonetheless right that experimentation with direct and deliberative democracy cannot provide grounds for renewing democratic theory or practice? In the context of the result of the Brexit referendum, democrats have had recent occasion to lament the use of plebiscites to address complex issues of public policy on which voters are sharply divided. Indeed, the 'deliberative turn' in democratic theory has been taken in large part because of dissatisfaction with public will formation in both representative and direct democratic institutions and practices (see for example Offe, 2017, on the Brexit referendum and the case for citizen deliberation). It is precisely because substantive issues of public policy cannot be reduced to binary choices, and that citizen preferences can be constrained, coerced and manipulated in unequal democracies, that an expansion of deliberative democracy is required – or so its protagonists conclude.

It is important not to restrict the discussion of direct democracy to plebiscites, however. In recent decades, there has been an explosion of citizen participation in decision making, particularly, but not exclusively, of participatory budgeting in local authorities (Sirianni, 2017; see also Chapter Six in this book). Political parties have responded to the manifest problems of declining party membership, lower voting turnout and increasing distrust by embarking on a wave of democratic experimentation – in what has been termed a 'second wave of democratic reform' (Farrell, 2014). This has included measures to open up politics to greater transparency and scrutiny (such as Freedom of Information); decentralisation and devolution of power, including the extension of directly elected mayors; expanded citizen engagement and direct participation in public authority policy making and budget setting; the opening up of political parties to new members and registered supporters; and the election of leaders by primary contests. The use of new digital technologies has tended to widen the scope of these reforms and accelerate their take-up (Simon et al, 2017).

To regard these as 'foolish reform movements' that deliver power to interest groups and demagogues and result in self-defeating choices by the electorate (Achen and Bartels, 2016, pp 302–3) is arguably to generalise from recent US experience and a limited number of cases therein. Wider evidence on participatory budgeting in Europe and in US cities such as New York, Chicago and Boston paints a more impressive picture of citizen engagement and civic renewal (Gillman, 2016), while a more balanced account of citizens' referenda emerges from the record in states such as California, where ballots to increase taxes for valued public services, liberalise drug laws and increase environmental protection have passed in recent years. History teaches us that direct democracy brings with it risks and the possibility of elite capture and public manipulation, which requires careful attention to institutional design, including checks and balances. But for the example of a TV celebrity, Donald Trump, elected by party primary, we can offer the counterexample of the impeccably centrist insider, Emmanuel Macron; for Tea Party mayors and governors, we can contrast participatory budgeting in Paris or radical new forms of municipal democratic experimentation in Portugal and Spain, and other European countries. The empirical record of direct and participatory democracy is more mixed and its history more contingent than realist critics acknowledge.

A similar story can be told about deliberative democracy. Here again we have seen a profusion of democratic experimentation across the world in recent decades, from local citizens' juries, to state-level deliberations, national citizens' assemblies and constitutional conventions (Farrell, 2014; Fishkin and Mansbridge, 2017). Deliberative democrats argue that we now have compelling evidence to support the claims that deliberative democracy is practicable and realistic, not utopian; inclusive, not elitist; communicatively diverse, and not simply dominated by rationalist 'talk'; oriented towards pluralistic, workable agreements, rather than consensus; and able to overcome the hurdles of social division, power inequality and polarisation. Catalogued in this way, these claims attest to the fact that deliberative theorists have sought to address – in both theory and empirical practice – the main criticisms levelled against citizen deliberation. The weight of this evidence may not have set 'controversies to rest' over deliberative democracy, as Nicole Curato and her fellow authors have recently argued (Curato et al, 2017). But the innovation in deliberative democratic practice, its spread across different jurisdictions and the empirical findings from this experimentation suggest it cannot be readily dismissed as politically inconsequential or 'undermined by what has been learned since the Enlightenment about human cognition and social life' (Achen and Bartels, 2016, p 301).

Perhaps the most serious challenge to deliberative democracy is that of scaling up or 'designed coupling' (Hendriks, 2016) with the institutions of mass democracy. The record of translating the outcomes of citizens' assemblies, such as those held in Canada, Iceland and the Republic of Ireland into political change is undeniably poor (with the notable recent exception of the referendum to amend the constitution on abortion rights in Ireland). How processes of deliberation 'dock' into representative democratic institutions remains uncertain and necessarily subject to local or national variation. Should they be initiated by citizens and parties, or by governments? Engage politicians and parties, or exclude them? Restricted to constitutional and democratic reforms, or ranging widely across social and political issues (Setälä, 2017)?

A central issue is that, if the recommendations of deliberative assemblies are not binding on elected authorities, how is the circuit back into formal politics to be closed? Opponents of deliberative democracy believe this represents a fundamental dilemma. If deliberation is purely consultative, it is harmless but not worth the fuss. If it is institutionalised and given real decision-making teeth, it undermines healthy political competition and empowers vested interests (Shapiro, 2017).

Whether you agree with the assessment will depend in part on your view of what constitutes a robust democracy. Ian Shapiro (2017) valorises the aggregation of interests and policy programmes into competition between two parties in a majoritarian system, designed to ensure that whomsoever can win the battle of ideas can implement their agenda. Whatever else its merits, this looks redolent of an industrial society class politics, coupled with a Westminster first-past-the-post electoral system. Most advanced democracies now have multiparty politics and proportional voting systems, with plural sites of power. Reconfiguring these democracies to engage citizens in a mix of deliberative, direct and representative democratic institutions, and addressing the systemic dysfunctions and inequalities that plague democracy, may be a simultaneously more realistic and radical democratic agenda.[1]

Realist political theory: resignation or radicalism?

Can realists really be radicals? In his widely cited survey of the literature, William Galston (2010, p 408) identified four key 'building blocks' of realist political theory that he considered to be 'particularly strong': the injunction to take politics seriously as a particular field of human endeavour, and not to treat it as a branch of ethics; the proposition that civil order is the *sine qua non* for every other political good (or what the philosopher Bernard Williams called the 'first question of politics'); the emphasis on the study in history and not in abstraction of different political institutions and regime types; and the call for a more complex moral and political psychology, recognising that irrationality, difference and conflict are pervasive in human affairs.

It is not difficult to see how these building blocks can lead to an accommodation with the status quo, rather than a radical democratic agenda. If conflict is ubiquitous, order and stability can become the limit of our aspirations, rather than the starting point of any recognisably political project. If equality, justice or liberty can only be constituted as 'ideal' theories, we cannot seek their realisation in real history or actual politics. If irrationality, human passions and coercive power are universal, perhaps they are enduring and immutable − essential to history, rather than changing with it or taking different forms, depending on the institutional structures of society. And if these are fixed human traits and characteristics of any human society, do they not place limits on the feasible, constraining our ambitions (Finlayson, 2017)?

Yet realist political theory need not lead us down these conservative, even nihilist paths. Liberal realists can accept the lack of normative consensus in society and reject the search for 'regulative ideals' to animate politics, but nonetheless argue that liberal goals − holding power accountable, and securing liberty, equal opportunities and the

---

[1]   In recent years, deliberative theorists have taken a 'systemic turn' to address the deliberative qualities of political systems as a whole (Owen and Smith, 2015).

diversity of human flourishing – can be promoted in a wide range of social and political institutions. Liberal realists claim that 'the conflicts that would otherwise be endemic to human nature can be provisionally adjudicated through institutions and practices' and that each of these 'may be subjected to normative critique to the extent that it excludes important sectors of society from its benefits, is unfairly rigged by powerful actors, or displays systematic and excessive bias with regard to the range of interests it promotes' (Sabl, 2017b, pp 366, 370).

Alternatively, in radical democratic vein, those realist thinkers associated with 'agonism' (Honig, 1993; Mouffe, 2013; Honig and Stears, 2014) seek to harness contestation and conflict rather than contain or disperse them. They see passions, disputations and unreasonable demands giving voice to marginalised and excluded groups and providing a wider repertoire for political struggles. Contingency and arbitrariness open up new spaces and sites for politics. As Marc Stears has summarised the optimism of this view, 'To act politically in the knowledge of disagreement and struggle is to keep open the possibilities of genuine free expression and, with Nietzsche, to celebrate the possibility of forging new realities through the struggle of the old ones' (Stears, 2007, p 546).

Seeking to radicalise realism beyond liberalism, Mouffe argues that agonistic confrontation is the very stuff of democracy: democratic institutions secure non-violent conflict, turning enemies into political adversaries. Too much consensus leads to apathy and disaffection. Politics is always and forever a struggle for hegemonic dominance between 'us' and 'them'. It is collective, not individual; affective not rational; and oriented towards achieving social transformation, not the maintenance of the existing order (Mouffe, 2013).

There are some continuities here with the empirical realist insistence on the group nature of politics and the role of emotions and social identities in shaping political behaviour, although for Mouffe antagonism is constitutive of any social order; she does not rest her argument on individual or group psychology. Arguably, her position suffers from a similar reductionism and myopia to the historical institutions that structure political struggles between social classes or groups as the empirical realism of Achen and Bartels. Nonetheless, the political conclusions she draws are very different. Mouffe privileges the construction of a radical popular 'we' over the diversity of identities and aspirations that can be pursued – collectively or otherwise – within liberal democratic institutions and practices. Her self-conscious progressive populism is a far cry from Madisononian American realism.

Of greater political potential perhaps is Bonnie Honig's (2017) work on 'public things'. For Honig, public things are those objects, institutions and infrastructures that are publicly owned or subject to public oversight or use: libraries, parks, prisons, universities, transportation networks, power supplies and so on. These are things upon which democracy is constitutively dependent: democracy is 'rooted in common love for, antipathy to, and contestation of public things'. Without them, democracy is reduced to procedures, polling and policing – all necessary but not sufficient for democratic life. Public things do not simply take care of our needs, but also 'constitute us, complement us, limit us, thwart us, and interpellate us into democratic citizenship' (Honig, 2017, pp 4–5).

Privatisation and the reduction of the values of public institutions to the pursuit of efficiency or market competition therefore denude democracy of the public objects upon which it depends. Active citizenship must be mobilised around their defence, sustaining the infrastructure of citizenship and contesting its depletion. Here then is a radical democratic agenda replete with tangible objects of public love: from national parks to urban public spaces, clean water supplies, green energy systems, public universities and veterans' homes. In the United Kingdom, it would embrace the National Health Service, the BBC, ancient woodlands, public utilities and the like.[2] These are all arenas in which 'public work' and the everyday engagement of citizens with the maintenance and repair of their civic institutions takes place (Ober, 2008; Boyte, 2011).

From this brief sketch, it is clear that a democratic politics which draws upon the insights of realist political theory need not acquiesce to the status quo or surrender to apparently immutable human traits that inhibit any projects of progressive political change. We can find in 'real' history and politics claims for justice, recognition and equality. These values are elaborated, nurtured and advanced in real political struggles, not simply imposed from outside of history. Indeed, a realist refusal to acknowledge that democracy is sustained by anything other than a mutual interest in avoiding violence may precisely misjudge how far the defence of democratic institutions rests on deeper norms or commitments – to freedom, equality or the common good. In other

---

[2] This list can potentially grow to include many other commonly owned resources such as land, housing and renewable energy facilities. See Chapter Fourteen in this book.

words, pessimistic realists may be denuding democracy of the normative resources upon which its defence against authoritarian assaults depends.[3]

Realists are also attentive to systematic concentrations of power. Accordingly, they give substantial weight to how the rules of the game in a democracy are configured and to the ways in which the realm of democratic politics can be expanded, rather than closed down by technocratic or market imperatives. Erring towards the view that powerful interests and forces will always be at work at different sites of power – whether in the state, market or community – draws renewed attention to questions of political inequality, democratic accountability and whether the norms governing different realms of public life can prevent the domination that results from concentrations of power. It can also equip democrats with realistic insights about their opponents: in political struggles, you have to know what your enemy is up to.

Conclusion

A democratic agenda informed by realist thinking should find room for direct and deliberative democracy, alongside representative institutions. Recent reforms of political parties to open them up to new members, registered supporters and primary contests represent a response to processes of (state-centric) hollowing out. Seeking to row these back under the guise of political responsibility and effective government is likely to weaken democracy, not strengthen it. Similarly, the extension of deliberative democracy and attention to how citizens form political preferences and engage in debate in wider society need not be premised on excluding emotions and passions from politics, or privileging deliberation over political contest, and the formation and enactment of political programmes. Civic and democratic innovations can supplement and enrich political action, as long as we are realistic about how they are structured, their relationship to formal institutions of representative democracy and constitutional law, and the ever-present threat of elite capture (Tam, 2018).

Yet whatever their modalities, the success of democratic reforms will depend in large part on the reduction of socioeconomic inequalities. A common thread in most recent democratic theory – from empirical to liberal and radical realists, civic republicans to liberal democrats – is that economic inequality corrodes political equality and fosters oligarchy. State-citizen cooperation should therefore not be confined to guiding

---

[3]   I am indebted to Marc Stears for this point.

government activities, but must extend into reforming power relations and resource distribution across society.

References

Achen, C. H. and Bartels, L. M. (2016) *Democracy for Realists*, Princeton, NJ: Princeton University Press.

Beramendi, P., Häusermann, S., Kitschelt, H. and Kriesi, H. (eds) (2015) *The Politics of Advanced Capitalism*, New York: Cambridge University Press.

Boyte, H. (2011), 'Constructive politics as public work', *Political Theory* 39 (5): 630–660.

Crouch, C. (2004) *Post-Democracy*, Cambridge: Polity.

Curato, N., Dryzek, J.S., Ercan, S.A., Hendriks, C.M. and Niemeyer. S. (2017) 'Twelve key findings in deliberative democracy research' in Fishkin, J.S. and Mansbridge, J. (eds) *The Prospects and Limits of Deliberative Democracy*, Special Issue of *Daedalus, Journal of the American Academy of Arts and Sciences*, 146 (3): 28–38, Cambridge, MA: MIT Press.

Farrell, D. (2014) '"Stripped down" or reconfigured democracy', *West European Politics* 37 (2): 439–455.

Finlayson, L. (2017) 'With radicals like these, who needs conservatives? Doom, gloom, and realism in political theory', *European Journal of Political Theory* 16 (3): 264–282.

Fishkin, J. S. and Mansbridge, J. (eds) (2017) *The Prospects and Limits of Deliberative Democracy*, Special Issue of *Daedalus, Journal of the American Academy of Arts and Sciences* 146 (3), Cambridge, MA: Daedalus.

Fukuyama, F. (1992) *The End of History and the Last Man*, London: Penguin.

Galston, W. (2010) 'Realism in political theory', *European Journal of Political Theory* 9 (4): 385–411.

Gillman, H.R. (2016) *Democracy Reinvented: participatory budgeting and civic innovation in America*, Washington, DC: Brookings Institution Press.

Hendriks, C. (2016) 'Coupling citizens and elites in deliberative systems: the role of institutional design', *European Journal of Political Research* 55 (1): 43–60.

Honig, B. (1993) *Political Theory and the Displacement of Politics*, New York: Cornell University Press.

Honig, B. (2017) *Public Things: democracy in disrepair*, New York: Fordham University Press, Kindle edition.

Honig, B. and Stears, M. (2014) 'James Tully's agonistic realism', in Tully, J., *On Global Citizenship: James Tully in dialogue*, London: Bloomsbury Academic.

Iversen, T. and Soskice, D. (2009) 'Distribution and redistribution: the shadow of the nineteenth century', *World Politics* 61 (3): 438–486.

Lee, C. (2015) *Do-It-Yourself Democracy: the rise of the public engagement industry*, New York: Oxford University Press.

Lee, C. and Romano, Z. (2013) 'Democracy's new discipline: public deliberation as organizational strategy', *Organisation Studies* 34 (5–6): 733-753.

Mair, P. (2013) *Ruling the Void: the hollowing out of Western democracy*, London: Verso.

Miller, D. (2016) 'In what sense must political philosophy be political?', *Social Philosophy and Policy* 33 (1–2): 155-174.

Mouffe, C. (2013) *Agonistics: thinking the world politically*, London: Verso, Kindle edition.

Ober, J. (2008) 'The original meaning of "democracy": capacity to do things, not majority rule', *Constellations* 15 (1): 3-9.

Oesch, D. and Rennwald, L. (2018) 'Electoral competition in Europe's new tripolar political space: class voting for the left, centre-right and radical right', *European Journal of Political Research*, doi:10.1111/1475-6765.12259

Offe, C. (2017) 'Political deliberation and the adversarial principle', in Fishkin, J. S. and Mansbridge, J. (eds), *The Prospects and Limits of Deliberative Democracy*, Special Issue of *Daedalus, Journal of the American Academy of Arts and Sciences* 146 (3), Cambridge, MA: Daedalus.

Owen, D. and Smith, G. (2015) 'Survey article: deliberation, democracy, and the systemic turn', *The Journal of Political Philosophy* 23 (2): 213-234.

Runciman, D. (2018) *How Democracy Ends*, London: Profile Books.

Sabl, A. (2015) 'The two cultures of democratic theory: responsiveness, democratic quality, and the empirical-normative divide', *Perspectives on Politics* 13 (2): 345-365.

Sabl, A. (2017) 'Review symposium: elections and responsive government', *Perspectives on Politics* 15 (1): 157-158.

Sabl, A. (2017b) 'Realist liberalism: an agenda', *Critical Review of International Social and Political Philosophy* 20 (3): 366-384.

Schäfer, A. and Streeck, W. (eds) (2013) *Politics in the Age of Austerity*, Cambridge: Polity.

Setälä, M. (2017) 'Connecting deliberative mini publics to representative decision-making', *European Journal of Political Research* 56: 846-863.

Shapiro, I. (2017) 'Collusion in restraint of democracy: against political deliberation', in Fishkin, J. S. and Mansbridge, J. (eds), *The Prospects and Limits of Deliberative Democracy*, Special Issue of *Daedalus, Journal of the American Academy of Arts and Sciences* 146, (3), Cambridge, MA: Daedalus.

Simon, J. et al (2017) *Digital Democracy: the tools transforming political engagement*, London: NESTA.

Sirianni, C. (2017) 'Review essay, civic innovation: yesterday, today and tomorrow', *Perspectives on Politics* 15 (1): 122–127.

Stears, M. (2007) 'Review article: liberalism and the politics of compulsion', *British Journal of Political Science* 37: 533–553.

Streeck, W. (2017) *Buying Time: the delayed crisis of democratic capitalism* (2nd edn), London: Verso.

Tam, H. (2018) *Time to Save Democracy: how to govern ourselves in the age of anti-politics*, Bristol: Policy Press.

Williams, B. (2005) *In the Beginning Was the Deed*, Princeton, NJ: Princeton University Press.

3

The Importance of Collective Control

Anna Coote

If the aim is to build more cooperative relationships between citizens and the state, much depends on how far citizens are willing to engage in the process of change – especially those who are least active and vocal in political decision making.

It is rarely just apathy that makes people reluctant to engage. More often, it is a well-founded scepticism that anything one says or does can make a useful difference – and this feeling is particularly widespread among those who are poor and powerless. It is part of an exclusionary process, driven by unequal power relationships across economic, political, social and cultural domains, and characterised by unjust distributions of resources, capabilities and rights (Popay, 2010, p 295). The problem is intensified when people are invited to engage in decisions – often by well-intentioned public authorities – only to find that nothing changes as a result. At this point, scepticism combines with 'consultation fatigue' (Richards et al 2007, p 16), to produce a cynicism about the chances of anything called 'engagement' or 'participation' being more than a cheap trick. These feelings give rise to two significant barriers to cooperation: people lack confidence in their own ability to make a difference; and they distrust the efficacy of the process (of building cooperation) and the motivations behind it.

Both problems can be traced to the distribution of power and, particularly, control. Degrees of confidence and trust are strongly influenced by how far people control what happens when they engage with the state. Understanding what constitutes control and what enables people to exercise it is therefore vital to renewing state-citizen cooperation. Whatever the aims or intentions of public authorities, whatever methods of engagement and decision making they employ, they will fail unless they start from here.

In this chapter I focus first on control: how it is defined, its component parts, how it is generated and the implications for systems change. I then turn to the concept of the commons and the process of commoning – by which I mean claiming and controlling a range of resources that are essential for meeting human needs – and explore the implications for policy and practice.

Defining control

The terms 'power' and 'control' are sometimes used interchangeably. For the purpose of this chapter, I take 'power' to mean the ability to carry out a desired goal despite resistance and 'control' to mean exercising or constraining power over someone or something. Unsurprisingly, control is complex. It operates at multiple levels and in different ways: individual and collective, real and perceived, direct and indirect. There is a fundamental distinction between 'actual control, or the objective control of conditions present in the context and the person, and perceived control, or an individual's belief about how much control is available' (Mann, 1986; Skinner, 1996, p 551; Helzer and Jayawickreme, 2015, p 654).

In their review of evidence connecting control and health, Whitehead and colleagues draw together a range of terms that are used to describe control. At the individual level these include: autonomy; control over one's destiny; ontological security; a sense of coherence; and power to exert one's influence to effect change. Collective control has been described in terms of community empowerment, cultural continuity, collective efficacy, power with (rather than over) others and a range of interacting 'social protective factors' including community capacity and competence, social cohesion, social capital and collective efficacy (Whitehead et al, 2016, p 53).

I am mainly concerned here with collective control exercised locally, and with control shared between citizens and the state, for four reasons. First, when people seek to improve their local living conditions, they are likely to achieve more by acting together than by acting alone. Secondly, I take the goal of renewing state–citizen cooperation to be more about public authorities relating to citizens in groups than dealing with them one by one. Thirdly, building collective control locally provides a necessary foundation for building cooperative relationships between citizens and state at regional and national levels. And, finally, cooperation implies shared control.

Understanding the components of control

What is it, then, that gives rise to collective control? What does it consist of and how do groups of people develop it? Drawing on a range of overlapping theoretical perspectives, we can understand control in terms of capabilities, critical awareness and agency. Control is generated when people have the practical means and functioning capacity that enable them to lead the kind of life they have reason to value, and to do this at a communal level by acting together (Sen, 1999; Papaioannoi, 2016, p 306). At the same time, it is important that people build and share knowledge about the barriers and opportunities they face, and consciously determine to address them (Freire, 1970; Woodall et al, 2012, p 743). When people have the necessary capacity, consciousness and intent, they must be able to 'enact a process that drives change', whether directly or indirectly (Ling and Dale, 2013, p 4).

Building on this theoretical framework, the New Economics Foundation (NEF) has developed a dynamic model of control for the practical purpose of evaluating a programme funded by People's Health Trust, 'Local Conversations'. The programme seeks to address the underlying causes of health inequalities by enabling disadvantaged communities to take control of decisions and actions that affect their daily lives (Coote, 2016). In the model shown in Figure 3.1, collective control comprises a range of interacting components. In order to exert control, people must be *socially connected* with others who live in their locality, with whom they can build a sense of belonging and trust, mutual support and solidarity. They need *knowledge, understanding and skills*, so that they become aware of local conditions and their underlying causes, of local power structures, possible routes to change and how to take effective action. They must have *resources*, such as access to money and other assets including places to meet. They must be able to exert *influence*, to have their views heeded as well as heard, and respected by those in positions of power. And they must have *confidence* that together they can make or influence changes that they consider desirable.

These components of control interact dynamically, as Figure 3.1 indicates. The *experiences* of actual control interact with *feelings* of being in control and the two can reinforce each other. Where a group achieves positive changes, this can not only improve local conditions, but also strengthen the components of control and increase the sense of being able to effect change. Conversely, where positive change doesn't happen, any sense of control can drain away as disappointment and cynicism set in.

Figure 3.1: NEF's dynamic model of control

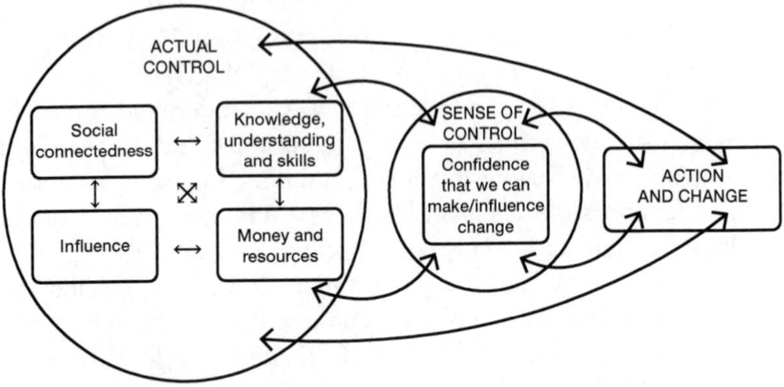

Source: New Economics Foundation, http://www.peopleshealthtrust.org.uk/news/blog/what-do-we-mean-when-we-talk-about-control

Overlapping ideas are reflected in the World Bank's framework of empowerment – which identifies four elements: access to information; inclusion and participation; accountability; and local organisational capacity (World Bank, 2016). Further insights come from researchers evaluating Communities in Control (CiC). This is a major UK programme exploring 'whether community empowerment helps people living in disadvantaged circumstances to live the longer, healthier lives enjoyed by better off groups' (Popay, 2018). They identify conditions required for control to be exercised across three dimensions: through structural means that enable people to decide and act collectively ('power to'); by building capacity within the group ('power within'); and by making alliances with others ('power with').

In the CiC study, the emergence of collective control was found to be shaped through existing relationships between residents and the histories of their relationships with local organisations, as well as through tailored interventions by external bodies. The experience of developing collective control is described as 'unstable, subject to struggle, and part of a continuing, dynamic, nonlinear process' (Ponsford et al, 2015, p 64).

Control, health and inequality

The three studies mentioned here have drawn on mounting evidence that having more control over one's life is associated with better physical and mental health. In 2010, the Marmot review of health inequalities in England, *Fair Society, Healthy Lives*, declared that its central ambition was 'to create the conditions for people to take control over their own lives'. This exhaustive and influential study of the underlying determinants of health recognises control both as a product of favourable living conditions and as a factor contributing to better health: 'If the conditions in which people are born, grow, live, work, and age are favourable, and more equitably distributed, then they will have more control over their lives in ways that will influence their own health and health behaviours, and those of their families' (The Marmot Review, 2010, p 18). It recommends that 'Political, civic and managerial leadership in public services should focus on creating the conditions in which people and communities take control, to lead flourishing lives, increase health expectancy and reduce disparities in health expectancy across the social gradient' (The Marmot Review, 2010, p 152). This underlines the importance of renewing citizen–state cooperation. If public authorities want to create the appropriate conditions, they can only do so by working *with* the people concerned: they cannot to it *to* them. That means sharing control.

The Marmot Review explores ways in which unequal social and economic conditions influence people's health and life expectancy. Since control is one of the underlying determinants of health, it follows that it ought to be accessible to people in equal measure – not monopolised by those with deeper pockets and sharper elbows. This matters for the quality of state–citizen cooperation as much as for the health of the population. Those who are excluded and marginalised are least inclined to cooperate with the state, usually for good reason, as I noted at the start of this chapter. So the challenge is to break out of the negative cycle whereby people who are poor and powerless have less control over their lives and destinies than those who are better off, and consequently tend to have poorer quality of life and lower levels of health, as well as less confidence that they can change things for the better and deeper distrust of public authorities.

The aim is then to reshape patterns of influence into a 'virtuous circle', where greater equality of control helps to reduce health inequalities and build a healthier democracy. Efforts to strengthen citizen–state cooperation will need to ensure not just more control for citizens but more equal control among them. This involves tackling inequalities through social and economic measures, including access to decent jobs and adequate income, and to education, health and other public services (the 'social wage'). It involves interventions that are designed to be inclusive, that reach out to those who are excluded and marginalised, and that specifically aim to build the capacity of such groups, to enable them to participate and take control (Coote, 2011, p 288). There is a wealth of experience of how this may be achieved, some of which is captured in Figure 3.2. Shared control is integral to the process.

Figure 3.2: Guidance for public authorities seeking to engage marginalised groups

- Identify those whose voices are seldom heard and locate them, using outreach and other community development techniques.
- Meet marginalised groups on their own territory and on their own terms, rather than trying to include token representatives in other participative exercises.
- Let marginalised groups define their own agendas and ways of working – respect their wisdom and experience and treat them as equals.
- Share their language – literally and metaphorically.
- Consider more creative methods for communicating and working together – for example, using artwork, theatre and song instead of the normal stuff of meetings.
- Invest in co-ordination and facilitation and in building and sustaining networks.
- Keep on reaching out – one-off gestures won't help.
- Feed back, reflect, learn and continue to improve ways of sharing responsibility.

Changing public authorities

In order to build control among the people they are supposed to serve, public authorities themselves must change. They must learn to cede power to others, to share control, to see people as assets, not just problems to be fixed, to respect and value wisdom based on lived experience, to take risks and to embrace changes not of their own choosing.

The essence of a cooperative relationship is mutual trust and reciprocity, and being able to bring together different kinds of knowledge and skill so that these complement each other. This means developing appropriate methods of engagement, learning to co-produce decisions and actions, and changing systems to support cooperation and shared control. I will touch briefly on each of these themes.

Methods of engagement

There is a growing body of knowledge about deliberative dialogue and participatory decision making, discussed in more detail elsewhere in this book (see, for example, the chapters in Part Two). Methods include citizens' juries, deliberative workshops, public forums and assemblies, as well as online discussions and forums; these often overlap in their approach, and are deployed by public authorities to engage people in decisions that affect their lives. They are usually regarded as a way of grounding and guiding the work of elected representatives, rather than pre-empting them, and enriching rather than supplanting representative democracy.

At best, they are informed by a nuanced understanding of the risks and opportunities of engagement and participation; they involve a broadly representative sample of people affected by the matter in hand, including marginalised groups, and manifestly influence subsequent decisions and actions: participants can gain real control in the process. At worst, they are superficial or token gestures that seek to co-opt public opinion and fend off dissent: participants often feel manipulated and out of control. So one important measure of an authority's capacity to change is how far it is genuinely committed to – and engaged in – sharing control through appropriate forms of deliberative dialogue and participatory decision making, not as an occasional exotic experiment, but as a standard or default approach.

Co-producing decisions and actions

The currency of a good idea is quickly debased when the language used to describe it is applied too widely and indiscriminately. This is a problem for co-production, now in popular usage across the UK public sector. The principles of co-production nevertheless remain a valuable guide for those seeking to improve the quality of state–citizen cooperation by sharing control. It goes beyond participative methods of engagement to the substantive business of getting things done.

Drawing on work by Elinor Ostrom, on early experiments with time banking, and on long traditions of mutual aid and community development (Chapter Seven in this book), co-production has been developed as an approach to policy and practice that brings together professionals and others working in public authorities, and members of the public (citizens and residents) who have different interests, knowledge and experience. Rather than those in the former group doing things to or for those in the latter group, they work together to produce ideas, insights, decisions, services and other activities, outputs and outcomes (Parks et al, 1981, pp 1001-11; Cahn, 2001; Boyle et al, 2010; Coote, 2011, pp 291-300).

Co-production is, essentially, about sharing responsibility and control between people who are regarded – and treat each other – as having equal worth and being able to make contributions of equal value to a shared enterprise. It recognises that people have different attributes and make different contributions. Thus, the codified knowledge of professionals can be combined with the experiential knowledge of citizens. The relationship is reciprocal, with each side of the partnership benefiting from the exchange and recognising that its own success in the shared venture depends on what the other can contribute. While it may involve a great variety of activities, processes and tools, co-production is said to be recognisable where it exhibits most or all of the features in Figure 3.3 (Doyal and Gough, 1991, ch 14; Boyle et al, 2010).

Figure 3.3: Defining features of co-production

- Recognising people as assets: transforming the perception of people from passive recipients of services and burdens on the system into one where they are equal partners in designing and delivering services.
- Building on people's existing capabilities: altering the delivery model of public services from a deficit approach to one that provides opportunities to recognise and grow people's capabilities and actively support them to put these to use with individuals and communities.
- Mutuality and reciprocity: offering people a range of incentives to engage, which enable us to work in reciprocal relationships with professionals and with each other, where there are mutual responsibilities and expectations.
- Peer support networks: engaging peer and personal networks alongside professionals as the best way of transferring knowledge and supporting change.
- Blurring distinctions: blurring the distinction between professionals and recipients, and between producers and consumers of services, by reconfiguring the way services are developed and delivered.
- Facilitating rather than delivering: enabling public service agencies to become catalysts and facilitators of change rather than central providers of services themselves.

Source: Boyle et al (2010, p 9)

Notably for this discussion, co-production implies radical change for public authorities, as the last two features in Figure 3.3 indicate: the dividing line between 'them' and 'us' (providers and recipients of services) begins to dissolve, while public servants take on enabling, brokering and facilitating roles. Efforts have been made by some public authorities to integrate the principles of co-production into their commissioning frameworks, through which they contract providers of publicly funded services. This can include co-designing the commissioning process itself, as well as making it a condition that contractors co-produce services (Slay and Penny, 2014).

There are countless examples of how co-production has empowered people and groups, and improved their wellbeing (Boyle et al, 2010; NESTA et al, 2012; Gallagher and Duneen, 2016). But how far co-production can help to transform the relationship between citizens and state will depend on how it is implemented, how it affects those involved, and how deeply it is embedded in organisational systems. It can be a genuinely empowering process, or one that chiefly provides cover for austerity measures by seeking to substitute public services with unpaid labour.

The UK Care Act 2014, for example, provides statutory guidance to local authorities, saying they should 'actively promote participation in providing interventions that are co-produced with individuals, families, friends, carers and the community'. However, the Act coincided with deep cuts in public funding for local authorities, greatly diminishing the capacity of publicly funded services to play their part in social care. If people are left to themselves to deliver social care, with inadequate public resources to support them, they will end up *doing* more, but with little or no *control* over the overall quality of care, or over their own time and autonomy. The reciprocal feature of co-production breaks down.

Changing systems

The fact that it is possible to use participative engagement and co-production in ways that are either more or less conducive to enhancing collective control and state–citizen cooperation highlights the importance of paying attention to the systems within which public authorities and people interact.

A 'system' can be thought of as a configuration of interacting, interdependent parts that are connected through a web of relationships (Holland, 2000). 'Systems thinking' acknowledges that these configurations can cause problems, even when they are well intentioned, and that problems can be solved by changing systems. It looks beyond actors and institutions to focus on relationships and interconnections, recognising that systems are dynamic and non-linear, and that changes can ripple through systems continuously (Burns, 2014). 'Systems change' is a process of radically transforming 'thinking, assumptions and ways of working'; it calls for 'new facilitative forms of leadership and extensive collaboration' and involves a continuous process of 'innovation, reflection and learning' (Hough, 2014).

Broadly, any effort to enhance collective control and/or build state-citizen cooperation will need to adopt a systems perspective, taking account of the complex web of material elements, interconnections, goals, meanings and power relations that interact dynamically within a system; as well as anticipating non-linear change, feedback loops, and unintended and indirect consequences (Burns, 2007; Meadows, 2008). The NEF model of control in Figure 3.1 reflects at least some of this ambition.

For a public authority, the point is not just to try to change bits of itself – a policy, a department, a commissioning protocol or a particular cohort of workers, or even a leadership team (although these things may be necessary) – but to recognise the whole system within which it operates, and the component parts. It will then need to work out a plan – ideally co-produced with citizens – to change the system so that it supports cooperation and shared control, and is able to sustain that support in the medium and longer term.

Taking control of essential resources

The goal of people taking control over their lives and destinies has been a strong theme in the work of the New Economics Foundation. It reflects a commitment to building an economy that serves the interests of people and the planet, as a viable alternative to the neoliberal model, where human and natural resources are treated as throughputs in an economic system whose main objective is to increase productivity, profits and GDP (gross domestic product) growth. Being a throughput is not a recipe for empowerment or sustainability.

This goal has prompted us to study not only what control means and how it can be enhanced – which I have discussed – but also what it is that people need to control. We have drawn inspiration from growing movements to claim and control 'the commons'. This refers to resources that are life's necessities. They include natural resources such as land, water, air and sources of energy; cultural resources including access to digital platforms; and social resources, meaning the relationships and activities through which we help each other participate and flourish in society. We argue that none of these are simply nice to have: they are the means by which we meet basic human needs. Accordingly, they should not be appropriated by those who have wealth and power, but held in common so that they are accessible to everyone, by right, now and in future. This is a 'whole systems' perspective, which recognises that social, environmental and cultural resources are not separate but interdependent: they are all essential to human survival and wellbeing and, as such, we argue, they should be held in common, subject to similar claims and expectations (Mattei, 2012; Coote, 2017; Gough, 2017, pp 38-63).

There are multiple ways in which the concept can be realised in practice. Examples include managing land through local trusts for the benefit of local people, building affordable homes that are controlled by the people who live in them, and taking water supplies, local energy generation, telecommunications and bus services into shared ownership at municipal level. Social wealth funds are a form of commons (where surpluses produced by wealth-generating enterprises are invested for the common good). In the social sphere, parent-led childcare cooperatives and community-led social care systems and time banks are expressions of the same idea: shared control of essential resources for the benefit of all (Coote, 2017).

Our main focus at NEF has been on a 'social commons' that reasserts and safeguards the collective ideal. This was firmly embedded in the post-war welfare settlement but has been severely eroded by market rules, privatisation and a consumerist ethos of individualism, competition and choice. The collective ideal stands for pooling resources, sharing risks, looking after each other and making sure that every one of us has an equal chance to flourish and participate – not just now, but into the future.

In a nutshell, the idea of a social commons implies equal rights of access to resources required for meeting social needs. It calls for a radically different set of mechanisms for deciding how needs are defined and for designing and delivering services and other activities to meet them. Control shifts to the local level and is shared between people with professional expertise and those whose wisdom is drawn from everyday experience. The principles of co-production take centre stage. Decisions are shaped through democratic dialogue. Local initiatives are fostered and supported by public authorities. Care is generated through relationships rather than transactions. There is room for enterprise but not for profiteering. And, critically for this discussion, the role of state institutions is transformed so that they become champions and guarantors of shared ownership and control, and of equal access and standards of care, as well as fair distribution of tax revenues.

The idea of the commons throws up a number of practical and political challenges and it is beyond the scope of this chapter to explore these in detail (some are dealt with by Pat Conaty in Chapter Fourteen). I will focus here on the relationship between 'bottom-up' and 'top-down' politics, which bears upon the question of state–citizen cooperation – touching briefly on three issues: management, decision making and the role of the state.

Management of the commons

One longstanding critique of the commons is that resources that are freely available to all will soon be exhausted because everyone will take what they want regardless of the needs of others. This has been called the 'tragedy of the commons' and has been used for many years to justify private ownership of land and other essential resources. However, as Elinor Ostrom has famously demonstrated, this it is largely a myth. Ostrom sets out eight specific design principles for effective management of 'common pool resources' (CPRs). One is that people who use resources must be able to participate in decisions about how to manage them; another is that higher level authorities should recognise and support the self-determination of communities involved in claiming and controlling resources (Ostrom, 1990).

Making decisions about the commons

If, as Ostrom proposes, people who use common resources are to participate in decisions about how to manage them, how should this be done? For the purpose of building a social commons, NEF has proposed a three-way dialogue that combines laypeople with professionals and other experts, and with democratically elected representatives. It combines elements of participatory and representative democracy, rather than forms of direct democracy or plebiscite.

The model of a constitutional convention could be adapted for the purpose, building on practical experience in the UK, such as the Scottish Constitutional Convention, which paved the way for the creation of the Scottish Constitution, and from other countries including Ireland, Iceland, Canada and the Netherlands (Kroll and Swann, 2015).

Figure 3.4 suggests how locally generated initiatives and multiple local conversations could feed into people's assemblies at regional level, which would in turn inform and shape parliamentary action to facilitate and support the process of building the social commons across the country. Control is anchored locally. Decisions about local needs and ways of meeting them are generated through deliberative dialogue, with local conversations informing people's assemblies. Resources are distributed, standards set and rights of equal access are ensured through legislation and public institutions. The state works with and for the people 'to enable us all to work together, share risks and pool resources, in order to claim, build and secure access to life's necessities' (Coote, 2017, p 14).

The role of the state

For some, the commoning movement is anti-statist. It starts from the premise that people are best left to their own devices to run their lives and neighbourhoods, with little or no interference from the state. For others (with whom I agree), the state has a crucial role to play, not least because it is the only vehicle that can promote and safeguard equality between different groups and geographical areas. Without that vehicle, there may be more 'commoning' but there will be less social justice (Mestrum, 2015).

Figure 3.4: A three-way dialogue for building a social commons

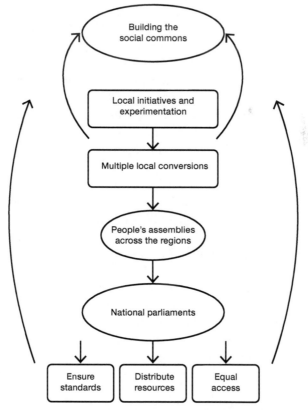

Source: Coote (2017)

This calls for a new kind of partnership between assertive local action and a transformed public realm. To realise the ideal of the commons at scale, public authorities will need to be open and democratic, and shaped through democratic dialogue, and to operate in multiple layers, with lines of authority following the principles of subsidiarity. They will ensure fair and equal access and decent standards, and they will distribute public funds to make this possible. The people who work in them will see their role as facilitators, enablers and co-producers of the common good.

These are ambitious goals and they are certainly not going to be realised swiftly. However, inspiration can be drawn from a number of European cities. For example, in Barcelona, in northern Spain, the radical party Barcelona En Comú, which at the time of writing has a majority in the city government, promotes what it calls a 'collaborative economy'. This includes many hundreds of cooperatives and other community-led and public interest organisations, such as Guifi.net, an internet access enterprise and Som Energia Coop, a green energy cooperative, which promotes 'locally generated, clean, sustainable electricity' for ordinary homeowners (Bollier, 2016; Van Kouwen, 2016).

In Bologna in northern Italy, the city government has introduced a pioneering regulation for 'the care and regeneration of urban commons'. This envisages the city as 'a collaborative social ecosystem' where the local state hosts a large number of self-organised, shared ventures that aim to serve the common interest. There are more than 90 different 'pacts of collaboration' between citizen groups and the Bolognese government, which specify the scope of each project and respective responsibilities. 'These fall into three categories: living together (collaborative services), growing together (co-ventures) and working together (co-production)' (Bollier, 2015; see also LabGov, 2014).

The Flemish city of Ghent has endorsed an ambitious 'commons transition plan', which considers in detail how to build a 'partner' city – one that enables and empowers three developments: 'commons-oriented civic initiatives'; 'generative market forms', which sustain the commons and create livelihoods for the core contributors; and 'facilitative types of support from civil society organisations'. The Ghent plan includes a model of 'poly-governance', with state, markets and civil society working together to support and scale up the commons ideal (Bauwens, 2017).

These initiatives illustrate the importance of devolved powers (cities in England, for example, with the possible exception of the Greater

London Authority, would be unable to replicate their approach). Even with devolved powers, they are not enough to supplant or even threaten the dominant paradigm. But they certainly chip away at conventional wisdom about how political and economic systems should operate. All three cities show a willingness to support local residents in claiming, building and controlling local resources. They point towards a new kind of politics where people are in control, supported by the state, and where state-citizen cooperation is the norm.

Conclusion

In this chapter I have argued that the issue of control is central to the challenge of strengthening state-citizen cooperation. I have focused on collective control, exploring what it means, why it matters and how it is generated. Control operates at multiple levels and in different ways: individual and collective, real and perceived, direct and indirect. It impacts on health and equality as well as on the democratic relationships. The determinants of control interact dynamically and can reinforce each other to create negative or positive cycles.

For this to happen, public authorities themselves must change, for example by developing appropriate methods of engagement, learning to co-produce decisions and actions, and changing systems to support cooperation and shared control.

Examples of shared control can be found in 'commoning' movements, where people get together to claim and control resources that are essential for human survival and wellbeing. The theory and practice of the commons brings into sharp relief the relationship between 'bottom-up' and 'top-down' politics, which is central to state-citizen cooperation. Inspiration can be drawn from pioneering cities such as Bologna, Barcelona and Ghent, where city governments are changing systems to champion and support local initiatives that put local people in control. These initiatives are far from perfect and subject to much criticism, so they should not be idealised. Nevertheless, they provide some useful pointers towards building a 'virtuous circle', where greater control, shared more equally among citizens, can reduce inequalities in wellbeing and build a healthier democracy.

References

Bauwens, M. (2017) 'A commons transition plan for the city of Ghent', P2P Foundation. https://blog.p2pfoundation.net/a-commons-transition-plan-for-the-city-of-ghent/2017/09/14

Bollier, B. (2015) 'Bologna, a laboratory for urban commoning'. www.bollier.org/blog/bologna-laboratory-urban-commoning

Bollier, B. (2016) 'Barcelona's brave struggle to advance the commons'. www.bollier.org/blog/barcelonas-brave-struggle-advance-commons

Boyle, D., Coote, A., Sherwood C. and Slay, J. (2010) *Right Here, Right Now*, London: NEF and NESTA.

Burns, D. (2007) *Systemic Action Research: a strategy for whole systems change*, Bristol: Policy Press.

Burns, D. (2014) 'Systemic action research: changing system dynamics to support sustainable change', *Action Research* 12 (1): 3-18.

Cahn, E. (2001), *No More Throwaway People: the co-production imperative*, Washington, DC: Essential Books.

Coote, A. (2011), 'Equal participation: making shared social responsibility work for everyone', *Trends in Social Cohesion* (23): 288-290. https://neweconomics.org/uploads/files/Building-a-New-Social-Commons-WEB-version.pdf

Coote, A. (2016) 'How communities build control', New Economics Foundation. http://neweconomics.org/2016/11/communities-build-control/?_sf_s=dynamic+model+of+control

Coote, A. (2017) 'Building a new social commons', New Economics Foundation. https://neweconomics.org/uploads/files/Building-a-New-Social-Commons-WEB-version.pdf

Doyal, L. and Gough, I. (1991) *A theory of human need*, Basingstoke: Palgrave.

Freire, P. (1970) *Pedagogy of the Oppressed*, Continuum.

Gallagher, M. and Duneen, R. (2016) *Seeing is Believing: co-production case studies from Wales*. Version 6, 12 January. www.goodpractice.wales/SharedFiles/Download.aspx?pageid=96&mid=187&fileid=78

Gough, I. (2017), *Heat, Greed and Human Need: climate change, capitalism and sustainable wellbeing*, Cheltenham: Edward Elgar.

Helzer, E. G. and Jayawickreme, E. (2015) 'Control and the "good life": primary and secondary control as distinct indicators of well-being', *Social Psychological and Personality Science* 6 (6): 653-660.

Holland, J. H. (2000) *Emergence: From chaos to order*, Oxford: Oxford University Press.

Hough, J. (2014) 'Changing systems for people with multiple needs: Learning from the literature', New Economics Foundation. www.fulfillinglives-ng.org.uk/wp-content/uploads/2014/10/Systems-change-summary-final-w-logos.pdf

Kroll, J. and Swann, J. (2015) 'We the people: constitutional decision making through citizen-led deliberative processes', Electoral Reform Society. www.electoral-reform.org.uk/wp-content/uploads/2017/06/We-the-people-citizen-led-constitutional-conventions.pdf

LabGov (2014) www.labgov.it/2014/10/31/bologna-regulation-on-public-collaboration/

Ling, C. and Dale, A. (2013) 'Agency and social capital: characteristics and dynamics', Community Development Journal 49 (1): 4-20.

Mann, M. (1986) The Sources of Power, Cambridge: Cambridge University Press.

The Marmot Review (2010) Fair Society, Healthy Lives: strategic review of health inequalities in England post-2010. www.parliament.uk/documents/fair-society-healthy-lives-full-report.pdf

Mattei, U. (2012) 'First thoughts for a phenomenology of the commons', in Bollier, B. and Helfrich, S. (eds) The Wealth of the Commons. http://wealthofthecommons.org/essay/first-thoughts-phenomenology-commons

Meadows, D. (2008) (ed Wright, D.) Thinking in Systems: a primer, Hartford: Chelsea Green Publishing.

Mestrum, F. (2015) The Social Commons: rethinking social justice in post-neoliberal societies, Brussels: Global Social Justice.

NESTA, New Economics Foundation and Innovation Unit (2012) People Powered Health Coproduction Catalogue. https://media.nesta.org.uk/documents/co-production_catalogue.pdf

Ostrom, E. (1990) Governing the Commons: the evolution of institutions for collective action, Cambridge: Cambridge University Press.

Papaioannou, T. (2016) 'Marx and Sen on incentives and justice: implications for innovation and development', Progress in Development Studies 16 (4): 297–313.

Parks, R., Baker, P., Kiser, L. Oakerson, R., Ostrom, E., Ostrom, V., Percy, S., Vandivort, M., Whitaker, G. and Wilson, R. (1981) 'Consumers as coproducers of public services: some economic and institutional considerations', Policy Studies Journal 9 (7): 1001-1011.

Ponsford, R., Collins, M., Egan, M., Lewis, S., Orton, L., Salway, S., Townsent., A., Halliday, E., Whitehead, M. and Popay, J. (2015) 'Development of a framework for identifying and measuring collective control as a social determinant of health: findings from an evaluation of a natural policy experiment in empowerment', *The Lancet*, 386: S64.

Popay, J. (2010) 'Understanding and tackling social exclusion', *Journal of Research in Nursing* 15 (4): 295–297.

Popay, J. (2018) 'Communities in control study', School of Public Health Research. http://sphr.lshtm.ac.uk/our-research/projects/health-inequalities-communities-in-control-study/

Richards, C., Blackstock, K. L. and Carter, C. E. (2004) *Practical Approaches to Participation*, SERG Policy Brief No 1, Series Editors: C. E. Carter and C. L. Spash, Aberdeen: Macaulay Institute.

Sen, A. (1999) *Development as Freedom*, Oxford: Oxford University Press.

Slay, J. and Penny J. (2014) *Commissioning for Outcomes and Co-production: a practical guide for local authorities*, New Economics Foundation. http://b.3cdn.net/nefoundation/974bfd0fd635a9ffcd_j2m6b04bs.pdf

Skinner, E. (1996) 'A guide to constructs of control', *Journal of Personality and Social Psychology* 71: 549-570.

Van Kouwen, S. (2016) 'The Commons Collaborative Economy explodes in Barcelona', Cities in Transition. https://citiesintransition.eu/publicatie/the-commons-collaborative-economy-explodes-in-barcelona

Whitehead, M., Pennington, A., Orton, L., Nayak, S., Petticrew, M., Sowden, A. and Whit, M. (2016) 'How could differences in 'control over destiny' lead to socio-economic inequalities in health? A synthesis of theories and pathways in the living environment', *Health and Place*: 51-61. http://eprints.whiterose.ac.uk/97671/1/1_s2.0_S1353829216000241_main.pdf

World Bank (2016) 'What is empowerment? Overview', PovertyNet. http://web.worldbank.org/WBSITE/EXTERNAL/TOPICS/EXTPOVERTY/EXTEMPOWERMENT/0,,contentMDK:20272299~pagePK:210058~piPK:210062~theSitePK:486411,00.html

Woodall, J., Warwick-Booth, L. and Cross, R. (2012) 'Has empowerment lost its power?', *Health Education Research* 27 (4): 742-5.

4

Deliberative Engagement with Complex Policies

Simon Burall

> The democratic method is that institutional arrangement for arriving at political decisions in which individuals acquire power to decide by means of a competitive struggle for the people's vote. (Schumpeter, 1976, p 269)

Nick Pearce has shown that the scope for democracy to embrace deliberative engagement is highly contested (Chapter Two of this book). Even if the sweeping rejection of participatory democracy by theorists such as Christopher Achen and Larry Bartels (2016) does not command general assent, much of the current thinking about democracy still appears to rest on Joseph Schumpeter's narrow conception of the 'democratic method'.[1] The foundation of this view is that elections allow voters to make their interests clear for politicians and civil servants to act on. This assumption is flawed, not least because party manifestos cover a wide range of public policies, from the economy, education and health to the environment and foreign policy, for example. Within each of these domains, the manifestos of all parties are a mixture of concrete proposals, broad sketches of an approach to policy and even broader political philosophy. It would be a very rare voter who agrees with every policy contained within.

Furthermore, legislatures such as the UK Parliament are elected for five-year terms. As the distance between the last election and the next widens, the likelihood of voters' interests changing increases. It

---

[1]   The quote from Schumpeter was first published in 1942.

is difficult to see how, even a couple of years after an election, elected representatives are supposed to ascertain their voters' interests in response to the latest unexpected event.

It is therefore impossible for the few bytes of information transmitted by voters' crosses on their ballot papers to convey the complexity of their interests across all the proposals contained within any party's manifesto. This does not mean we should toll the bell for representative democracy. Elections are important for determining broad political direction. They are also important as the ultimate accountability mechanism, putting the power to reject poorly performing governments or politicians into the hands of citizens. However, they are only one component of a functioning democracy.

Democracies develop a wide variety of mechanisms for collecting a clearer signal about the interests of their citizens. These include a well-functioning and plural media, a robust and diverse civil society, lobby groups, statutory consultations and more informal public engagement processes, for example. However, such mechanisms tend to privilege the loudest voices and magnify emotions at the expense of facts. This in turn reduces complex policy decisions about, for example, the impact of autonomous vehicles on national transport policy, or how to deal with climate change, to binary oppositional arguments. This means that the extremes of the debate drown out the tensions and trade-offs required to ensure that the majority of voters' intentions and interests are taken into account.

We need to find other ways to draw out and engage with voters' competing preferences and interests in order to inform and influence the wide range of highly complex and technical policy decisions required for the functioning of a modern economy.

In this chapter I will examine what can actually be achieved with properly structured deliberative engagement, particularly in relation to complex policies concerning scientific prediction and technological innovation, where a number of emerging applications, for example artificial intelligence, genome editing and even changes to energy generation and storage systems, have the potential to pervade many aspects of our lives and disrupt economic systems, healthcare, transport, and even the way we relate to each other and the state. It draws on over a decade of experience in the UK and internationally of using these techniques. It then explores their limitations and outlines a possible approach for institutionalising such processes in order to strengthen democratic control. And if they can be made to work in facilitating public deliberations and decisions over complex scientific and technological development, they will clearly have much to offer in helping to settle a wide range of other public policy issues as well.

The Sciencewise experiment

The Sciencewise programme was established by the UK Government in 2004 to develop public engagement processes on topics as diverse as nanotechnology, synthetic biology, climate change and data science (Warburton, 2011). It is also part of a wider global movement to engage the public more effectively in policy relating to scientific innovation, encompassing the pioneering Danish Board of Technology, and newer kids on the block such as Australia's newDemocracy foundation.

Specifically, Sciencewise supports a particular form of deliberative public engagement called public dialogue. Sciencewise dialogue projects are commissioned by government departments interested in understanding not only *what* the public thinks about a specific scientific innovation, but also *why* they think it and *how* they balance the trade-offs which will appear as applications resulting from the innovation emerge. In short, they open up policy makers' understanding of a wider range of views, perspectives and questions that relate to specific policy decisions as well as wider attitudes to public perspectives about the relationship between science and society.

Such projects involve between 50 and 200 members of the public recruited to represent the broad demographics of the UK. The participants meet at least twice for a day at a time. They hear evidence about the scientific innovation from scientists and policy makers working on the issue. They deliberate with their peers and the experts in small groups as they learn about the issue and engage in the moral, social and ethical issues it raises. Their responses to the sets of policy questions relating to the technology form one element of the evidence the commissioning government department will use as it develops policy to guide the development, regulation or licensing of the technology.

The programme is unusual in carrying out longitudinal evaluation of its dialogue projects, and revisiting policy areas even a decade after projects have finished in order to understand their ongoing impact. As a result, it can provide evidence of some significant impacts on public policy (Postle et al, 2015), demonstrating that well-conceived and executed public engagement processes can bring public voice to the heart of policy making. The 2012 Sciencewise-sponsored public dialogue on mitochondrial transfer demonstrates this perfectly.

Mitochondrial transfer: public voice informing complex and controversial policy

Mitochondria are present in nearly every cell in the human body and are responsible for turning the various components of our food into the forms of chemical energy used by the body. Around 1 in 4,300 people in the UK are affected by a disorder caused by mutations to mitochondrial DNA (Gorman et al, 2015).

Treating this requires taking the nucleus from an egg containing defective mitochondria and transferring it to an egg with healthy mitochondria from a second woman. The resulting embryo contains DNA from the mother, father *and* the person who donated the healthy mitochondria. This process affects the child that is born *and* the child's descendants. Such changes therefore raise significant ethical issues. At the time of the dialogue, the 1990 Human Fertilisation and Embryology Act prevented the modification of DNA in order to provide treatment which would affect such individuals and their descendants. The act covered the DNA involved in the inheritance of our unique characteristics in the nucleus of the cell, as well as mitochondrial DNA.

Policy makers were not at all certain that the public would support such a change to the act and, if so, under what conditions. Given this, in March 2012 the then Secretary of State for Health, Andrew Lansley, along with the Human Fertilisation and Embryology Authority (HFEA), commissioned a public dialogue as part of a wider suite of engagement activities. The aim was to provide evidence about the public's views on the social and ethical issues involved in changing the law to allow the creation of eggs containing DNA from three people for the purposes of treating the disorder.

The public dialogue consisted of three sets of deliberative workshops. The workshops took place in Newcastle, Cardiff and London over the course of two days. Participants were recruited to represent a range of demographic criteria including age, gender, socioeconomic status and family circumstances. Scientists attended the first set of days in each area to provide scientific and technical input, while bio-ethicists attended the second. In common with all deliberative dialogues of this sort, the workshops were highly interactive; significant time was given over for deliberation between participants, and between participants and experts (Sciencewise, 2014).

In common with all Sciencewise public dialogues, an independent Oversight Group involving a range of stakeholders with the full spectrum of views on the topic was established. This group was responsible for overseeing the process and advising on and checking materials for bias before they were used (Sciencewise, 2014).

Speaking after the public engagement had finished, and in reference in particular to the public dialogue element of the engagement, Professor Lisa Jardine, Chair of HFEA, said, 'Perhaps surprisingly, the public supported the new techniques if it could prevent serious illness. They had little objection to its being approved for clinical use as long as it was scrupulously overseen by an appropriate regulatory body' (Sciencewise, 2014, p.1).

The report of the dialogue fed into an HFEA paper published to inform the decision by the Authority in March 2013. The HFEA was clear about the central role of the dialogue participants' views in its advice in the paper, saying that the dialogue, 'helped enormously to formulate the policy advice we gave Government. [It p]rovided a serious backbone to that assessment', and that it 'directly fed into law potentially being changed' (Sciencewise, 2014, p.2).

In February 2015, Parliament approved the regulations for changes to mitochondrial DNA to be allowed. These changes include the strict safeguards and oversight the public discussed during the public dialogue.

World Wide Views and global policy making

Not every issue can be solved nationally. One such issue is obviously climate change, a challenge requiring concerted local, national and international action to mitigate its effects and adapt to the change that is inevitable.

Article 6 of the UN Framework Convention on Climate Change (UNFCCC) commits member governments to promote 'public participation in addressing climate change and its effects and developing adequate responses' (United Nations, 1992). The Danish Board of Technology (DBT), working with civil society partners across the world, developed the World Wide Views (WWViews) process (World Wide Views, 2018) to support governments to deliver on this commitment.

On 6 June 2015, a coalition of civil society organisations ran WWViews for a third time focusing on climate and energy. This process was jointly initiated by the secretariat of the UNFCCC, DBT, Missions Publiques and the French National Commission for Public Debate. It was supported by the French Government, which was hosting the 21st annual conference of the parties to the UNFCCC in November 2015.

The process consisted of 97 day-long deliberations in 76 countries across five continents. In total, around 10,000 citizens were involved.

The process took place on the same day, starting at 9am in Fiji and finishing 27 hours later in Arizona, USA. Countries taking part ranged from Afghanistan to Zimbabwe, including 31 in Africa, 26 in Europe, 21 in Asia Oceania and 19 in the Americas (Bedsted et al, 2015).

As with the mitochondrial transfer dialogue described above, the citizens were selected to participate based on the demographics of their respective countries and regions.[2] They were provided with balanced information, as well as about the international discussions on policy measures to deal with climate change. The process was designed to be cheap to organise in order to make it feasible for any country to participate regardless of income. It aimed to ensure that there was a clear link to policy making by addressing issues of immediate relevance to policy makers in order to ensure that citizens' voices were more likely to be heard. At the end of the process, following significant deliberation between participants in each country, participants voted on 34 common questions. This was to ensure that the results were clear and comparable across continents and countries so that they were easy to communicate to policy makers.

Once the process was completed, national and regional partners, experts and civil society representatives came together in Copenhagen to analyse the results. The results were clear: participants strongly supported political action to limit the global temperature increase to 2 degrees Celsius above pre-industrial levels. A full 97% of the participants wanted the Paris agreement to include a long-term goal for zero emissions by the end of this century.

The results from the process were launched in September 2015 (World Wide Views, 2015). As with deliberative processes of this kind, the results provided important insights into citizens' perspectives on the different policy choices facing governments. They helped politicians to understand which options the public supported and which they did not, where they thought politicians were not going far enough, and where they were going too far. Critically, the process helped develop a better understanding of *why* the participants came to these conclusions.

If deliberative processes can help to engage citizens in assessing and shaping complex scientific policies, they can be of use in policy development generally. The online database Participedia provides details of many more examples.

---

[2]   No special educational attainment was required, and trained facilitators ensured explanations were jargon-free and any complex ideas were presented in terms the lay public could understand.

Nonetheless, politicians, civil servants and the media can be sceptical about the value of such processes despite the national and international examples where such deliberative processes have improved the policy-making process. Some of this scepticism results from the particular features of such processes; they are small scale, time bound, difficult to communicate to the wider population and can seem relatively expensive. This does not reduce their utility, but rather points to the need to explore how to increase deliberation more widely in our democracy. This question is particularly pressing given the growing democratic deficit in many areas of public policy.

Deliberative systems – deliberative capacity

The processes highlighted above draw their inspiration from a number of places. The tools and techniques they use when working with participants in the deliberative workshops are inspired by, and often replicate, those used in community development, stakeholder engagement and conflict resolution. They are also rooted in deliberative democracy theory, which is, in part at least, a reaction against the Schumpeterian view of democracy as a competition for votes as the expression of voters' interests. The next section focuses instead on one aspect of this theoretical conceptualisation of democracy.

Australian academic John Dryzek (2009) defines deliberative capacity as 'the extent to which a political system possesses structures to host deliberation that is authentic, inclusive, and consequential' (p.1382). He notes that such capacity does not reside in specific institutions or governance processes, but can be found in different ways across the whole of the governance system. Critical to his definition of deliberative capacity is that the deliberation results in reflection by its participants which is not coerced from them, connects to more universal principles (of human rights for example), exhibits reciprocity and is consequential (Dryzek, 2009).

These last two elements of his definition are vital to ensure when thinking about the role of the public in policy making. Reciprocity means that deliberative capacity is determined by the extent to which the wide variety of views in a democracy are both visible to all participants *and* interact, thus providing the opportunity for changing perspectives in light of new evidence or a better understanding of the needs and interests of others. For deliberation to be consequential it must have an impact on collective decisions or social outcomes. While this impact could be direct, it doesn't have to influence explicit 'policy decisions', but could instead affect the wider public debate and context in which the decisions are being made.

Dryzek notes that deliberation of the kind that increases the deliberative capacity of the system can take place in different 'sites' within the system. In later work, Dryzek identifies seven of these sites, or spheres: private; public; empowered; transmission; accountability; meta-deliberation; and decisiveness (Stevenson and Dryzek, 2014). These sites can be mapped onto the UK's democratic system and doing so highlights the low deliberative capacity of our democracy and the fragility of the connection between different groups of citizens, and citizens and the government (Burall, 2015).

This theoretical framework helps to shine a light on the challenge that faces the kinds of mini-publics which I have explored above. They can, and should, be viewed positively when they impact, sometimes significantly, on individual policy decisions. They are also, when well run, highly deliberative; they include and make visible a wide range of perspectives and are designed to allow participants to reflect on their own views and change them when faced with different perspectives and new evidence.

However, what such processes are unable to do, except on extremely rare occasions, is to influence the wider public debate. They therefore have very limited, if any long-lasting, impact on the deliberative capacity of the system as a whole. This means that the types of deliberative interaction between participants, and between participants and experts, are not replicated more widely within the system. As a result, neither the deep and complex interaction with the tensions and trade-offs such decisions can create nor their varying impacts on different individuals and communities are taken into account in the wider debate or in subsequent policy decisions. This in turn means the majority of individuals and communities not involved in the dialogue may feel that their interests are not considered and the wider impact on their lives of many technological developments have excessively negative effects.

Given this, while such mini-publics are useful stopgap measures to plug the gap in the poor transmission mechanisms between the public and empowered spaces in Dryzek's deliberative system, they are not enough (Burall, 2015). Therefore, the key question to which this chapter is attempting to develop an answer is what policies can public bodies, civil society organisations and others interested in increasing the quality of our democracy adopt in order to increase the deliberative capacity of the system as a whole?

Networks and power distribution

The core change that government needs to make is to approach public engagement from a very different angle. The current model of engagement starts from the point of view of the government. In all of the examples highlighted above, government has identified a policy decision which it needs to take, and a key element of the evidence it needs is what the public thinks about a specific technological application and the narrow policy decision relating to this. The framing of the policy problem, and the questions posed to the public, are from the starting point of the government's perspective.

The net effect of this is that it tends to treat the public as individuals disconnected from wider society who have not thought about the particular policy question. In doing so it both removes many of the perspectives and views that the public might bring to the table by narrowly framing the issues to be discussed and ignores the ways the public may already be engaging and taking action (Chilvers, 2017). It therefore disempowers participants and the wider public.

However, we know that the public is far from disengaged from the issues the government is grappling with. The public is not an undifferentiated mass, collectively unaware and disengaged from the wider debates about the policy decision under discussion. For all but the most esoteric scientific research there are industry lobby groups and membership organisations actively engaging in the issues raised by the policy decision under discussion.

Members of the public also don't wait for government to raise policy questions before they start discussing them; they are talking about the local environment and climate change, recent medical advances and even genetic modification, robots, autonomous vehicles and artificial intelligence at home, in the pub and at community events, for example. In addition, they don't act as individuals independent of each other; they are active members of workplace networks, local football clubs, in residents' associations and other such community organisations. Even those whom people in power characterise as disengaged are part of, and highly active in, community and wider networks (Brodie et al, 2011).

In my experience of working with government to design and implement projects to engage the public, a large part of the problem stems from misunderstanding the much overused term 'stakeholder'. When government bodies talk about engaging with stakeholders, what they mean is organisations and individuals with a particular interest in a specific issue. Such organisations and individuals will have more detailed knowledge about the issue than others not working on it, and certainly than the lay public. They will often be lobbying the government to make changes to laws and regulations relating to the issue. Government contrasts this active, self-interested and knowledgeable set of stakeholders with the public, which as a result becomes conceived of by government, in practice if not in theory, as the undifferentiated mass described above.

Recasting the relationship between stakeholders and the public

A useful working definition of stakeholders is: 'individuals and groups that can affect or are affected by an organisation's policies and/or actions' (Blagescu et al, 2005, p 20).This definition makes it clear that the public are also stakeholders of any decision taken by a government body; some individuals may be deeply affected by the decision because they are, for example, heavy users of a service which will change because of implication of a new scientific discovery, but the public as a whole is also affected because it is taxpayers' money which is being spent, or a new technological innovation which will change our transport system or the way we relate to each other and wider society, for example.

However, it also isn't helpful to think of the public in the same way as those with a specific interest in the policy decision under discussion. They rarely have the time, resources or technical knowledge to engage in the same way, even though they can and do have a contribution to make which is as valuable as those 'formal stakeholders'.

Drawing on the analysis above, that the public cannot be thought of in the same way as 'formal stakeholders' and nor can they be seen, given the networks that individuals are deeply embedded in, as an undifferentiated mass. There is a more productive way of conceiving of the different groups which government should be engaging with.

Figure 4.1 The stakeholder-public spectrum

Formal stakeholders	Wider civil society and	The public
Have specific interest	community groups	Members of public
and knowledge about	Have interest in an	engaged as
the issue.	issue unrelated to the	individuals at home
Lobbying government	specific policy	and in the workplace,
for changes to	decision.	for example.
policy/law.	Members of the public	
	involved as supporters,	
	activists, members or	
	users.	

Combining these two analyses suggests that there are, in fact, a number of different publics which the government could and should be engaging with.

Towards the left of the spectrum are the already engaged and interested publics, often polarised in opinion, but reflecting only a portion of the wider set of public perspectives on the issues raised by a technology. Towards the middle and left are the more (from the perspective of the government's specific policy focus) latent publics (Mohr et al, 2013). These latent publics are actively engaged in different issues, but are able to engage in debates about the impacts of scientific innovation only if they are 'activated' by making the issues more relevant to them.

In short, there is a public debate, sometimes quite sparse, about every policy decision the government is considering, but the government is very bad at tapping into it. Members of the public are highly networked and part of an interconnected communications and discussion system that government could tap into and engage with. To do this it would need to think about the problem of public engagement in terms of strengthening existing, and creating new, networks and see part of its role as building deliberative capacity rather than just extracting specific information about public views to inform narrow policy decisions.

A new approach to engage diverse publics

This framing, that there are multiple publics, provides the nucleus around which a new way of engaging the public can crystallise.

Given that most publics are already engaging with issues about the impact of a wide range of policies at least in a general way, the question moves from 'how do we engage the public to find out what they think?' to 'how do we find out what different publics are already saying about the issue and engage in the conversation with them and their networks?'

Let us focus again on the example of scientific innovations, and consider how the government will need to develop a way of understanding evolving public views in relation to technologies that will have the kind of pervasive and disruptive impact described at the start of this chapter. It will need to identify the gaps in its knowledge about public perspectives, and target publics which appear to be disengaged from the wider societal debate.

One way for the government to do this would be to create an Office for Public Debate with the specific mandate to strengthen democratic control by developing a more plural and effective deliberation and debate, which informs and impacts on policy and practice, about the relationship between technological innovation and society in general, and specific technologies in particular. This body should not be a passive observer of the public debate; it will need to be actively engaged in it and play a number of different roles:

1. *Connecting the existing public debates to the scientific and policy debates.* The science of highly disruptive technologies often moves very fast. As a result, the calls for effective policy, regulation and licencing will often move with equal speed. One role for any new body will be to provide authoritative and neutral information about both the science and policy as they develop. This will need to be in a variety of forms for the different publics depending on whether they are latent or active stakeholders. It will need to correct factual misunderstandings which are affecting the debate. If it does this effectively then it will build a resource of evidence and materials that publics will use to inform their own debates.

2. *Connecting the public to experts.* The development of the wider debate will happen quickly. Publics will discuss and debate the impacts of technologies and the direction they want them to move in lectures, science cafes, on personal and professional blogs, as well as on social media. They will also discuss it in ways that may not be visible to policy makers and scientists, whether this is in the pub, at work or in the parent and toddler group. The new body must create a framework for understanding the range of views and communicate this to policy makers and scientists who are not actively engaged in this wider debate. It will also need to correct the misconceptions that policy makers have about the public's perspectives on the development of the technology. In doing this, it will build up a set of resources and evidence about the public's views on specific technologies and the relationship between scientific innovation and society more generally. This will be invaluable for informing policy making, pointing the way to where future engagement is needed, as well as supporting the body in its third role.

3. *Engaging in the wider debate.* There will be gaps in the public conversation. The body will need to identify publics which are unengaged, actively engage them, as well as asking unanswered questions of those already engaged. The networks of scientists and policy makers will be as imperfect as those of the public. The body will need to create connections between publics with different perspectives as well as connecting policy makers and scientists to groups of the public with relevant perspectives. This will help to develop a group of scientists, policy makers and publics that are better

able engage more widely in order to promote a more effective and better informed societal debate.

This new body will need to demonstrate its trustworthiness to all sides of the debate if it is to be taken seriously and have a chance of fulfilling the three roles laid out above. Ensuring that it has a properly balanced membership will therefore be important. Members will need to commit to supporting the body to develop an open debate over which they have limited control. The body will have to represent the principles of open government, transparency, participation and accountability (Open Government Partnership, 2011). Its funding will have to be such that it can fulfil these principles, and carry out what will be a substantial workload while demonstrating its independence from the funders.

The global Open Government Partnership and other models

The sketch above is not a theoretical and highly aspirational model for a glorified government listening unit charged with listening in on stakeholder and citizen conversations. Attempts to create such models are becoming more prevalent; though none have such an explicit focus on building deliberative capacity as is proposed above, they are shifting the government from the centre of decision making to a position of being an important actor in a much wider network of debate and policy development.

One example is the global Open Government Partnership with which my own organisation, Involve, has worked closely in the UK. The UK Government, as a member of this partnership with 75 member countries, is committed to creating a biennial national action plan aimed at developing concrete, time-bound commitments to make the UK Government more accountable and responsive to citizens.

At the core of the process for developing the UK's national action plan is a relationship between the Cabinet Office and the UK Civil Society Network on Open Government, a network of over 700 not-for-profit organisations[3] working both nationally and locally either directly on issues relating to open government, transparency, participation and accountability, or more widely on public service delivery. The Cabinet Office and Involve jointly coordinate a process by which both government departments and civil society organisations

---

[3]   For update details about the membership of the UK Civil Society Network on Open government see: https://www.opengovernment.org.uk/networks/uk/

propose ideas for stretching open government commitments and work together to develop them into final proposals which are then signed off by ministers and those civil society organisations from the network which played an active role (Hughes and Burall, 2014).

By the time the 2013 National Action Plan (Cabinet Office, 2013) was published, the benefits of this more open, collaborative process were obvious. For example, the active involvement of the members of the civil society network meant that alternative expertise and perspectives were introduced into the process. This in turn meant that links were made to other national and international initiatives which the government would not have identified had it been developing the plan alone. This meant that the commitments were more robust and better evidenced, and therefore more likely to achieve their intended outcome. A perhaps unexpected impact of the process was that the active and constructive involvement of civil society organisations meant that civil servants were more confident in advocating the benefit of what were, in some cases, challenging commitments for the government to be making. The partnership approach adopted in developing the commitments carried on into their delivery, ensuring civil society involvement throughout implementation and therefore a better chance of success (Hughes and Burall, 2014).

Proposals for structures and processes have also been made for other areas of policy making. For example, recent mapping of public engagement with the development of a low carbon energy system has shown that it is considerably more varied than is often assumed and includes significant examples of citizen-led and grassroots engagement and action outside any involvement with government (Pallet et al, 2017). Recognising the multiplicity of citizens' engagement with the issues requires a more holistic and joined-up engagement strategy. This in turn has led to the proposal for an

> open access 'observatory' which continually updates evidence of UK energy public engagement [which] would be a major step forward in ensuring all actors are better informed. It could also advise on good practice for different forms of engagement and how they can be more effectively responded to. (Chilvers et al, 2017, p 1)

Conclusion

The systematic lack of deliberative capacity identified above cannot be filled quickly. It will only be filled by governments actively seeking out alternative voices. Many citizens currently adopt a position of rational disengagement; all of their previous experience of democratic debates and government consultations has taught them that their views will be ignored so it is better to expend precious time and energy in other parts of their lives.

Government bodies, working with civil society partners, must demonstrate they are listening and acting on what they are hearing. If they do, the public will become more confident that it is worth engaging with government-backed exercises to seek out informed opinions. We have many of the pieces in place to develop stronger democratic control over both scientific innovation and wider public policy issues. The key challenge will be to help those in government to change its perspective about the public, its role in developing policy, and its ability to engage and empower different publics.

References

Achen, C. H. and Bartels, L. M. (2016) *Democracy for Realists*, Princeton, NJ: Princeton University Press.

Bedsted, B., Mathieu, Y. and Leyrit, C. (2015) *World Wide Views on Climate and Energy: results report*, Denmark: Danish Board of Technology Foundation, Missions Publiques and the French National Commission for Public Debate.

Blagescu, M., Las Casas, L. and Lloyd, R. (2005) *Pathways to Accountability: the GAP framework*, London: One World Trust.

Brodie, E., Hughes, T., Jochum, J. Miller, S., Ockenden, N. and Warburton, D. (2011) *Pathways through Participation: what creates and sustains active citizenship*, London: Pathways through Participation.

Burall, S. (2015) *Room for a View*, London: Involve.

Cabinet Office (2013) *Open Government Partnership UK National Action Plan 2013–2015*, London: Cabinet Office.

Chilvers, J. (2017) 'Expertise, professionalization, and reflexivity in mediating public participation: perspectives from STS and British science and democracy', in Bherer, L., Gauthier, M. and Simard, L. (eds) *The Professionalization of Public Participation*, London: Routledge, 115–138.

Chilvers, J., Pallett, H. and Hargreaves, T. (2017) *Public Engagement with Energy: broadening evidence, policy and practice*, London: UK Energy Research Centre.

Dryzek, J. (2009). 'Democratization as deliberative capacity building', *Comparative Political Studies* 42 (11), 1379–1402.

Gorman, G. S., Schaefer, A. M., Ng, Y., Gomez, N., Blakely, E. L., Alston, C. L., Feeney, C., Horvath, R., Yu-Wai-Man, P., Chinnery, P. F., Taylor, R. W., Turnbull, D. M. and McFarland, F. (2015) 'Prevalence of nuclear and mitochondrial DNA mutations related to adult mitochondrial disease', *Annals of Neurology* 77 (5): 753-759.

Hughes, T., and Burall, S. (2014) *Story of the UK National Action Plan 2013–15*, London: UK Open Government Network.

Mohr, A., Raman, S. and Gibbs, B. (2013) *Which Publics? When?: Exploring the policy potential of involving different publics in dialogue around science and technology*, London: Sciencewise.

Open Government Partnership (2011) Open Government Declaration. www.opengovpartnership.org/open-government-declaration

Pallet, H., Chilvers, J. and Hargreaves, T. (2017) *Mapping Energy Participation: A systematic review of diverse practices of participation in UK energy transitions, 2010–2015*, London: UKERC.

Postle, M., Fleet, D., Turley, A., Ylioja, P., Da, S. and Macnaghten, P. (2015) *Evaluation of the Sciencewise Programme 2012–2015*, London: Sciencewise.

Schumpeter, J. (1976) *Capitalism, Socialism and Democracy*, London: George Allen & Unwin.

Sciencewise (2014) *Mitochondrial Replacement Case Study*, London: Sciencewise.

Stevenson, H. and Dryzek, J. (2014) *Democratizing Global Climate Governance*, Cambridge: Cambridge University Press.

United Nations (1992) *United Nations Framework Convention on Climate Change*, Article 6 (a iii), New York: United Nations.

Warburton, D. (2011) *Evaluation of Sciencewise-ERC, Final Report*, London: Sciencewise.

World Wide Views (2015) *Launch of the WWViews on Climate and Energy Results Report*. Strong public support for political leaders to commit to ambitious climate action now. http://climateandenergy.wwviews.org/wp-content/uploads/2015/09/WWViews-Results-Report-press-release-final.pdf

World Wide Views (2018) *The World Wide Views Method*. http://wwviews.org/the-world-wide-views-method/

5

The Road to Empowerment

Hazel Blears and David Blunkett

Despite all that has been written about the proven value of reconnecting state institutions with the citizens they serve, many people may still remain unconvinced because of their assumptions about the nature of political power. For them, people do not seek out political power to give it away. And once they have got it, they will hold on to it tightly. Far from being ready to engage in cooperative decision making or sharing power with communities, politicians are on this view bound by circumstance to go it alone.[1] Anyone trying to persuade them to change course would be deemed naïve in not appreciating what it is like to get into government and run it.

The only naivety, we have to say, is to suppose this is how politics actually works. Some politicians may want to act without having to involve too many other people; some may indeed think of the public as relevant only when their votes are needed at election times. But many, at all levels of government, are concerned with the views of their constituents, and want to understand and respond to them more effectively. We ourselves have entered politics so that we can leverage the power of government to improve people's lives. We know we did not get everything right, but our abiding interest has always been to learn to serve the public better. And the most important thing we

---

[1] F. A. Hayek went so far as to argue that the more a government seeks to do for the public, the more power it will accumulate and exercise unilaterally without giving the people any real say, and it will inevitably lead to oppressive rule. But our experience in politics has taught us that there is an empowering alternative to Hayek's much flaunted 'road to serfdom' (2001).

learnt is that the power to advance the common good, far from being diminished, is greatly multiplied through being shared with citizens.

The best of the civil service and officials at local level share this endeavour. But human nature is what it is, and all too many still fall into the trap of being defensive about pulling down the barriers to public and democratic participation (Blunkett, 2001).

We came to value empowerment as a result of having to steer our way through the challenges of managing competing demands and tackling diverse problems with limited resources. Shaped by our own experiences of growing up in working class communities, encountering exclusion in all its debilitating forms, we wanted to ensure that the voices of ordinary people were heard, and their ideas taken on board. Too many policies, programmes and plans had failed in the past because they were designed by those who had not bothered to engage with the people who were meant to benefit from them. And such failures were not just a tremendous waste of public money, they increased the anger and cynicism of local residents who were ignored and left with no role to play in shaping their community.

With the increasingly polarised politics of today, there is growing anger among people who feel excluded from influence and decision making. Against this backdrop, the sense of powerlessness can all too easily manifest itself in distrust, suspicion, bigotry and alienation. But it does not have to be like this. It is not abstract theory but concrete political experience which taught us that by involving people and empowering them to shape their own futures, we can share responsibility and rediscover the value and pleasure of working and learning together, cooperating in mutual organisations and renewing the bonds of solidarity which make us all stronger.

The participatory alternative

A just and democratic society must be safeguarded from widespread inequality of power and resources. But this should not be interpreted to mean that public services such as healthcare, education, transport and housing must be organised and delivered to everyone in every area in the same way. Provisions need to adapt to different needs, and this will not happen unless the people who are meant to be supported by these services have a meaningful say about their design and accessibility. This in turn calls for reciprocity between state and citizens with each playing their part with mutual respect and responsibility.

The tension between top-down uniformity and bottom-up diversity is not new. The Fabian tradition descending from Beatrice and Sydney

Webb holds that the state should take control and look after the people, including the working class who are too poor or not well educated enough to deal with the many problems they face. By contrast, there is a mutualist strand that came down via thinkers like G. D. H. Cole which placed a premium on the active involvement of ordinary people and their organisations such as friendly societies, cooperatives, credit unions, community associations and trade unions. As Cole (1961, p 337) said:

> A socialist society that is true to its egalitarian principles of human brotherhood must rest on the widest possible diffusion of power and responsibility so as to enlist the active participation of as many as possible of its citizens in the tasks of democratic self-government.

The ultimate problem with top-down control is that it is too inflexible to respond to changing needs, but oversensitive to loud voices and secret lobbying. In health and education, highly centralised budgets have ended up creating a postcode lottery, not because of democratic engagement and local decision making, but because of centralised processes that reinforced inequality and intergenerational disadvantage by concentrating new resources, and modern facilities, where the loudest voices and demographic expansion demanded.

Conversely, in policing and justice the pressure was to provide identical budgets and identical services everywhere. This was inappropriate when comparing a poor, densely populated inner-city community afflicted by high levels of serious crime and antisocial behaviour with a rural, middle class community with different issues, different problems and far less likelihood of being a victim of crime.

In housing, while the demolishing of the slums of squalid and insanitary back-to-back houses in the 1960s/1970s was welcomed, the creation of monolithic tower blocks in inner-city areas that were supposed to be 'streets in the sky' led in reality to too many isolated and frightening places where none of the architects who designed them would ever dream of living. The problem was compounded by council landlords insisting that all dwellings would be painted the same colour, where there was no choice over the configuration or equipping of kitchens, and where improvements would only take place when unilaterally imposed. No wonder Right to Buy was so popular when it gave council tenants a chance to take control of their own homes. But the transfer of homes with modest rent out of the public sector with no replacement meant that there would be a growing shortage.

An alternative would have been for Tenant Management Organisations and housing cooperatives to be given the opportunity to work with residents to improve the services for their homes.

Indeed, the essence of the participatory alternative is to have the know-how to steer clear of the marketisation trap (which has in housing saddled some with negative equity and left many others with no prospect of finding somewhere they can afford to rent), and move us forward to where public provisions are made stronger and dependable because they are shaped in partnership with the people they are meant to serve. This partnership will be developed through empowering citizens to take decisions about the priorities and direction of local public services, giving people ownership and a stake in the running of public services and above all devolving power and opportunity within public services to local communities (Blears, 2003; Blunkett, 2003a).

We have never been under any illusion that there will be resistance to this in various quarters. However, we see that not as a reason to concede, but as a challenge that must be overcome if government is ever to fulfil its function more effectively. As David Marquand said in the run–up to the 1997 election, a new community politics must be:

> bottom–up not top-down, it must shy away from universal solutions and all embracing formulae, it will run with the grain of human ignorance, it will be an extraordinary difficult and demanding politics requiring levels of humility and openness from which the political class of today falls abysmally short. (Quoted in Blears, 2003, pp 4–5)

As others in this book have argued,deliberative cooperation with citizens goes far beyond current concepts of community consultation. In working class areas, it is still the professionals who are in charge regardless of how much consultation is conducted. The consultation model helps local people become more aware about local political processes but does not alter the underlying power structures. Being asked what you think is fine but real ownership comes from being involved in the planning, financing, organisation, delivery and evaluation of a public service.

The state model of public ownership gives us theoretical control without any real efficacy. Public buildings such as libraries, museums, town halls; public institutions such as schools, colleges and parks; and public services from health to social services are supposed to 'belong' to all of us because they are under the control of the state. Yet in most cases we neither have nor feel we have any real influence over them.

Nationalisation of the kind exercised by the Labour Government of 1945 may have been the best solution for the social and economic problems of the time. State ownership of major sections of industry in peacetime was a natural progression of their control by the state in wartime. It belonged in a world of monolithic national institutions and bodies, of rationing and of controls, and of a uniform population. But now we need to anchor public ownership in different non-state forms of social ownership, underpinned by mutuality, employee participation and cooperative enterprise. Leaving things to the so-called free market where exploitation and injustice can go unchecked is not the answer, and nor is resting on the idea that Whitehall alone knows best.

Partners with empowered communities

So how should those in government share power and responsibility in solving public problems with those who have put them there? The key is empowerment. We are well aware that this is a much used and abused word. But it captures the essence of what needs to be done. It goes much further than simply involving people in discussions about their future. People have to genuinely believe that their involvement will make a difference. It is therefore essential that politicians and officials are clear, transparent and above all honest about plans that will affect communities.

To make empowerment real, there are three aspects that need to be addressed. First of all, people need to learn the relevant skills. We are not just talking about schools and adult education supporting citizenship development, but also politicians and public officials at all levels learning how to seek and support citizens' input. Next, we must change policies and practices so that barriers are removed and citizens have more meaningful opportunities to engage, consider and shape the development of public actions. Last but not least, we want communities to have the confidence and capacity to work with each other and with public bodies to design and deliver local solutions wherever that is possible (Blears, 2004; Blunkett, 2001).

Neither of us had a detailed blueprint for taking our agenda forward. We knew that we must learn from testing out different approaches, trying out new arrangements and adapting to fast-changing circumstances. Over the last 20 years, inside and outside government, we have discovered that much can be achieved so long as we recognise there are always further lessons to learn.

On citizenship education, with the help of the indefatigable Bernard Crick (1998), political literacy was placed on the school curriculum in England. It is vital that young people learn why democratic politics has to be participatory as well as representative, and how collective power is needed as a counterweight to the power of wealth, privilege and elite connections. Above all, they should understand that politics is a messy business, where people who get engaged at whatever level will inevitably have to compromise and find acceptable and workable solutions that take account of other people's views and the need to make incremental steps in pushing forward with radical ideas.[2] Although, as James Weinberg and Matt Flinders argue (see Chapter Eleven of this book), the potential of citizenship education has not been fully realised, it nonetheless provides a basis for more effective delivery in the future.

Beyond schools, we promoted active citizenship learning among adults through what became the Take Part programme. With learning hubs spread around the country, public service users, community activists and government officials were able to improve their understanding of each other's perspectives, and how prevailing practices should be changed to meet people's needs. Many involved in the programme have continued to help bridge the gap between state and citizens, and some have gone on to share its approach with citizens in other countries from the US to Colombia (see Chapter Thirteen in this book).

From 2003 on, we took forward the Together We Can programme for civil renewal. It committed 12 central government departments (including those for health, environment, trade and industry, transport, constitutional affairs, the Treasury, and of course the Home Office where we were in charge at the time) to undergo a culture change by opening more of their policies and practices to input from citizens and community groups. The actions that were consequently taken ranged from the development of patient and public involvement in shaping health services, the evaluation and support of dialogue processes to inform science and technology policy,[3] transfer of power and resources to neighbourhoods, support for rural communities in assessing and identifying affordable housing needs, to involving local communities in extending the use of school facilities, making the police more responsive to local concerns through neighbourhood policing, bringing rail operators and communities together to develop community rail partnerships, and involving communities in setting sustainability goals and strategies (HM Government, 2005).

---

[2]   This view has been reinforced by the House of Lords Select Committee on Citizenship and Civic Engagement in 2018.

[3]   It led to the establishment of Sciencewise (see Chapter Four in this book).

People were not 'consulted' and left without further feedback. They were involved in ongoing planning that reflected their informed concerns, and could experience the changes that were brought about.[4] The work we promoted was not limited to within central government departments either. We sought out external partners to increase the reach of empowerment activities. For example, we developed the Guide Neighbourhoods initiative to enable residents and community groups that were demonstrating success in how they engaged and influenced public policies affecting them to act as consultants to others ambitious to follow the same path. This was a significant departure from the usual pathway of giving large sums of public money to international consultancies, instead facilitating communities to link up with and partner each other in a learning enterprise (McCabe et al, 2007).

Local government is another major partner for building cooperative relations with citizens (Blunkett and Green, 1981; Blunkett and Jackson, 1987; Blunkett, 2003b; and Chapter Eight in this book). We collaborated with a number of forward-thinking local authorities to set up the network of Civic Pioneers, these being councils that would prioritise the adoption of tried and tested engagement practices, venture to experiment with innovative approaches in community empowerment, and actively share their lessons with others across local government. Rather than central government issuing directives on what local authorities were to do, we enabled them to share their success stories with each other, and exchange lessons on what would not work so well (Gaffney, 2005; DCLG, 2008b).

Enabling communities to take control

As we reflected on the progress that was being made and the roadblocks that were still in the way, we were aware that increasingly we must turn our attention to the challenge of expanding communities' capacity to be effective civic partners. In her introduction to the White Paper, *Communities in Control*, Hazel Blears stated:

> With the right support, guidance and advice, community
> groups and organisations have a huge, largely latent, capacity
> for self-government and self-organisation. This should be

---

[4] A summary of the progress made was given in the 2005/2006 annual review of 'Together We Can', which contained reports from the Secretaries of State and Ministers of the 12 Government Departments in question (HM Government, 2006; see also Tam, 2011).

the hallmark of the modern state: devolved, decentralised, with power diffused throughout our society. (DCLG, 2008a, p iii)

From Aristotle's (1905) observation that 'if liberty and equality, as is thought by some, are chiefly to be found in democracy, it will be best attained when all persons alike share in government to the utmost' (p. 156), to Article 21 of the Universal Declaration of Human Rights in 1948 which sets out citizens' rights to take part in government, the principle of enabling all to have a real and equal say in how they are governed will only be realised to the extent people can acquire and exercise that power in practice. The core theme of *Communities in Control* was thus to devise support and reforms that can help more people:

- Become more active as citizens;
- Find relevant information they can understand and use in dealing with public issues;
- Have a real say in influencing the decisions made by elected representatives and appointed officials;
- Hold to account the people who exercise power in their locality;
- Get swift and fair redress when things go wrong and make sure it doesn't happen to anyone else;
- Stand for public office and get the support needed;
- Take on and run local services with others in the community.

The measures that were taken forward to achieve these objectives fell into four broad categories. The first group was concerned with investing in the development of community capacity and infrastructure. For example, a £70 million Community Builders Fund was established to help independent multipurpose community-led organisations in providing suitable, accessible community spaces for people to come together to plan and run local activities to meet local needs. There was further support to establish 14 pilot schemes to promote the development of community land trusts to enable local people to build and run their own housing provision (see Chapter Fourteen in this book).

Building on earlier ideas on expanding community control of public facilities (Blears, 2003) and the findings of the independent review of community assets (Quirk, 2008), funding was provided for the setting up of an Asset Transfer Unit in the community sector, to give advice and support to public sector bodies and local community organisations on how to identify and transfer underused public land and buildings (such as community centres, street markets, swimming pools, parks or a disused school) to community ownership, not only to facilitate local control but also to establish an asset base for groups to generate long-term income to fund projects to meet local needs.[5]

The second group of measures were directed at identifying, evaluating and promoting empowerment techniques and practices that should be more widely adopted. A dedicated empowerment fund was set up to support national third-sector organisations to learn more about, experiment with and implement innovative empowerment initiatives. In parallel, the National Empowerment Partnership was established to promote the sharing of good ideas and effective practices within regions and across the country (Sender et al, 2011).

Studies were commissioned to review and publicise specific approaches. For example, the impact of the Take Part programme was examined and widely disseminated (Miller and Hatamian, 2011; see also Chapter Thirteen in this book). The potential benefits of participatory budgeting (a process enabling communities to discuss and prioritise local public spending) and how they could be realised through a number of factors were scrutinised and promoted with the help of online advice and a dedicated team based in an external charitable organisation (SQW et al, 2011; for more on participatory budgeting, see Chapter Six in this book).[6]

In the third group was direct support for organisations dealing with different target groups and issues. These included grants to the Young Foundation for the development of the Uprising Leadership Programme for young people from diverse backgrounds to become effective community and political leaders;[7] support for the Community Development Foundation to help community development workers expand the reach of their work in enabling more local people and groups to engage with public decisions and activities; funding for Planning Aid to support local people in contesting complex planning applications so they would not be at a disadvantage with the professional planners acting on behalf of developers or the local authority; and more extensive roll-out of neighbourhood management, particularly in deprived areas, so that more people can access support for feeding

---

[5] The Asset Transfer Unit advised on the use of asset locks to make sure transferred assets can only be utilised for the public good, and not private gain.

[6] For the resources developed in support of this technique see: www. participatorybudgeting.org.uk/

[7] The programme was to become an independent charity in 2013.

their views into joined-up local services covering health, policing and transport.

Public agencies that were part of the criminal justice system were given the policy steer and practical guidance to involve witnesses and victims of crime more closely and ensure that the system was transparently supportive of them. They were also advised on adopting community justice practices which enabled local people to decide what tasks offenders on work orders should undertake; while local forums were encouraged to discuss and help shape community safety priorities.

Finally, there were a range of measures to strengthen the role of local government in empowering local participation. Following on from the report of the Councillors Commission, advice was disseminated both on how current elected councillors could do more to facilitate citizen participation, and how future councillors should be more representative demographically of the constituents they served (DCLG, 2007; see also Chapter Twelve in this book).[8] There were plans to place certain duties on local government in support of community empowerment. Some, such as the attempt to formulate a statutory mechanism to require local authorities to give a satisfactory response to communities seeking redress when local services fell below acceptable standards, did not at the time find a way forward.[9] Others, such as the creation of new legislative powers and duties on local authorities to promote democracy and to extend the existing duty to involve local people in key decisions to cover more areas of public services, did find their way onto the statute book, only to be repealed after Labour lost power in 2010. But the aim of helping community organisations take on public services by factoring in social and environmental values as well as economic ones did secure support down the line when it was incorporated into a private member's bill that was to pass and become the Public Services (Social Value) Act 2012.

The retreat from empowerment

Far from being over-idealistic about how effective state-citizen cooperation can be brought about and entrenched, we are all too aware of the barriers to advancing it, and the difficulty in sustaining

---

[8]   Jane Roberts was the Chair of the Councillors Commission.

[9]   The main difficulty was finding a formulation that would not undermine local authorities by opening them up to endless demands, reasonable or otherwise, to change what they had done, or to make too many allowances so that redress would not reliably be provided in the vast majority of cases.

it. Even when we were Cabinet Ministers, we knew that some policies could take too long to implement, new legal duties were not always desirable or feasible, and the funding available to us had to be targeted at a limited number of areas and issues or else they would be spread too thinly to have any real impact. After 2010, we heard the rhetoric of the Big Society even as we witnessed the decimation of the community sector, the funding shortages that plagued local groups, and the closing down of national support organisations such as the Community Development Foundation, Community Matters, the Community Sector Coalition, People Can (previously Scarman Trust), the Urban Forum and countless others.

In truth, echoes of support for the principles we have long advocated sounded increasingly hollow, while massive cuts in funding for local government and third-sector organisations proved fatal for any hope that communities could be in control of their destiny. Instead many people were diverted into thinking they could take back control by leaving the European Union while the government tried to seize even greater power without any form of parliamentary check-and-balance. Local people and their councils have been left to pick up the pieces of fractured and underfunded services. The inevitable result has yet again been disappointment, anger and cynicism.

Learning together

Despite the widespread sense of alienation, however, one of the most important things we have learnt about power sharing is that we do not have to wait until those with political power are willing to engage in it. Many of the best ideas and practices for state-citizen cooperation are generated by people outside government – activists, organisers, residents, who help their communities unite and speak with a more powerful voice, and promote engagement, build assets and strengthen their shared social capital.

We should take stock of what has been achieved so as to be ready to press for what is yet to be accomplished. Changing circumstances provide threats and opportunities. The exponential rise of digital communication and social media has brought people together, but has also increased intolerance, hatred and distrust. We live in the most connected society that has ever existed and yet people feel overwhelmed by being disconnected and we have an epidemic of loneliness. Part of the answer may lie in people coming together by connecting digitally in a positive way, agreeing on social action, working cooperatively and enjoying the sense of achievement in putting their own skills and talents together with others and creating something more than they can alone.

Early in the development of social media the campaign across international boundaries, Make Poverty History, was able to mobilise millions of people in the cause of debt redemption for sub-Saharan Africa and the beginnings of a serious dialogue on climate change. Whether in taking on some of the great giants who provide the platform for social media and the operation of the World Wide Web, or joining together to force change from international providers of goods and services such as energy companies, the potential of linking empowered citizens as consumers to create a culture in which change is forced upon the otherwise extremely powerful has the potential to be transformational. This collective action could empower individuals against exploitation by unfair markets and overbearing and authoritarian states. From simple replicas of joining together, as the Trade Union movement did all those years ago, to 'buy' cheaper energy, through to the not so new technique of boycotts, the potential for mutual action has been transformed (Blunkett, 2012).[10]

Raising finance through peer-to-peer lending such as Crowdfunding and Kickstarter, the expansion of Investing for Impact, the success of community share issues and the rise in community-owned assets are all encouraging manifestations of a new generation becoming involved in diverse forms of mutual support and taking responsibility for their common wellbeing. This vast potential is being explored by the Co-operative Group in harnessing the power of collective action to advance the public good.

There will never be enough public resources to do all the things that need doing. It is therefore imperative to spend the public money we have as effectively as possible, and to try and create sustainable and affordable solutions to the demands we face. The pressures on public services from health and social care to housing, transport and education are immense. The pressures on individuals and families to live and work, to support their families and to manage their budgets are increasing, and their inability to change the circumstances around them can be debilitating.

---

[10] The publication of *In Defence of Politics Revisited* (Blunkett, 2012) not only commemorated the 50th anniversary of the publication of Bernard Crick's *In Defence of Politics* (2005) [originally published in 1962], but sought also to update the concept of people engaging both as consumers as well as citizens in counterweight to increasingly powerful and unaccountable global forces.

We have a choice. We can develop even bigger monolithic public service solutions and push them top-down onto communities. Or we can tap into the energy, ideas, creativity and innovation of not so ordinary people and learn together to develop a genuinely collaborative approach to tackle the many challenging issues that face us today.

We are still optimistic and believe cooperation between state and citizens is the best way forward. For example, we are both involved with the Well North programme (see www.wellnorth.co.uk). This is operating across ten areas of the North of England in those places where, despite many public interventions, some of the most intractable problems of poor health, inadequate housing, low educational attainment and lack of well-paid and satisfying work are still prevalent. At its heart, Well North is about empowering local people to devise their own solutions, providing backup, support, guidance and help and sharing ideas across the ten areas.

Local authorities linked to core institutions (universities and foundation trusts) such as the experimentation in Preston, have a lot to teach us. It is essential to develop procurement policies which not only involve and engage local people but actually save money, inspire people to want to innovate and encourage people to believe that something 'real' can happen. While the jury is still out on devolved city regional initiatives (particularly Greater Manchester, Merseyside and West Midlands), there are very many important local experiments taking place which need to be evaluated and scaled up.

Providing resources to develop the capacity, what is often called social capital, as well as the individual learning pathway, is fundamental to ensuring that communities can take control of the way they are governed. To be able to use the inherent social assets which constitute the survival of the most deprived neighbourhoods, and engage with adult and lifelong learning, requires the development of programmes, such as those at the Northern College and many other adult learning institutions, to build confidence and capability.

The lessons we want to share from our own experience is that the past teaches us what might work for the future. There is no need to reinvent the wheel. But there is the challenge to apply sound techniques under rapidly changing circumstances. We should evaluate best practice from the past, share experience from the moment and scale up what works in a way that empowers those committed and interested to make it work within their own particular economic, social and cultural environment.

References

Aristotle (1905) *Politics*, New York: Cosimo Classics.

Blears, H. (2003) *Communities in Control*, London: Fabian Society.

Blears, H. (2004) *The Politics of Decency*, London: Mutuo.

Blunkett, D. (2001) *Politics and Progress*, London: Methuen Books.

Blunkett, D. (2003a) *Civil Renewal: a new agenda*, London: Home Office.

Blunkett, D. (2003b) *Active Citizens, Strong Communities: progressing civil renewal*, London: Home Office.

Blunkett, D. (2012) *In Defence of Politics Revisited.* https://gruposhumanidades14.files.wordpress.com/2014/01/david-bucklett-in-defence-of-politics-revisited.pdf

Blunkett, D. and Green, G. (1983) *Building from the Bottom: Sheffield experience*, London: Fabian Society.

Blunkett, D. and Jackson, K. (1987) *Democracy in Crisis: the town halls respond*, London: Hogarth Press.

Cole, G. D. H. (1961) *A History of Socialist Thought, Vol V, socialism and fascism 1931–1939*, London: Macmillan.

Crick, B. (1998) *Education for Citizenship and the Teaching of Democracy in Schools*, London: Qualifications and Curriculum Authority.

Crick, B (2005) *In Defence of Politics*, London: Continuum.

DCLG (Department for Communities and Local Government) (2007) *Councillors Commission: report with recommendations on how to improve the democratic role of elected local councillors and facilitate citizen participation*, London: DCLG. http://webarchive.nationalarchives.gov.uk/20121029115445/http://www.communities.gov.uk/documents/localgovernment/pdf/583990.pdf

DCLG (Department for Communities and Local Government) (2008a) *Communities in Control: real people, real power* (White Paper), London: DCLG.

DCLG (Department for Communities and Local Government) (2008b) *Civic Pioneers Case Study Review*, London: DCLG. http://webarchive.nationalarchives.gov.uk/20120920044846/http://www.communities.gov.uk/documents/communities/pdf/1108568.pdf

Gaffney, M. (2005) *Civic Pioneers: local people, local government, working together to make life better*, London: Home Office. http://webarchive.nationalarchives.gov.uk/20120920061439/http://www.communities.gov.uk/documents/communities/pdf/152002.pdf

Hayek, F. A. (2001) *The Road to Serfdom*, London: Routledge.

HM Government (2005) *Together We Can: the government action plan*, London: Home Office (Civil Renewal Unit).

HM Government (2006) *Together We Can: annual review 2005/2006*, London: DCLG. http://webarchive.nationalarchives.gov.uk/20120919132719/http://www.communities.gov.uk/documents/communities/pdf/151402.pdf

McCabe, A., Purdue, D. and Wilson, M. (2007) *Learning to Change Neighbourhoods: lessons from the Guide Neighbourhoods Programme*, London: DCLG. http://webarchive.nationalarchives.gov.uk/20120920045010/http://www.communities.gov.uk/documents/communities/pdf/changeneighbourhoodsreport.pdf

Miller, S. and Hatamian, A. (2011) *Take Part: final report*, London: Community Development Foundation.

Quirk, B. (2008) *Making Assets Work: the Quirk Review of community management and ownership of public assets*, London: DCLG. http://webarchive.nationalarchives.gov.uk/20120920045030/http://www.communities.gov.uk/documents/communities/pdf/321083.pdf

Sender, H., Khor, Z. and Carlisle, B. (2011) *National Empowerment Partnership (NEP) Programme: final evaluation report*, London: Community Development Foundation.

SQW, Cambridge Economic Associates, Geoff Fordham Associates (2011) *Communities in the Driving Seat: a study of participatory budgeting in England: final report*, London: DCLG.

Tam, H. (2011) 'Rejuvenating democracy: lessons from a communitarian experiment', *Forum* 53 (3): 407–420.

PART TWO

What is Required for Effective Engagement

6

Lessons From Democratic Innovations

Graham Smith

In telling ourselves the story of democracy, we refer to heady principles of political equality and popular control. But the extent to which either of these principles is enacted in democracy as a *practice* is open to question. Social and economic differentials across society have a significant bearing on citizens' capacities to effect political change. As our societies become ever more unequal, so too does the distance from the ideal of democracy. For those committed to forms of participatory democracy, the cognitive dissonance between the principles and practice of democracy is unacceptable.

Various strategies for democratising the practice of democracy find their expression in contemporary politics. The promotion of democratic innovations – institutions designed specifically to increase and deepen the participation of citizens in the political decisions that affect their lives – is one such strategy that sits alongside complementary tactics such as associative democracy, basic income, reform of campaign financing, regulation of media ownership and the like.

We have enough evidence to know that democratic innovations can be effective in engaging and mobilising citizens in ways that have significant effect on political decision making and outcomes. We can point to Ireland, where the recommendations from the Irish Convention on the Constitution that ran from late 2012 to early 2014 and included both randomly selected citizens and selected politicians led to a national-level referendum that amended the constitution to introduce marriage equality (Elkink et al, 2017; Suiter et al, 2018). The Irish Citizens' Assembly, which followed in the Convention's wake in 2016, led to changes in the constitutional status of abortion, again following a popular vote. Alternatively, we can look to Latin America, where there is strong evidence that participatory budgeting (PB) across a number of municipalities has been effective in reversing longstanding differentials in participation. The broad mobilisation of disadvantaged groups, especially the poor, has led to more equitable redistribution of public goods and improvements in social wellbeing in areas such as health care and infant mortality rates (Baiocchi, 2003; Wampler 2007; Touchton and Wampler, 2014).

However, we need to be careful about the claims that we make about the current practice of democratic innovations. The tendency – as I have just done above – is to pick out exemplary cases; to focus on success stories. Such examples show us what is possible through participatory processes. But this selection bias means that we often fail to consider the lessons that need to be learned from the more mundane application of participatory processes and failures of attempted democratic innovation (Spada and Ryan, 2017), in particular their misuse and abuse by public authorities. This chapter will argue that while we have developed a fairly sophisticated understanding of how the design of democratic innovations can affect the democratic qualities of participation, we have less insight into the broader context and conditions under which democratic innovations are effective. Particularly pertinent for this book is the need for a better understanding of the role of the state and other public institutions. The interface between the state and citizens as mediated by democratic innovations needs further attention if we are to ensure that strategies to promote democratic innovations fully respect the time and efforts of citizens engaged in such processes.

This chapter begins with a discussion of the slippery concept of democratic innovations, providing a brief overview of the variety of forms that such participatory processes take. This variety can make it difficult to draw generalisations, as different designs have different democratic effects. We then move to a discussion of the context and conditions under which democratic innovations are established and sustained. Emerging research shows the importance of not only focusing on the design of participatory processes, but also the broader social and political context, in particular the actions and motivations of public authorities, in understanding the impact and outcomes of these processes. The final section of the chapter asks what can be done to ensure that strategies to embed democratic innovations are more effective, in particular the need to focus attention on broader participation infrastructure and the ways in which democratic innovations can be institutionalised into the political system.

Defining democratic innovations

The term 'democratic innovations' has entered the lexicon to describe a class of 'institutions that have been specifically designed to increase and deepen citizen participation in the political decision-making process' (Smith, 2009, p 1). While I am implicated in the adoption of this term and it is nearly impossible to reverse common usage, it is a slightly unfortunate classification for at least two reasons. First, it is not obvious why the term 'democratic innovation' should be reserved for participatory institutions only. After all, there are plenty of innovations in democratic practice that are not designed specifically to engage citizens in political decision making. It would be hard, for example, to argue that the recent establishment of an independent Commissioner for Future Generations in Wales was not a democratic innovation in this broader sense. The term democratic innovation has been appropriated to capture too limited a range of institutional developments in democracies. Secondly, the focus on 'innovation' in citizen participation may be too limiting. Initially I used this term to focus on participatory bodies that represent a departure from the traditional institutional architecture of contemporary democracies (Smith, 2009). But the boundary between democratic innovations and more mundane forms of public participation is not clear-cut. The term 'democratic innovations' has been used expansively to capture all forms of institutionalised public participation in the decision-making processes of public authorities; at other times the idea of 'increasing and deepening citizen participation' entails a more limited class of participatory process.

This second way of interpreting the term resonates with the strong normative commitment of many academics, activists and practitioners to establish a more participatory and deliberative politics. It resonates with Fung and Wright's (2003, p 15) categorisation of empowered participatory governance that 'abides by three general principles: (1) a focus on specific, tangible problems, (2) involvement of ordinary people affected by these problems and officials close to them, and (3) the deliberative development of solutions to these problems'. Elsewhere, Fung (2003, pp 340–41) distinguishes this category of empowered participatory process from those that have a more educative, advisory or collaborative problem-solving function.

Yet even if we take the more normatively driven approach to distinguishing democratic innovations from other participatory processes, there is still much to learn from the broader class of participatory democratic institutions. If we are to develop a critical understanding of what works, when and under what conditions, we must draw insights from more mundane participatory processes and failures in the practice of participatory institutions as much as from those that are deemed a success.

However we define democratic innovations – whether using the expansive or more limited conception – it is clear that we are talking about a class of institutions which display considerable variety. While their common feature is the institutionalised participation of citizens, designs vary. These have a differential effect on participants and broader democratic outcomes. I have considered these differences in relation to four key democratic goods – inclusiveness, popular control, considered judgement and transparency – and the institutional good of feasibility that recognises the costs that participation can place on both citizens and public authorities (Smith, 2009). If we take the good of inclusiveness, for example, we can see that participatory budgeting and randomly selected mini-publics such as the Irish Citizens' Assembly contribute to its realisation in very different ways.

The original Porto Alegre model of PB rests on open assemblies in which citizens are able to make demands for investment in their localities. Separate forums of representatives elected from within these assemblies collate and prioritise the various demands and establish rules for the distribution of resources. The rules of the PB tend to prioritise investment in poorer areas, with the likelihood of investment affected by the number of participants any locality can mobilise to vote for representatives. This sophisticated incentive structure mobilises participants from more socially and economically marginalised communities, in so doing reversing the typical inequalities of participation. In contrast, the application of random selection (often using quota sampling) in mini-publics ensures a diverse body of citizens that reflects the sociodemographic and attitudinal characteristics and variations across society. Facilitation ensures a degree of fairness in deliberation that is rarely achieved by other participatory designs. Similarly, other goods are enacted to a greater or lesser extent depending on the design characteristics of these democratic innovations.

This approach to analysing democratic innovations followed in the footsteps of Fung (2003), who explored the functional consequences for the quality of democratic governance of different designs. He highlighted four clusters of contributions of empowered participatory governance, related to the character of (1) participation and deliberation, (2) information pooling and individual transformation, (3) popular control and state capacity and (4) political effects. His broader framework generated similar insights: design choice has significant implications for how these characteristics are expressed in practice. Later work by Fung (2006) placed democratic innovations within a 'democracy cube', defined by the dimensions of (1) participation, (2) influence and (3) communication and decision mode. This made the same point in a visually arresting manner. Our research clearly shows how the design of democratic innovations affects the experience and impact of citizen participation and the balance of how different democratic and institutional contributions or goods are realised.

While the insights from these studies are sound and the approach continues to influence much subsequent academic work, their main limitation is that typically they analyse only a small number of exemplary cases where the enactment of democratic goods is particularly impressive. These exemplary cases tend to be face-to-face forms of engagement. This means that our knowledge of the broad field of democratic innovation and empowered participatory governance is skewed. We have relatively little systematic knowledge of the more extensive categories of mundane cases and cases that would be seen as failures from a democratic perspective (Spada and Ryan, 2017). Additionally, our knowledge of the impact of rapidly evolving digitally enabled forms of participatory governance – whether wholly online or hybrid (a mix of online and face-to-face) – remains patchy.

Linking design to context and outcomes

While we continue to develop more systematic knowledge of the importance of design to the democratic performance of democratic innovations, this does not provide a full explanation of the conditions under which democratic innovations are established and sustained and have an impact on the political process. The systemic turn in deliberative democracy pushes us to move away from the consideration of single institutions – in this case democratic innovations – in isolation and to better understand the implications of the ways in which they are integrated within the political system (Mansbridge et al, 2012; Owen and Smith, 2015). This means not only paying attention to the design of democratic innovations, but to issues such as the mode of 'coupling' between participatory processes and centres of political power (Burall, 2015; Hendriks, 2016).[1] Democratic innovations are a

---

[1]   While most of the work on deliberative systems is highly academic in nature, in *Room for a View: democracy as a deliberative system*, Simon Burall (2015) draws on this literature to make the case to practitioners for taking a systemic perspective on their activities.

form of 'governance-driven democratisation' (Warren, 2009) in that they are typically (although not always) organised or sponsored by public authorities.

If we are to see the spread of empowered (rather than more mundane) participatory governance, then we need to better understand the conditions under which public authorities are willing to establish such institutions and respond to citizens' decisions and recommendations. The tendency to focus on exemplary cases means that our knowledge base is skewed towards those cases where elected or appointed officials have been minded to establish democratic innovations and to implement their recommendations and proposals. This runs against a fairly extensive literature that suggests widespread lack of interest or even active resistance among most elected and appointed officials towards citizen participation. This often stems from the perception that citizens are cognitively incapable of dealing with complex policy issues and a concern that devolving power to citizens threatens, for politicians, their authority and, for civil servants, their professional knowledge and status (Newman et al, 2004; Petts and Brooks, 2006; Ganuza et al, 2016; but see also Chapter Eight in this book). That many examples of participatory governance are poorly designed and executed not only disappoints and alienates citizens, but provides succour to those who are sceptical of the participation agenda.

Returning to our earlier examples, we can see that there were particular – but different – sets of conditions that led to the establishment of both participatory budgeting in Porto Alegre and mini-publics in Ireland. PB was originally established in Porto Alegre in 1989 by the newly elected Workers' Party mayor who was ideologically committed to participatory democracy, but also recognised in PB a mechanism through which he could, first, legitimise pro-poor, redistributive policies in a city council where the Workers' Party was in the minority, secondly, challenge established patterns of clientelism and corruption, and third, build more long-term electoral support. The mayor was also able to exploit extensive demands and pressure from civil society for more transparent and participatory forms of political decision making.

While the novel design of PB, in particular its division of labour between making demands and rules was a critical element its success in Porto Alegre, just as important was the mayor's willingness to engage in significant restructuring of the city bureaucracy. A centralised planning office was established to provide relevant technical support and to coordinate the administration's response to decisions from the PB process. As Rachel Abers argues, the pre-existing planning office was 'too deeply entrenched in bureaucratic habits and technocratic ideology to carry out the innovative and politically charged projects that the government was hoping to implement' (Abers, 2000, p 77). Secondly, the mayor created a community relations department which played an active role in mobilising participants and associations and supporting citizen representatives. Finally, investment in a computerised project management system ensured a degree of transparency through the provision of information on the status of projects and the budgets of city agencies.

What then happened as PB spread to other Brazilian and Latin American cities and into Africa, Asia, Europe, North America and Oceania? A number of municipalities followed a similar path to the early Porto Alegre experience, including experimentation with expanding the reach of the PB process to new policy areas and establishing committees and procedures (including quotas) to promote the interests of women, young people, indigenous people and other politically excluded groups (Cabannes, 2004). The development of digital channels of engagement also helped broaden participation: La Plata in Argentina combines offline, online and remote (SMS) voting, which in its 2010 cycle directly engaged 10% of the local eligible population (Peruzzotti et al, 2011).

However, this is not the whole story. Paolo Spada and Matt Ryan (2017) show that across Brazil, on average only half of the PB processes established survive for longer than four years. The transnational movement that has seen forms of PB spread to over 1,000 cities worldwide has led in many cases to the diminishment of basic tenets of its practice in the process of transfer and diffusion. Too often, in its adaption to local conditions, what has been implemented under the name of PB has not reflected earlier Latin American experience and in many cases would be difficult to classify as examples of empowered participatory governance (Ganuza and Baiocchi, 2012; Sintomer et al, 2012). Political leaders have not been willing to give citizens power over significant proportions of municipal budgets or to reorganise state infrastructure to support public engagement and the implementation of the public's decisions.

The Irish use of randomly selected bodies in constitutional decision making tells a different story about enabling conditions (Elkink et al, 2017; Suiter et al, 2018). The Convention on the Constitution emerged from coalition negotiations between Fine Gael and Labour to establish a government following the 2011 general election. All the main political parties had included the need to review the Irish Constitution within their manifestos, but had proposed different convention designs – some involving randomly selected citizens; others more traditional stakeholder models. Fine Gael had been influenced by an earlier academic-led citizens' assembly experiment (Farrell et al, 2011) and their negotiations with Labour yielded a novel compromise solution, with the Convention on the Constitution combining two-thirds randomly selected citizens and one-third politicians. The perceived success of the Convention led to the later creation of the Irish Citizens Assembly. This second body followed the more traditional mini-public design, involving only randomly selected citizens. This design choice may well have been motivated by the desire of politicians not to be involved in decision making about the constitutional status of abortion – a highly controversial issue in Ireland, but one on which there was pressure for politicians to act from both civil society and international organisations.

Preceding the Irish use of random selection was a large number of applications of mini-publics around the world since the development of citizens' juries in the US and planning cells in Germany in the 1970s. Other mini-public models have emerged, including deliberative polls, consensus conferences, reference panels and G1000s, alongside the high-profile citizens' assemblies. All share the application of forms of random selection and facilitated deliberation (Setälä and Smith, 2018). There are celebrated cases where these mini-publics have been carefully coupled with formal decision-making processes. For example, in Canada, the governments of both British Columbia and Ontario committed themselves to referendums on the recommendations that emerged from citizens' assemblies they had established to consider new electoral systems. In both cases, there are resonances with the Irish situation – politicians had been unable to come to an agreement on electoral reform (Fournier et al, 2011).

An interesting recent development is the insertion of citizens' juries in the Oregon initiative process – the Oregon Citizens' Initiative Review (CIR). There has long been concern about the quality of information that citizens receive before voting on ballot measures that if passed become law. In 2008, the civil society organisation Healthy Democracy Oregon ran a pilot project to show how a mini-public could provide credible information to the public before voting. In the process adopted by the State Government in 2011, a citizens' jury is established by the Citizens' Initiative Review Commission to consider particular ballot proposals. The jury holds public hearings to engage directly with campaigns for and against the measure and policy experts. Following in-depth deliberations, the panel drafts a Citizens' Statement that highlights their most significant findings on the measure. This Statement is made available to the public in the official voters' guide produced by the government and sent to every household to inform their judgements. But these examples are relatively rare exemplary cases of integration into the political process. Most deliberative mini-publics have been at best consultative bodies – and there is little systematic evidence of their impact on political decision making.

What we tend to see, then, in the exemplary cases, is a combination of intrinsic and instrumental motivations on the part of political leaders faced with a challenging political context. In Porto Alegre, this was the difficulty of establishing a redistributive agenda against entrenched interests; in Ireland, intractable constitutional issues where the political leaders were unwilling or unable to act. In those contexts where both PB and mini-publics have been less entrenched, these motivations appear to be absent.

In an attempt to understand the differences in 'where, when, why, how and to what effect' participatory processes are established, Tina Nabatchi and Lisa Blomgren Amsler (2014) have articulated an analytical framework that incorporates context, sponsors, design and outcomes. Their framework begins with the broad context and setting – not just the legal framework, but also factors such as the scale and size of the polity, political culture and presence (or absence) of civic assets. This context has a role in shaping, first, who sponsors and convenes participatory processes and their motivations; second, the characteristics of participatory design; and finally, the outcomes of the process that vary from impacts on individual participants to community capacity and government and governance. In presenting their framework, Nabatchi and Amsler are pushing scholars to consider the relationship between how and why participatory processes are established, how and why they are sustained and the broad set of impacts and outcomes that follow.

Jens Newig and colleagues, as part of the EDGE (Evaluating the Delivery of Environmental Governance using an Evidence-based Research Design) project, have drawn similar distinctions between context, design and results in trying to understand the effectiveness of different approaches to participatory environmental governance. Their work takes a step forward in two ways. First, they are drawing on a more extensive set of processes, collecting data on hundreds of cases from published studies in academic and policy literatures. Secondly, they have established a series of hypotheses that link aspects of the design of participatory governance to the environmental standard of outputs, acceptance of outputs by stakeholders and implementation of and compliance with the output (Newig et al, 2018).

The Participedia project has taken a different approach to data collection on the diversity of participatory processes that goes beyond the analysis of published work and encompasses participation in any policy area. Recognising that knowledge of participatory processes is held by diverse groups, Archon Fung and Mark Warren developed a platform to crowdsource data from different communities of interest around the world – whether researchers, public officials, practitioners, activists or participants (see Fung and Warren, 2011). Now on the third iteration of the platform and involving research groups from a variety of countries and continents, at the time of writing Participedia houses over 800 case entries. The sheer variety of entries expands our imagination regarding the range of participatory designs and may lead to new approaches to defining the boundaries and categories that make up the field of activity. Early exploitation of both the quantitative and qualitative data housed on Participedia suggests that there is potential to improve further our understanding of how context, design and outcomes are related (Smith et al, 2015; Gastil et al, 2017). The LATINNO platform has similar ambitions. Developed by Thammy Pogrebinschi, it houses thousands of cases from across Latin America, with data for each case on context, institutional design and impact.

A different approach has been taken by the Cherrypicking project, led by Joan Font, which aims to understand the fate of proposals that emerge from participatory processes: what explains the apparent selective adoption of proposals by public authorities? Font and colleagues generated a series of hypotheses to test whether variables associated with context, process design and proposal characteristics explained whether public authorities implemented proposals. Adopting a sophisticated methodology, they followed the fate of over 600 proposals from 39 processes from municipalities in three regions of Spain (Font et al, 2016).

While there was no evidence that contextual factors had an effect on which proposals were selected, there was evidence that design characteristics were significant: proposals from participatory budgeting were more likely to be adopted than from other designs and the quality of the process had a positive impact. However, it is proposal-level variables that have the strongest explanatory power: the existence of support among elected and appointed officials, the extent to which a proposal challenged existing practices of the authority and its overall cost were all strongly predictive of implementation. From a democratic perspective, this is worrying: public authorities are listening selectively or cherry-picking the recommendations from citizens that reinforce their existing preferences and ways of working (Font et al, 2017). The research team's focus is on the more mundane, everyday use of participatory processes, but gives us clear evidence of the challenges facing those who wish to embed more effective forms of empowered participatory governance.

Where there is even less systematic work is on the conditions under which public authorities are motivated to institutionalise participatory processes. Where studies exist, they tend to focus on participatory budgeting, which is not surprising given its global diffusion. The first systematic comparative analysis was undertaken by Brian Wampler (2007), who analysed eight contrasting cases from Brazil to identify the conditions under which citizen empowerment and enhanced government accountability were institutionalised. He was able to show how the interaction between mayoral support for the delegation of authority to citizens and the response of civil society organisations led to quite different participatory outcomes: what he termed institutionalised, informal and contested, co-opted and emasculated participatory democracy.

Matthew Ryan and I have proposed an approach to analysing the institutionalisation and sustenance of participatory processes using new developments in qualitative comparative analysis (Ryan and Smith, 2012). In an exploratory study, we aimed to explain when and why forms of PB are institutionalised that give citizens control of budgetary decision making. We use four explanatory conditions: civil society demand, participatory leadership strategy, fiscal independence and bureaucratic support. The initial findings show that there are different pathways to institutionalising more extensive citizen control, with different combinations of the explanatory conditions. While there are cases such as Porto Alegre where all four conditions are present, we can also find unusual pathways where, for example, the application of democratic innovations is driven by bureaucratic actors in the absence of political leadership and civil society demand.

While Wampler's study could rely on primary field research because it is limited to eight cases, other more extensive studies rely on published data – or in the case of Participedia, on those interested in participatory governance to upload data. This creates methodological challenges because there are academic and practitioner incentives to present institutions that display novel characteristics and/or have had meaningful impact. Even the Cherrypicking project that collected data direct from the field relied on public authorities or media outlets having published material on a participatory process before it could be included in their dataset. Practitioners and officials in particular are often loath to publicise examples of failure (Spada and Ryan, 2017). This caveat aside, these research projects typically encompass a far broader range of cases, often across a variety of types of participatory processes, when compared to earlier studies that tend to focus on a small number of exemplary cases. In so doing they give us more insight into the conditions under which democratic innovations are likely to be effective.

What is to be done?

What can be done to promote the more effective institutionalisation of democratic innovations? How can we move from a few widely celebrated cases to more extensive application of empowered participatory governance?

For Nabatchi and Matt Leighninger (2015) our focus needs to be not just on creative design of democratic innovations, but on strengthening participatory infrastructure – in other words investing in the democratic system to enable high-quality and meaningful participation. They highlight three specific elements of that infrastructure which require particular attention: (1) empowering and activating leaders and networks; (2) assembling participation building blocks; and (3) providing systemic support. Participation leaders and networks cut across different institutions and groups in the public, private and civil society sectors that convene, organise and fund democratic innovations. The building blocks of a participatory infrastructure are varied and go beyond the design of a single democratic innovation. They include institutions and processes to disseminate information, gather input and data, support discussion and connections, enable small-scale and large-scale decision making and encourage public work. These are the building blocks of a broader participatory culture or system.

Finally, they point to the need for systemic support that generates 'incentives for participation leaders, opportunities for training and skills development, adequate financial and other resources, clear policies and procedures, and reliable evaluation measures and benchmarks' (Nabatchi and Leighninger, 2015, p 67). Their call for investment in the infrastructure of democracy resonates with that of Carmen Sirianni and Lewis Friedland (2001), who make the case for enhanced civic innovation: building the capacity of civic organisation and networks to connect citizens to public life through advocacy, policy design, education and service delivery. Too often the decision to sponsor, organise and respond to democratic innovations is at the discretion of elected or appointed public officials: the development of participatory and civic infrastructure aims to protect against such arbitrariness.

We are witnessing more extensive codification of participation – local and national laws that require participatory processes under particular conditions. In Peru and the Dominican Republic, for example, PB is mandatory for municipalities under national law. However, law can only take us so far – what is then implemented under the name of PB varies considerably. It is instructive that in Porto Alegre activists were resistant to the codification of the process, arguing that this would be a break to creativity and further innovation of PB. But that arguably left the process vulnerable to a less supportive incoming mayor when the Workers' Party lost control of the city. PB in its birthplace was weakened substantially.

An emerging institutional development may offer one strategy for ensuring higher quality forms of participatory governance: autonomous public organisations dedicated to public participation (APOPPs) (Bherer et al, 2014). APOPPs are created by governments with the mandate to organise or oversee democratic innovations in legally specified areas of policy. The Oregon Citizens' Initiative Review Commission is one such APOPP. Other examples include the former Danish Board of Technology (Teknologiraadet), French National Commission on Public Debate (Commission nationale du débat public), Montreal Board of Public Consultation (Office de consultation publique de Montréal) and Tuscany Participatory Authority (Autorità regionale per la garanzia e la promozione della partecipazione). While APOPPs remain relatively rare, and they have achieved different levels of success, their institutionalisation is one way to establish and ensure more independent and recurrent practices of participatory governance. The degree of autonomy and visibility enjoyed by APOPPs protects them to some extent from day-to-day political pressures, ensuring a level of quality and oversight of participatory arrangements and a competent authority to promote the outcomes of democratic innovations within decision-making processes.

Simply putting in place laws and institutions will not be enough, however. Hearts and minds need to be changed – and budgets need to be focused on creating the participatory infrastructure to support democratic innovations. This points to the need to develop a movement to promote more effective citizen participation. There is a challenge here though in developing the constituency for democratic innovation. Most civil society organisations have particular policy goals they are aiming to achieve. Campaigning and mobilising for process change is more challenging – 'What do we want? Randomly selected mini-publics! When do we want them? Now!' does not quite have the same ring as most activist causes.[2] PB is an interesting case as it combines a

---

[2]   Although see the work of the Sortition Foundation.

demand for democratic participation with explicit redistribution and social justice concerns. Here we do find coalitions of participation and social justice activists. But compare this to randomly selected mini-publics where civil society activists are often suspicious of a process that delegates power to a cross-section of citizens – where activists can only act as witnesses, but not participate in the deliberations and decision making. Evidence from mini-publics points towards more progressive recommendations when compared to more traditional political processes, suggesting that this suspicion is not well founded.

There is also a potential tension with the growing professionalisation of public participation. This is a positive development in that participatory skills and knowledge are being developed and diffused and standards and quality considered. Yet it also means that there are organisations (private and non-profit) competing for contracts from government (Lee, 2015). This can generate the challenging situation in which organisations need to win short-term contracts to run one-off participatory initiatives, but at the same time know that structural change is necessary to achieve more sustained and effective participatory culture and institutions. The balance sheet can preclude or demote the necessary work on system change.

In the US, organisations such as National Coalition for Dialogue and Deliberation (NCDD) and the Deliberative Democracy Consortium (DCC) are doing interesting work in bringing together different elements of the participation network and leaders from across sectors and policy silos. We also see the emergence of progressive movement parties that are committed (most of the time) to developing a more participatory politics, such as Podemos in Spain. These actors aim not just to promote one-off participatory initiatives, but rather to embed the broader participatory culture and infrastructure that is necessary to ensure the sustenance and ongoing impact of democratic innovations.

Conclusion

Exemplary cases of democratic innovations spark our imagination and offer succour to those of us who wish to see the empowerment of citizens through the development of a more participatory and deliberative politics. But we cannot generalise from these relatively rare cases of empowered participatory governance – too often public participation is ill conceived, poorly organised and lacking in meaningful support from elected and appointed officials. Our challenge is to better understand the conditions under which democratic innovations can be effectively institutionalised. This is an agenda that crosses academic, practitioner and activist boundaries. We need to collect and marshal the data and evidence more effectively. And we need to build the participatory infrastructure and shape hearts and minds such that democratic innovations become an established part of our democratic practices and culture.

References

Abers, R. N. (2000) *Inventing Local Democracy: Grassroots Politics in Brazil*, Boulder and London: Lynne Rienner.

Baiocchi, G. (2003) 'Participation, activism and politics: the Porto Alegre experiment', in Fung, A. and Wright, E.O. (eds) *Deepening Democracy: Institutional Innovations in Empowered Participatory Governance*, London: Verso, 45–76.

Bherer, L., Gauthier, M. and Simard, L. (2014) 'Autonomy for what? Comparing the role of autonomous public organizations dedicated to public participation', paper presented at European Consortium for Political Research Joint Sessions, Salamanca, 10–14 April.

Burall, S. (2015) *Room for a View: democracy as a deliberative system*, London: Involve.

Cabannes, Y. (2004) 'Participatory budgeting: a significant contribution to participatory democracy', *Environment and Urbanization* 16 (1): 27–46.

Elkink, J. A., Farrell, D. M., Reidy, T. and Suiter, J. (2017) 'Understanding the 2015 marriage referendum in Ireland: context, campaign, and conservative Ireland', *Irish Political Studies*, 32 (3): 361–381.

Farrell, D., Byrne, E., O'Malley, E. and Suiter, J. (2011) *Participatory Democracy in Action: a pilot*. Dublin: We the Citizens.

Font, J., Pasadas del Amo, S. and Smith, G. (2016) 'Tracing the impact of proposals from participatory processes: methodological challenges and substantive lessons', *Journal of Public Deliberation* 12 (1): Article 3.

Font, J., Smith, G., Galais, C. and Alarcón, P. (2017) 'Cherry-picking participation: explaining the fate of proposals from participatory processes', *European Journal of Political Research* 57 (3): 615–636.

Fournier, P., van der Kolk, H., Carty, R. K., Blais, A. and Rose, J. (2011) *When Citizens Decide: lessons from citizen assemblies on electoral reform*, Oxford: Oxford University Press.

Fung, A. (2003) 'Recipes for public spheres: eight institutional design choices and their consequences', *Journal of Political Philosophy* 11 (3): 338–367.

Fung, A. (2006) 'Varieties of participation in complex governance', *Public Administration Review*, Special Issue, 66 (s1): 66–75.

Fung, A. and Warren, M. E. (2011) 'The Participedia Project: an introduction', *International Public Management Journal* 14: 341-362.

Fung, A. and Olin Wright, E. (2003) *Deepening Democracy: institutional innovations in empowered participatory governance*, London: Verso.

Ganuza, E. and Baiocchi, G. (2012) 'The power of ambiguity: how participatory budgeting travels the globe,' *Journal of Public Deliberation* 8 (2): Article 8. www.publicdeliberation.net/jpd/vol8/iss2/art8

Ganuza, E., Baiocchi, G. and Summers, N. (2016) 'Conflicts and paradoxes in the rhetoric of participation', *Journal of Civil Society* 12 (3): 328-343.

Gastil, J., Richards Jr, R. C., Ryan, M. and Smith, G. (2017) 'Testing assumptions in deliberative democratic design: a preliminary assessment of the efficacy of the participedia data archive as an analytic tool', *Journal of Public Deliberation* 13 (2): Article 1.

Hendriks, C.M. (2016) 'Coupling citizens and elites in deliberative systems: The role of institutional design', *European Journal of Political Research*, 55 (1): 43-60.

Lee, C. W. (2015) *Do-It-Yourself Democracy: the rise of the public engagement industry*, Oxford: Oxford University Press.

Mansbridge, J., Bohman, J., Chambers, S., Christiano, T., Fung, A., Parkinson, J., Thompson, D. F. and Warren, M. E. (2012) 'A systemic approach to deliberative democracy', in Parkinson, J. and Mansbridge, J. (eds), *Deliberative Systems*, Cambridge: Cambridge University Press.

Nabatchi, T. and Amsler, L. B. (2014) 'Direct public engagement in local government', *The American Review of Public Administration* 44 (4_suppl): 63S-88S.

Nabatchi, T. and Leighninger, M. (2015) *Public Participation for 21st Century Democracy*, Hoboken: John Wiley & Sons.

Newig, J., Challies, E., Jager, N. W., Kochskämper, E. and Adzersen, A. (2018) 'The environmental performance of participatory and collaborative governance: a framework of causal mechanisms', *Policy Studies Journal* 46 (2): 269-297.

Newman, J., Barnes, M., Sullivan, H. and Knops, A. (2004) 'Public participation and collaborative governance', *Journal of Social Policy* 33: 203-223.

Owen, D. and Smith, G. (2015) 'Survey Article: deliberation, democracy, and the systemic turn', *Journal of Political Philosophy* 23 (2): 213–234.

Peruzzotti, E., Magnelli, M. and Peixoto, T. (2011) 'La Plata; Argentina: multi-channel participatory budgeting', *Bertelsmann Stiftung, Reinhard Mohn Prize 2011 Entry*. https://participedia.net/sites/default/files/case-files/277_265_Case_Study_La_Plata.pdf

Petts, J. and Brooks, C. (2006) 'Expert conceptualizations of the role of lay knowledge in environmental decisionmaking: challenges for deliberative democracy', *Environment and Planning A* 38 (6): 1045–1059.

Ryan, M. and Smith, G. (2012) 'Towards a comparative analysis of democratic innovations: lessons from a small-n fsQCA of participatory budgeting', *Revista Internacional de Sociología* (RiS) 70 (Extra2): 89–120.

Setälä, M. and Smith, G. (2018) 'Mini-publics and deliberative democracy', in Bächtiger, A., Dryzek, J., Mansbridge, J. and Warren, M. E. (eds) *The Oxford Handbook of Deliberative Democracy*, Oxford: Oxford University Press.

Sintomer, Y., Herzberg, C., Röcke, A. and Allegretti, G. (2012) 'Transnational models of citizen participation: the case of participatory budgeting', *Journal of Public Deliberation* 8 (2): Article 9. www.publicdeliberation.net/jpd/vol8/iss2/art9

Sirianni, C. and Friedland, L. (2001) *Civic Innovation in America: community empowerment, public policy, and the movement for civic renewal*, Berkeley: University of California Press.

Smith, G., 2009. *Democratic Innovations: designing institutions for citizen participation*, Cambridge: Cambridge University Press.

Smith, G., Gastil, J. and Richards Jr, R. C. (2015) 'The potential of participedia as a crowdsourcing tool for comparative analysis of democratic innovations', *Policy and Internet* 7 (2): 243–262.

Spada, P. and Ryan, M. (2017) 'The failure to examine failures in democratic innovations', *PS: Political Science & Politics* 50 (3): 772–778.

Suiter, J., Farrell, D. M. and Harris, C. (2018) 'Ireland's evolving Constitution', in Blokker, P. (ed) *Constitutional Acceleration Within the European Union and Beyond*, London: Routledge, 142–154

Touchton, M. and Wampler, B. (2014) 'Improving social well-being through new democratic institutions', *Comparative Political Studies* 47 (10): 1442–1469.

Wampler, B., 2007. *Participatory Budgeting in Brazil: contestation, cooperation, and accountability*. University Park, PA: Penn State University Press.

Warren, M. E. (2009) 'Governance-driven democratisation', *Critical Policy Studies* 3 (1): 3–13.

7

The Potential of Community Development

Marilyn Taylor

There has been much discussion over recent years about the weakening of democracy and the public sphere. Commentators refer to a loss of trust in government, the rise of populism and the reduction in the role of politics, all of which have compromised the relationship between citizens and state. And they are critical of the rise of the New Public Management with its emphasis on technocratic approaches to public services. They call instead for new approaches to governing and for the development of deliberative forms of democracy (Dryzek, 2000; Fung and Wright, 2003) that see citizens as co-creators of our common world.

Recent research on 'empowered communities' in the UK has revealed similar concerns among practitioners working in and with communities in this country (http://localtrust.org.uk/our-work/empowered-communities/). In particular, respondents refer to the loss of opportunities for people to understand and reflect on the issues that matter to them and of spaces where critical thinking is encouraged and differences can be aired.

In 1984, Barber warned of the dangers of a 'thin' and minimalist democracy based on individual rights. Since then, the advance of neoliberalism, with its emphasis on marketisation, privatisation and individualism, is seen to have reconstructed the citizen as consumer (Boyte, 2008). Even innovations in participatory democracy – or at least their indiscriminate use – have attracted criticism (see, for example, Cooke and Kothari, 2001; Pateman, 2012). Boyte (2008, p 1) argues instead for a developmental approach to democracy that entails a shift from the citizen as a rights-bearing individual whose highest act is voting and demanding government be held accountable, or a citizen who deliberates and participates in civil society to the citizen as a co-creator of a democratic society and government as catalyst and enabler of civic action.

He advocates the cultivation of civic agency through 'organising', a collective approach with a strong focus on popular education. This, he argues, fosters a politics in which people are not empowered by leaders but rather empower themselves, developing skills and habits of collaborative action and also changing institutions and systems to make them more supportive of civic agency.

'Organising' is part of a wider tradition, broadly described as 'community development', which works with communities to identify and act collectively on issues of common concern. This chapter will discuss the approaches that have been taken within this wider tradition, the roles they can play in relation to democracy and the implications for the relationship between state and citizen. It will illustrate this with reference to UK policy and practice and will discuss the challenges that community development faces in seeking to deepen democracy and foster creative citizenship, challenges that are inherent in our understanding of democracy itself.

What is community development and what does it offer?

The National Occupational Standards for community development define it as a value-based process that 'enables people to work collectively to bring about positive social change. This long term process starts from people's own experience and enables communities to work together to:

- Identify their own needs and actions
- Take collective action using their strengths and resources
- Develop their confidence, skills and knowledge
- Challenge unequal power relationships
- Promote social justice, equality and inclusion in order to improve the quality of their own lives, the communities in which they live and societies of which they are a part. (www.esbendorsement.org.uk)

Several classifications of the different approaches to community development exist (see, for example, Rothman and Tropman, 1987; Smock, 2004; Gilchrist and Taylor, 2016) and practice may combine aspects of each. Broadly speaking, 'community-based' approaches work with communities themselves to foster the skills, capacity and relationships for people to take action to improve their situation and tackle local issues. 'Systems-based' approaches seek to work with the institutions and systems that affect people's lives and make them more responsive to local needs and aspirations. More radical, 'power-based' approaches focus on the structural causes of exclusion and inequality, mobilising communities to demand change.

These approaches have been shaped by a range of different traditions. Thus, as we shall see in the next section of this chapter, some UK scholars suggest that the roots of community development in their country lie in colonialism (Mayo, 1975). An influential critic of the values inherent in colonial traditions, with their imposed Western values and assumptions, was T. H. Batten, who advocated a non-directive approach based in education. In Scotland, community development was and continues to be framed as community education and learning (Scottish Education Department, 1975). In England, by contrast, community development's early progress was heavily influenced by social work, the discipline of key community development authors, until well into the 1980s (Thomas, 1983). Radical practice, meanwhile, has been influenced by the work of Saul Alinsky in the US in the 1940s and by Paolo Freire, whose 'critical pedagogy' supports shared and experiential learning in disadvantaged communities to challenge prevailing ideologies and develop an alternative vision for society (Smock, 2003).

So what can community development, thus broadly defined, contribute to the civic agency that Boyte calls for? In her address to the American Political Science Association Carol Pateman (2010, p 10) argued for 'changes that will make our own social and political life more democratic, that will provide opportunities for individuals to participate in decision making in their everyday lives as well as in the wider democratic system'. Community development has contributed to this vision by helping people in communities to identify common concerns and work together to address these: organising play groups, community gardens, festivals, litter picks, groups and many other self-help initiatives. It has supported them to gain control of local assets, from community buildings and land to energy. It has worked with communities to identify the external actors who have power over their lives – not only the local and national state but also private entities, such as landlords, developers and employers. It has supported them in their negotiations with these actors or in campaigns to challenge their behaviour. Examples include campaigns to tackle poor housing conditions, demand a say in redevelopment plans or protest the closure of local services from hospitals to local bank branches. It is also supporting communities in their attempts to reimagine local economies not only through asset ownership but through credit unions, community food ventures and a range of schemes to keep money local.

Butcher and colleagues (2007, ch 5) underline the centrality of action learning to community development, offering participants in community groups the opportunity to learn from each other through dialogue and debate, to be aware of alternative perspectives, locate their own concerns in a broader picture and to become politically aware in terms of both the analysis of their own situations and the tactics required to bring about transformational change. Essential to this is an understanding of power and the way that power operates to shape people's agendas and even the way they think about things (Lukes, 2005). Community development seeks 'to make power visible and to consider the tactics by which it can be reclaimed, negotiated or resisted' (McCrea et al, 2017, p 381). It has supported citizens in the 'invited' spaces of partnerships, working with or negotiating with the state. But it has also supported them in their own 'popular' spaces, either independently of the state or, in its more radical forms, campaigning against the state and other external actors.

The National Occupational Standards in England and other sources identify a range of values and principles that define community development. These include: people-led, collective, inclusive, and concerned with change, social justice and equality.

In principle, community development is *people-led*, starting from the concerns and hopes that citizens themselves express, rather than any external blueprint. It is essentially *collective*, building the networks and relationships that are needed to increase confidence and achieve change (Boyte, 2008; Gilchrist, 2009) – the social capital that Robert Putnam (1993) defines as essential to democracy. It seeks to be *inclusive*, acknowledging and respecting diversity, but also encouraging people to see what they have in common and establish common cause within and across communities.

At its best, therefore, community development provides people in communities with opportunities to practise democracy at a very local level and supports them in acquiring the skills, knowledge and confidence that they need to do so. As such it has the potential to provide 'a valued, and often rare, public space in which ordinary people "act together for the purpose of influencing and exerting greater control over decisions that affect their lives'" (Kenny, 2016, p 47, cited in McCrea et al, 2017, p 381).

This section has so far focused on the potential of community development but practice varies and McCrea et al (2017, p 381) counsel against the assumption that it is 'always a wellspring of authenticity or progressive politics'. They argue that 'its normative orientation towards solidarity and justice, however limited or compromised it may become in practice, imbues it with a distinctive moral and embedded force'. However, with others (Butcher et al, 2007), they underline the importance of a critical practice.

Critical practice

The need for a critical practice is highlighted by the complexities of community and of the relationship between state and citizen. McCrea et al (2017, p 380) argue that 'community is positioned at the interface of key tensions, including those between institutional politics and direct action and between diverse struggles for recognition, redistribution and representation'. In an earlier work, I have identified a number of similar tensions or 'balancing acts' that are inherent in the nature of community and power but also in democracy itself (Taylor, 2011, ch 12). These are tensions for which there are no blueprints or straightforward solutions, but which need to be constantly negotiated and renegotiated in community practice.

Diversity, recognition and inclusion

The rhetoric of 'community' is one of inclusion. But communities are diverse and may be fragmented – communities and networks are defined by who is 'out' as well as who is 'in'. Community groups can be insular and exclusive, while community development has, over the years, had to negotiate the claims for recognition of different identities and interests. It thus involves finding ways to understand and challenge prejudice and discrimination at the same time as building bridges across communities and identities. It also involves knowing when to respect difference and when to identify and work with the commonalities between different communities. This has been especially important with respect to race and gender but also applies to differences between generations (Chapter Nine in this book). The problem of how to engage young people is a hardy perennial for many community groups (Chapter Ten in this book).

Leadership, representation and participation

Action requires leaders who can take the initiative, but if community development is to live up to its principles, it needs to find ways of engaging with people across the whole community. This is especially important when it comes to negotiating with outside bodies, which are all too willing to accuse community leaders of being unrepresentative and unaccountable. A lot of the policy discourse about community seeks to identify, train and engage with community leaders. However, it is easy for community leaders who are negotiating with outsiders or taking on the management of assets to become divorced from the people on the streets around them. If civic agency is to be democratic, it needs to find methods of ensuring that leadership is shared and accountable, with a variety of ways for community members to engage and keep informed.

Scale

A further tension is the question of scale – what can be dealt with at local community level and what needs more broad-based action? Many community issues can be solved at community level – indeed, this may be the best way to address them. But there are elements in any community's life over which its members have little or no control and this requires them to join forces across boundaries, to find common cause and agree a common approach: 'Being realistic, you can't solve poverty by setting up a little group on Tuesday nights' (IVAR, 2018).

Scaling up and creating alliances may, therefore, be essential but it creates its own challenges of accountability and leadership. McAlevey (2016, p 10) emphasises the need to mobilise beyond the activist network, so that 'ordinary people help make the power analysis, design the strategy, and achieve the outcome' (p 10).

Institutional politics or direct action?

Community development is about change and social justice. But is this best achieved by working with the state or by exerting pressure from outside? Working on the inside carries the risk of co-option into a 'top-down' state agenda and losing a critical, independent edge. Dependence on government funding can lead to self-censorship and cooperation may fail to achieve the required results. Radical practice can be problematic too. Boyte (2008, p 4) contrasts organising with mobilising, which he argues can also be 'top-down':

> Find an enemy to demonise, stir up emotion with inflammatory language, create a 'script' that defines the issue as good vs. evil and shuts down critical thought ... Such approaches failed to address complex problems that require work across lines of difference, public judgment and imaginative collective action.

Both institutional politics and direct action have the potential to create change, although they play different roles (Craig et al, 2004). And research has found that maintaining an independent voice inside the 'invited spaces' of the system is most likely if it is based in people's own 'independent' or 'popular' spaces (Taylor et al, 2010). It will also depend on the political and institutional environment within which community development operates. The following sections will explore this further with reference to the changing policy environment in the UK.

The state and community development

Community development has been adopted by policy makers for a variety of reasons: to defuse tensions within communities; to address the crisis of legitimacy within the state and the political process; but also to encourage citizen responsibility and maximise community assets. It has sometimes been supported to *complement* the state and to inform state programmes, sometimes to work in *partnership with* the state. However, it has also been criticised for being *an instrument of the state*, while more recently the concern has been that government is using community development to *substitute for* the state.

As the previous section mentioned, the history of community development in the UK has been traced back by some to the colonial era, where it was deployed as an *instrument of the state* to encourage self-reliance and stave off unrest, as well as preparing the colonies for economic and political independence. Mayo (1975) traces similar 'colonial roots' in the US where community development was used to defuse black and minority ethnic unrest.

Early community development efforts in the UK were piecemeal and associated with post-war reconstruction, as intensive post-war slum clearance programmes displaced many communities to new neighbourhoods with few facilities. Energy went into building a sense of community in these new areas, encouraging self-help, promoting community activities and developing local support networks – a community-based approach, *complementing* and working *alongside* the state.

By the end of the 1960s, increasing urban unrest, racial tension and the realisation that the welfare state had not put paid to poverty led the UK government to introduce a more comprehensive range of community programmes. In doing so, it drew heavily on the US response to these problems – the War on Poverty (Marris and Rein, 1972) – combining a 'community-based' approach, which encouraged community activity, with a 'systems-based approach', which sought to coordinate local services and make them more responsive.

Community development had little government support in the 1980s, when the advance of neoliberalism under Margaret Thatcher's government espoused a more individualist approach. But it was to become mainstream with the election of New Labour in the UK in 1997, which launched the most comprehensive community programme since the 1970s (Social Exclusion Unit, 2001). The new government was driven by a concern to tackle social exclusion but also to promote civil renewal and was heavily influenced by a communitarian philosophy, promoting 'strong, empowered and active communities, in which people increasingly do things for themselves and the state acts to facilitate, support and enable citizens to lead self-determined and fulfilled lives' (Blunkett, 2003, p 43).

Partnership *with the state* was central to the New Labour approach. The government invested in programmes to support community involvement in such partnerships, to encourage and support community participation more generally, and to build capacity among policy makers and service providers as well as communities themselves (see Chapters Five and Thirteen in this book). While its initial focus was on the most disadvantaged neighbourhoods, one driver of change was its concern to address the democratic deficit more widely and encourage citizen and consumer engagement (Taylor, 2011). So, over time it expanded its community empowerment programmes beyond the most disadvantaged neighbourhoods to the country as a whole.

The Conservative-led Coalition Government elected in 2010 continued a number of New Labour themes, such as promoting the transfer of assets to the community and a range of community rights (to acquire buildings and land and to challenge existing service delivery), though with a different ideological badging. Under its Big Society banner, it too was keen to encourage people to take an active role in their communities. Perhaps surprisingly, though, one of the main vehicles it wanted to use was community organising. It may seem paradoxical for a Conservative Prime Minister to have endorsed a way of working with radical Alinskyan origins but politicians' interest had been captured not only by the success of Barack Obama's community organising politics in the US but also by the ability of Citizens UK – a UK organisation based on Alinsky's approach – to mobilise large numbers of people in its campaigns.

In the event, the government's Community Organisers Programme, which ran from 2011 to 2015, supported a less obviously radical community-based approach (Fisher and Shragge, 2017) and it has been extended under the Conservative administration elected in 2015. But a significant funder of community development now is the state-sponsored Big Lottery Fund (BIG), which, through Big Local, is investing over £1 million in each of 150 communities across England over a decade to 'help residents develop and use their skills and confidence to identify what matters most to them, and to take action to change things for the better, now and in the future' (localtrust.org.uk). It has recently partnered with government to create a Place Based Social Action fund to 'support local partnerships to come together to make a positive difference to their communities' (biglotteryfund.org.uk).

Many of the national programmes discussed here, while funded by central government, were channelled through local authorities or partnerships that included local authorities. Indeed, local government has itself also been a major funder of community development and a major employer of community workers. Even during the Thatcher years, a number of local authorities saw communities of place and interest as allies in their resistance to the neoliberal agenda and continued to fund community development. Currently, there is strong support in parts of the country for the development of new forms of co-production based on creative relationships between public services and citizen consumers (Durose and Richardson, 2016; see also Chapter Fourteen in this book).

The community development response

State support for community development has allowed it to thrive, but it also has its critics. In the 1960s and 1970s, for example, those involved in the Community Development Projects were critical of the assumptions behind the CDP programme, locating the sources of deprivation not in community pathology or the failures of systems and services, but in the structure of the capitalist economy itself. They advocated a more radical power-based approach, building coalitions with trades unions and social movements beyond the local to fight for change.

The New Labour policies some 30 years later were welcomed by those in community development. They gave communities both the place at the decision-making table they had fought for and the support they needed to underpin civic engagement, as well as devolving resources to local level. But they too had their critics, who argued that community development had been co-opted into a top-down agenda. While more was achieved for many of those involved than perhaps these critics allow (Lawless and Pearson, 2012), participants complained about the detailed monitoring requirements of a number of neighbourhood renewal programmes, while in too many parts of the country the rules of the partnership game were still dictated by state actors (Taylor, 2011). Existing cultures proved difficult to shift – something that the programmes of the 1960s and 1970s, both in the UK and the US, had also found (Marris and Rein, 1972).

In recent years, therefore, community development programmes have re-emphasised the need for a 'bottom-up, people-led' approach. They have also rejected what they see as the 'deficit model' of many programmes over the years, arguing that a focus on problems and deprivation risks stereotyping the very areas that these programmes seek to 'empower'. Asset Based Community Development (ABCD), which has been adopted by several English local authorities, is grounded in the work of Kretzmann and McKnight (1993) in the US and focuses on the assets and potential of communities themselves. On its website Big Local declares that 'It's not about your local authority, the government or a national organisation telling you what to do'. The Community Organisers Programme itself has stressed the need to listen to local people and 'not do for communities what they can do for themselves'. And the funders of these two programmes have been careful to adopt a 'hands-off' approach, resisting the monitoring requirements that attracted criticism in past programmes.

However, there have been criticisms of these approaches, too. The Community Organisers Programme was initially greeted with scepticism by people in the community field (Clarke and Newman, 2012; Fisher and Shragge, 2017), who saw it as part of a government agenda to cut public services and transfer responsibility for these to local communities. MacLeod and Emejulu (2014) have criticised the community-based model of ABCD for placing responsibility on disadvantaged communities and failing to recognise or address the external causes of the problems they face. In the event, and whatever the intention, organisers from the Community Organisers Programme have followed many different paths across the community development spectrum, from community-based to radical (Fisher and Shragge, 2017). Advocates of ABCD have defended themselves against the critique they face. But the language of the Coalition's Big Society and the support given to community activity takes its place, as we shall see, alongside a programme of austerity and public service cuts. In this situation, mainstream forms of community development will inevitably face the challenge that they are complicit in an agenda that expects the poorest and most desperate communities to fill in the gaps left by a rapidly retreating state.

Contemporary challenges for community development

So what is the potential of community development going forward? We have discussed the ongoing tensions that it has to negotiate. But there are a number of contemporary challenges – some to do with government policy, some not – which affect its ability to strengthen civic agency. Recent research (IVAR/Local Trust, 2018), based on interviews with people working in communities across the UK, has highlighted the following.

Austerity

The Coalition Government's aspiration to encourage people to take a more active role in their communities took its place alongside a brutal austerity programme introduced by the same government in the wake of the 2008 financial crash, which imposed major cuts to welfare benefits and public spending more generally. This has three implications for community development and civic action. Firstly, benefit cuts, insecure employment and depressed wages affect the capacity of people, particularly in the most disadvantaged communities, to become civic actors. In accordance with Maslow's hierarchy of needs (Maslow, 1943), their focus is on survival. In my own recent research, a Somali community worker explained that members of the Somali community might be holding down two or three jobs, which doesn't leave much time for engaging with others in the community, even at a social level:

> 'Many Somalis locally are struggling, going out early in the morning and coming back late in the evening. And what could a single mother do trying to bring up young children on her own? They might want to engage but would they have the time and capacity? They have to feed their children. They may be working Saturdays and Sundays.'[1]

---

[1] The observation was made in a research interview not published elsewhere.

Second is the impact that austerity, along with a neoliberal commitment to the withdrawal of the state, has had on the public services on which many in the most disadvantaged communities depend. A recent study commented on the importance of the investment in and support for communities that programmes like Big Local can offer, sustained over the long term and offering 'light-touch' community development support (Dobson, 2018, p 72). But its author argues that if such communities are to realise their potential, 'they also need reliable, effective, consistent and responsive public services'. Instead, there have been unprecedented cuts to local authority budgets, especially in the most disadvantaged areas (Beatty and Fothergill, 2013). This means that many services are being cut back with the expectation that communities themselves will fill the gap. There are undoubtedly circumstances when it is empowering for communities to take responsibility themselves, but only if they have the support, resources and capacity to do so. Instead, the communities that have least are expected to invest most in the future of local services (Dobson, 2018). Community development must not be expected to collude with the retreat of the state from its own responsibilities.

Thirdly, austerity has not only affected mainstream services. It has resulted in major funding cuts to community development at local authority level as well as direct financial and in-kind support to community groups. The UK exception is Scotland, where local authorities continue to be a more significant funder. Elsewhere, while independent charitable funders are expressing a welcome interest in place-based funding (Buckley et al, 2016), this cannot compensate for the loss of state support. Austerity has also cut a swathe through the community development infrastructure. The core funding support that characterised the New Labour era was withdrawn and most national infrastructure bodies have folded as a result. In Scotland, by contrast, where the devolved Scottish administration continues to invest, the national infrastructure has survived and seems to be thriving. Reductions in local authority support elsewhere in the UK mean that local infrastructure bodies too are closing, or turning to service delivery to fund their work, leaving the community organisations that depended on them with nowhere to go.

These cuts have been reflected in training provision. When Alison Gilchrist and I published the first edition of our *Short Guide to Community Development* in 2011, we included a list of 37 training providers, among them many universities. However, significant course closures mean that the table did not survive into the second edition (Gilchrist and Taylor, 2016). A few remain but training is now most likely to be provided as an element of the specific programmes and brands discussed earlier in the chapter.

Transience

The housing market has changed significantly over the past 50 years, with implications for the nature of the most disadvantaged communities. The relative proportions of social rented housing and private rented housing have shifted. Over the 50 years the proportion of households in social housing has fallen from 29% (peaking at 32% in 1981) to 15% – it is now the smallest tenure. Over the same period the proportion of households in the private rented sector fell from 20% to just 9% in the mid-1980s but since the mid-2000s has risen back to 20% (DCLG, 2017). This has made a significant difference to many disadvantaged communities. Whereas in the mid-to-late twentieth century, community development was often focused on large estates of rented social housing, with a relatively stable population, these estates now are more likely to house a significant proportion of housing units that have been bought by their tenants under 'Right to Buy' and then either sold on to private landlords or rented out directly. Many of the resulting tenancies are insecure and tenants may have to move on after six months. This makes it more difficult to get them to engage with, even identify with, the local community:

> In cases where neighbours are anonymous and do not stay long enough to develop any emotional connection to the place, they tend not to be committed enough to improve their own home, or to work with their neighbours and local agencies to improve the whole neighbourhood. (Manzo and Perkins, 2006, pp 335-6)

Rural areas have a different problem, as second homeowners and commuters take over available housing and prices rise beyond the reach of local people.

Disappearing spaces

A further challenge relates to the loss of spaces for what Jurgen Habermas (1984) defined as communicative action – the opportunity for citizens to engage in dialogue, reflect and learn. Wholesale changes in culture and industry mean that many of the institutions which offered these opportunities to working class people have been lost –

these would have included miners and working men's (sic) institutes, the unions, the chapels and so on. More recently the privatisation of public spaces, combined with cuts to public spending, means that spaces for spontaneous encounters – informal opportunities to encounter a diverse range of people, let alone to discuss and debate issues of common concern – are disappearing, while previously free spaces for more formal meetings and events are now charging or privatised. Social media offer alternatives but are not accessible to all and can trap people in 'bubbles' rather than allowing for the difficult conversations that are needed to resolve differences and challenge taken-for-granted assumptions.

Fragmented communities

Finally, the Brexit vote and the anti-immigrant sentiment that has been associated with it demonstrate a 'fear of the other' that has been whipped up by politicians and the media. The insecurity this fosters is fragmenting communities. Combined with the austerity that leaves communities feeling abandoned by those in power, this is fertile ground for populism and far-right organising (Kenny et al, 2018). In this situation, community development's political education role becomes ever more important and challenging.

Conclusion

Research commissioned by the New Labour government underlined the value of community participation and community involvement in delivering government policies and improving services (SQW, 2005; Pratchett et al, 2009), while evaluations of their flagship programmes also found evidence of improvement against key indicators (Lawless and Pearson, 2012). This chapter has discussed the various ways in which community development can underpin a strong vision of democracy and civic agency, in which people at local level can find their voices as citizens and act collectively together for transformative change.

It has also identified a number of tensions inherent in translating its principles into practice, which it argues are shared by democracy itself. It has discussed how the state supports but can also undermine its potential. And it has identified contemporary challenges that act as barriers to effective civic engagement. In the face of these changing times, the need for community development and the values that community espouses will become ever more important. At the same time, it will be essential for those who support and promote community development to engage in the kind of critical reflexivity that McCrea and colleagues (2017) and Butcher and colleagues (2007) advocate, challenging both their ongoing practice but also traditional assumptions about the nature of community and civic action.

References

Barber, B. (1984) *Strong Democracy: participatory politics for a new age,* Berkeley: University of California Press.

Beatty, C. and Fothergill, S. (2013) *Hitting the Poorest Places Hardest: the local and regional impact of welfare reform,* Sheffield: Centre for Regional Economic and Social Research, Sheffield Hallam University.

Boyte, H. (2008) 'Civic driven change and developmental democracy', in Biekart, K. and Fowler, A. (eds) *Civic Driven Change: citizens' imagination in action,* The Hague: Institute of Social Studies (see also www.iss.nl/cdc).

Blunkett, D. (2003) 'Civil renewal: a new agenda', The CSV Edith Kahn Memorial Lecture, 11 June.

Buckley, E., Cairns, B. and Taylor, M. (2016) *Working in Place,* London: IVAR.

Butcher, H., Banks, S., Henderson, P. with Robertson, J. (2007) *Critical Community Practice,* Bristol: Policy Press.

Clarke, J. and Newman, J. (2012) 'The alchemy of austerity', *Critical Social Policy,* 32 (3): 299–319.

Cooke, B. and Kothari, U. (2001) *Participation: the new tyranny,* London: Zed Books.

Craig, G., Taylor, M. and Parkes, T. (2004) 'Protest or partnership? The voluntary and community sectors in the policy process', *Social Policy and Administration,* 38 (3): 221-239.

Department of Communities and Local Government (DCLG) (2017) *50 Years of the English Housing Survey,* London: DCLG.

Dobson, J. (2018) *New Seeds Beneath the Snow? Big Local neighbourhoods in action,* London: Local Trust.

Dryzek, J. (2000) *Deliberative Democracy and Beyond: liberals, critics and contestations,* Oxford: Oxford University Press.

Durose, C. and Richardson, L. (2016) *Designing Public Policy for Co-production: theory, practice and change,* Bristol: Policy Press.

Fisher, B. and Shragge, E. (2017) 'Resourcing community organizing; examples from England and Quebec, *Community Development Journal* 52 (3): 454-469.

Fung, A. and Wright, E. (2003) *Deepening Democracy: innovations in empowered participatory governance,* London: Verso.

Gilchrist, A. (2009) *The Well Connected Community: a networking approach to community development* (2nd edn), Bristol: Policy Press.

Gilchrist, A. and Taylor, M. (2016) *The Short Guide to Community Development* (2nd edn), Bristol: Policy Press.

Habermas, J. (1984) *Communicative Action*, Boston: Beacon Press.

IVAR (2018) *Empowered Communities in the 2020s: IVAR research briefing 2 – countries dialogue*, London: IVAR.

IVAR/Local Trust (2018) *The Future for Communities: perspectives on power*, London: IVAR and Local Trust.

Kenny, S. (2016) 'Changing community development roles: the challenges of a globalizing world', in Meade, R., Shaw, M. and Banks, S. (eds) *Power, Politics and Community Development*, Bristol: Policy Press.

Kenny, S. (2018) 'Preface', in Kenny, S., McGrath, B. and Phillips, R. *The Routledge Handbook of Community Development*, London: Routledge.

Kretzmann, J. and McKnight, J. (1993) *Building Communities from the Inside Out: a path toward finding and mobilising a community's assets,* Evanston, IL: Center for Urban Affairs and Policy Research, Northwestern University.

Lawless, P. and Pearson, S. (2012) 'Outcomes from community engagement in urban regeneration: evidence from England's New Deal for Communities programme', *Planning theory and practice* 13 (4): 509–527.

Lukes, S. (2005) *Power: a radical view*, Basingstoke: Palgrave Macmillan.

MacLeod, M. and Emejulu, A. (2014) 'Neoliberalism with a community face? A critical analysis of Asset-Based Community Development in Scotland', *Journal of Community Practice* 22 (4): 430–450.

Manzo, L. and Perkins, D. (2006) 'Finding common ground: the importance of place attachment to community participation and planning', *Journal of Planning Literature* 20 (2): 335–350.

Maslow, A. (1943) 'A theory of human motivation', *Psychological Review*, 50(4): 449–458.

McAlevey, J. (2016) *No Shortcuts: organising for power in the new gilded age,* Oxford: Oxford University Press.

McCrea, N., Meade, R. and Shaw, M. (2017) 'Practising solidarity: challenges for community development and social movements in the twenty-first century', *Community Development Journal* 52 (3): 379–384.

Marris, P. and Rein, M. (1972) *Dilemmas of Social Reform*, New York: Atherton Press.

Mayo, M. (1975) 'Community Development: a radical alternative', in Bailey, R. and Brake, M. (eds) *Radical Social Work*, London: Edward Arnold, 129–143.

Pateman, C. (2012) 'Participatory democracy revisited', *Perspectives on Politics* 10 (1): 7–19.

Pratchett, l., Durose, C., Lowndes, V., Stoker, G. and Wales, C. (2009) *Empowering Communities to Influence Local Decision Making: a systematic review of the evidence*, London: Communities and Local Government.

Putnam, R. (1993) *Making Democracy Work*, Princeton, NJ: Princeton University Press.

Rothman, J. and Tropman, J. (1987) 'Models of community organisations and macro practice perspectives: their mixing and phasing', in Cox, F., Erlich, J., Rothman, J. and Tropman, J. (eds) *Strategies of Community Organization,* Itasca, IL: F. E Peacock, pp 3-26.

Scottish Education Department (1975) *Adult Education: the challenge of change* (The Alexander Report), Edinburgh: HMSO.

Smock, K. (2004) *Democracy in Action: community organizing and urban change*, New York: Columbia University Press.

Social Exclusion Unit (2001) *A New Commitment to Neighbourhood Regeneration: the Action Plan*, London: The Stationery Office.

SQW (2005) *Improving Delivery of Mainstream Services in Deprived Areas: the role of community involvement*, London: Communities and Local Government.

Taylor, M. (2011) *Public Policy in the Community,* Basingstoke: Palgrave Macmillan.

Taylor, M., Howard, J. and Lever, J. (2010) 'Citizen participation and civic activism in comparative perspective', *Journal of Civil Society* 6 (2): 145-164.

Thomas, D. (1983) *The Making of Community Work*, London: Allen & Unwin.

8

Community Action and
Civic Dialogue

Barry Quirk

Political commentators often portray democracy as a pathway for establishing an electoral majority for the purpose of governing. Used in this instrumental sense, democracy revolves around the conduct of political elites in finding a winning coalition for a programme of social change. But this is a terribly narrow and perverse interpretation of democracy's purpose. For in its widest sense, democracy is an ideal, a process and also an idea in action (Runciman, 2014). The rhythms and pulse of democracy can be found in the everyday life of each and every community. Democracy is not confined to the high arts of statecraft but instead it infuses the common and everyday life between us all.

Under this more rounded portrait, democracy involves people learning how to disagree with each other so that they can live together as equals without resorting to violence or competitive strategies of domination. In this fuller sense, democracy involves an open, emergent and deliberative style, as much as it requires formal and institutional foundations for governing. Open discussion and questioning are therefore central to the legitimacy of day-to-day democratic conduct (Quirk, 2011). This generates a corresponding need for political institutions themselves to adapt to open-ended change. This interlinked character of societal and governmental progress was powerfully described over 200 years ago by Thomas Jefferson (1816):

> I am not an advocate for frequent changes in laws and constitutions, but laws and institutions must go hand in hand with the progress of the human mind. As that becomes more developed, more enlightened, as new discoveries are made,

new truths discovered and manners and opinions change, with the change of circumstances, institutions must advance also to keep pace with the times. We might as well require a man to wear still the coat which fitted him when a boy as a civilised society to remain ever under the regimen of their barbarous ancestors.

While the nation state is usually thought of as the source and site of democratic and constitutional processes, the origin of our actual democratic practice is usually found in the locality in which we live. For it is at the local level where we encounter our first problems of collective action, and where we first learn how to deliberate together with others about what should be done to solve them. It is at the local level where we first attempt to reconcile the collective goals of a group of people with the wider public benefit for everyone in the area (Olson, 1971).

Rarely do we arrive at challenges with hard-boiled opinions as to what should be done. Instead we discuss with others; we learn from their views, values and preferences; and we ponder together on the best possibilities for the future. But the community in which we live is not merely a useful mechanism for us, it is often a strong part of our own identity too. Michael Sandel is rightly critical of what he calls the 'weak conception of community' where people who have shared goals simply regard cooperation between themselves as a necessary strategy for achieving these goals. Instead, Sandel suggests a strong conception of community. This strong conception stems from a sense of shared identity, which renders people's membership of a community not as instrumental, but as constitutive: 'Community describes not what they *have* as fellow citizens ... but also who they *are*, not a relationship they choose but an attachment they discover, not merely an attribute but a constituent of their identity' (Sandel, 1982, p 150; emphasis in original).

Forms of community action

Those of us with formal civic roles should be aware of our responsibility in helping community action enrich, and not undermine, democratic cooperation. Community actions tend to arise organically from people with regular connections through two differing types of sentiment. First, out of a supportive spirit of mutualism among people who have a shared sense of social aims;[1] and second, out of some form of power-related struggle with regard to formal political institutions and tussles over public resources and assets. The latter may take the form of some kind of community struggle, say, in defence of local amenities, facilities or services or to demand some new ones.

While community action can play an important part in developing democratic relations, it is not intrinsically progressive in character and its outcomes are not always ethically fair and socially just. Some community action involves capturing community and public assets for the social purpose of one small group. Others may, indeed, serve to focus energies on how to mobilise bias against progressive change. And some community action is focused squarely on preserving current amenity values and entrenching the existing positional advantage of one community relative to other communities.

There are very many examples throughout the country where the very energy of community action rubs against locally elected representative government. Unlike the local government system in some nations, UK local government is not constituted from below but constructed from above. Although its elected members are chosen by the local population following popular elections at ward level,[2] these political representatives seem at times to be engaged in a form of faux rivalry with community activists (see also Chapter Twelve in this book).

On occasions, it can seem as though the formal representative character of local democracy is contested by the actions undertaken by communities themselves. This need not be so, as the two can supplement each other. If communities embrace deliberative approaches, their decisions (through techniques such as community conferences, citizens' panels, citizens' juries and so on) can help to inform elected representatives who are then able to make better informed choices for the people (see Chapter Six in this book). The key issue here is whether those with positions in government adopt the appropriate approach to empower communities to engage in cooperative deliberations to help serve the common good.

---

[1] As for the arrangements for arriving at collective choices, the practical strategies may not be settled by any single discussion, but simply evolve over time. For example, in some fishing communities, in the absence of rules and regulations, people's everyday practices converged on tacit cooperation with each other so as to optimise fishing for everyone and not to overfish and so deplete all available resources (Ostrom, 1990).

[2] Each ward in England and Wales is composed of an average population of about 7,000 people, or some 5,000 voters on average. County councils have larger electoral areas called 'divisions'.

Contrasting approaches to empowering community action

Over the past 40 years, government attitudes to community action have changed considerably. In England in the late 1970s, it was an integral part of government strategies to revive 'inner urban areas'. These focused on changing the social fabric of places and reviving the economy and environment of localities. During the 1980s and 1990s a series of area-based, but nonetheless top-down, initiatives sought to revive inner-city areas throughout England that were subject to obvious urban stress and palpable socioeconomic deprivation. These initiatives included City Challenge, as well as area-based single regeneration budgets, which sought to change the conditions under which communities lived without engaging those communities in considering what changes were to be brought in.

In 1997, the newly elected Labour Government introduced a fresh approach to supporting local community action. This new approach, exemplified by initiatives such as New Deal for Communities, Neighbourhood Management and the cross-government Together We Can programme, was based on a more empowering model that relied on discussing options with local people, involving them in setting priorities and passing control over defined resources and specific public assets to community groups.

Local councils were encouraged to empower community action through fostering deliberative engagement, self-help and mutualism, and promoting cooperative behaviour among citizens, existing civil society groups and new community organisations. An independent review of community asset transfers, commissioned by the Labour Government, demonstrated through the adoption of a number of core principles and learning from in-depth case studies how community organisations could realise tremendous potential by taking on the management and ownership of community assets with support provided by the government and local councils (Quirk, 2007).

In opposition, David Cameron, the then Leader of the Conservative Party, devised a political approach to community around the notion of the Big Society. However, on the establishment of the Conservative-led Coalition Government following the 2010 General Election, it became clear that the Big Society concept had been minted before the global financial crash and that, at best, it sat awkwardly with the Cameron Government's far-reaching public sector austerity programme. The Big Society narrative focused on ways to expand social and community capital; but it became easily caricatured as a 'cover for cuts'. Despite the potential for broad appeal of a concept like 'Big Society', it was the earlier attempt to empower community action by the previous Labour Government that paved the way for real improvements to state-citizen cooperation, based on civic innovation, community enterprise and citizen engagement.

In the last two decades, the overall approach among UK local authorities to community empowerment has changed considerably. In the first instance, this was because of the growth of 'commissioning' approaches to securing local service outputs and trying to achieve desired local outcomes. The best of these approaches encouraged experimentation and innovation at the community level, but unfortunately the majority prefigured community outcomes too readily. In the second instance, the approach changed as a result of the public sector austerity programme that was applied disproportionately to local government budgets. With a cumulative reduction in local authority budgets in England of well over 40% over the decade to 2020 (Smith et al, 2016; Freeguard et al, 2018), it is perhaps unsurprising that many councils try to 'empower' community groups to perform those local functions that it can no longer finance directly. The combined effect of these two factors has led, in many parts of England at least, to an unfortunate form of municipalisation of community action.

However, there is little doubt that the rate of innovation and enterprise in the community sector has increased. The adaptive and resilient character of the community sector has been tested but there are very many examples of success. This has been energised by generational change, the power of modern networks and support from the more forward-thinking local authorities. The scope and spread of social innovation, the growth in the number of social entrepreneurs and the flourishing nature of local community enterprises all signal substantial changes to the nature of collaborative community action. The results can be seen in the growth of community-level start-ups supported by crowdfunding and the adoption of agile business models than was traditionally the case in this sector (see Chapter Fourteen of this book).

The digital world was supposed to witness the 'death of distance' such that global connections dominated local connections. However in the first wave of digital innovation (to 2010) what became evident was the growth of local community-level digital blogs and websites that enable the densification of local networks. In response to local critical incidents and to enable swifter community-level response on local issues, the second wave of digital innovation has witnessed growing evidence of increased localised social media networks and community-based virtual groups.

Local government's role in empowering community action

The Local Government Association in England (LGA, 2016) in its guidance to local authorities tries to overcome any bias towards conserving and capturing advantage by suggesting that councils need to place community action at the centre of their activities for four main reasons:

- Building community and social capacity – helping the community to share knowledge, skills and ideas.
- Community resilience – helping the community to support itself.
- Prevention – a focus on early access to services or support, engagement in design, cross-sector collaboration and partnerships.
- Maintaining and creating wealth – for example helping people into employment or developing community enterprises.

This guidance on community action builds on the work of the Young Foundation (2010), which outlined the cultural stance that councils needed to adopt if they were to develop an empowering style of community engagement. In this way, the LGA suggests a simple threefold approach:

- Create a culture of sharing problems and developing community-focused solutions across the council.
- Communicate the purpose of community action.
- Have a community action plan that runs through all council services.

This is important guidance, as it reminds councils that they are vehicles for community self-governance before they are instruments for central government functions and services. From being principally about functional service delivery in the 1970s and 1980s, UK local government has been rather swept up by the modernising ethos of the New Public Management (NPM) paradigm for organising government and the public sector, and has instead concentrated more on securing services or commissioning predetermined service outcomes. Turning councils' attention to their community self-governance role is a healthy corrective to the NPM ethos that has dominated local authority management over the past three decades.

If councils are to empower community action to help bring about genuine community self-governance, they need to recognise the profile and dynamics of the people who live and work in their local communities. Although the homes, the buildings, the fields or parks, the shops, the offices, the warehouses and factories, the roads and the railway lines may establish the contours of the landscape in which we live, our lives are given deeper texture by our day-to-day interactions among the social networks of our family, friends, neighbours and our wider community. In the early part of the twenty-first century throughout Europe and the US, more and more people live in the presence of social and cultural difference. While the cultural and economic collision of these differences is what gives large cities their vibrancy and their creative and innovative potential (Quirk, 2016), the economics of competitive individualism and the positional consumption of the wealthy can rub up against the harsh everyday realities of those trapped in conditions of urban poverty.

In some cities, the varied ethnicity of the population produces a form of 'super-diversity'. However, while diversity may have strong economic advantages, it may also prove socially challenging (Enos, 2017). Some researchers on ethnic integration have described a 'commonplace diversity' where people share public space but not private space. They may share the public realm of a neighbourhood, but they are unlikely to eat in one another's homes, or attend their neighbours' funerals (Wessendorf, 2013). Local government can play a leading role in supporting and facilitating community and neighbourhood events, which give people cross-cultural, intergenerational and other types of opportunities for transcending social habits and barriers. Simply framing opportunities to meet and get to know each other in relaxed surroundings over food and entertainment is very valuable. Such events build familiarity and trust that are essential for inclusive community action.

In an insightful account of the moral order, or the 'ethical operating system', in large cities Michael Ignatieff argues that a key problem for social cohesion is generating collaboration among strangers who do not share a common origin, religion or ethnicity. He suggests that:

> Transactional indifference, though there is plenty of this in any city, is not enough. People want their gaze returned. They want to hope for the kindness of strangers, no matter how rare it may be ... The ordinary virtues – trust, honesty, politeness, forbearance, respect – are the operating system of any community. (Ignatieff, 2017, p 52)

The key point here is that compromise, or simply connection, is found by people through close social interaction at the level of the local community. And these local compromises and connections are contextually informed and practically realised. They do not arise from theory or ideology. Ignatieff concludes his account by drawing upon a speech given in 1958 by the then 74-year-old Eleanor Roosevelt. On the tenth anniversary of the UN Declaration of Human Rights, she was asked to respond to a question about where universal human rights begin. She answered:

> 'Where do universal human rights begin? In small places, close to home – so close, and so small that they cannot be seen on any maps of the world. Yet they are the world of the individual person; the neighbourhood he lives in; the school or college he attends; the factory, farm or offices where he works. Such are the places where every man, woman and child seeks equal justice, equal opportunity, equal dignity without discrimination. Unless these rights have meaning there, they have little meaning anywhere. Without concerted citizen action to uphold them close to home, we shall look in vain for progress in the larger world.' (Quoted in Ignatieff, 2017, pp 196-7)

Roosevelt's response presents the case with real clarity. Concerted citizen action at the community level is the public essence of civic betterment. It does not require hundreds of people to be actively engaged; it happens when a small group of community actors identify ways of solving local problems through the energy of their collective action. These actors rarely wait to be invited by those who occupy positions of formal power; and they are seldom energised by being asked to be involved on some state-sponsored consultation exercise. Instead, by blending a sense of agency with a desire for solidarity, community actors can begin to strengthen the bonds of community and make change happen at the local level.

Local government has a vital role to play in creating the social conditions externally and institutional culture internally to make it more likely that community actors can find receptive partners in the public domain in pursuit of the common good. Councils should put a high premium on enabling people to interact across social groups and thereby bridge the diversity across and within their communities. It is at the local level that citizens first try to shape solutions to the social or public problems that confront them. And they attempt these solutions out of the often competing and conflicting perspectives that exist in their local communities. It is the practice of deliberation together with the practice of shaping solutions that gives us the real essence of democracy in action.

Civic dialogue

One of the key instruments in cultivating mutual respect and shared understanding is civic dialogue. While there are obviously conversations about issues of local and global import happening every day, dialogues about civic and local life can be framed, sponsored and supported by public institutions so as to assist communities in developing their own solutions to local problems. They can also assist public institutions to reframe their own approaches to policy challenges. Civic dialogue can therefore be engendered by citizens themselves, by civil society associations, by locally elected politicians and by public service providers (councils, police authorities, NHS commissioners and providers, among many others).

But in conditions of pluralism, the foundations of effective civic dialogue must involve clarity about the subjects under discussion so that participation is optimised and is made on as reasoned a basis as possible. Emotion will fuel participation and bring passion to the search for solutions. And emotion is an absolutely critical foundation for the political pursuit of equality, aspiration, compassion, patriotism and justice (Nussbaum, 2013). But cool reflective deliberation requires thoughtful and reasoned discussion about the nature of the problems to be solved. Hence reasonable levels of civic literacy are an important precursor to effective civic dialogue (Milner, 2002; Chapter Eleven in this book). Ideally it is also important that there is an open culture of public reason and that free and candid dialogue occurs among engaged and empowered citizens as well as with their governments (Habermas, 1984; Rawls, 1993).

This is why it makes little sense for governments (whether central or local) to press for community input into an issue if it is not ready to provide adequate, balanced and intelligible information to the public on which the issue can be considered. What's more, citizens need to be informed as to how best they can influence their government or make claims about what issues are in the public interest. This is difficult to achieve in national debates on issues which are reduced to a binary choice, as was the case in the UK-wide EU Referendum held in 2016.

The style of local public dialogue is therefore crucial if creative place-based solutions are to be found to contested public problems. Choose the subject poorly (say, by misdefining the public problem to be solved) and it will be difficult to engage people. Use a poor style of dialogue and people will not want to be involved. The character and nature of public dialogue is not set in stone. It can range from highly informal 'community conversations' or more formalised disputes between competing political parties. Social media platforms offer opportunities for wide citizen engagement and dialogue; but they also contain bias and problems that require detailed attention. Authorities need to beware that a well-framed open-ended dialogue about 'the future' is likely to draw much less attention and passion than a closed and more formulaic consultation exercise about proposals to close a well-loved local public facility. The latter exercise is less useful, though, both to the public and to the public institution that may be framing the nature of the problem to be solved.

Public policy problems arise from a range of different circumstances. In some cases, the market economy fails to provide much-needed services and goods at affordable prices. In others, problems stem from the failure of public services or crumbling public infrastructure. A key issue to consider is the nature of the dialogue that is being generated. Is the dialogue to be a classic debate between opposing arguments involving controlled discussions? Is it to be based on a subtler conversation using agreed concepts and evidence? Or is it to be genuinely open-ended and relying more on emergent ideas flowing from agreed approaches to concepts and evidence (Isaacs, 1999)?

Community engagement by statutory public authorities needs to move beyond the formulaic, passive arrangements that characterise too many existing approaches. They need to create a civic square of engaged participants that are keen to take part in emergent discussions about the future. Examples of good practice exist throughout the UK, among the best of which is The Deal by Wigan Council, in Greater Manchester. It was first devised in 2010 as a comprehensive approach to engaging people in both managing the pressures on Wigan's budgets and responding to local aspirations for service improvements. Unlike many in local and central government over the years who made cuts as they saw fit on the one hand and dismissed public demands as unrealistic on the other, Wigan Council involved local people on an ongoing basis to consider and prioritise options for service development and expenditure. The Deal covered a wide variety of projects and programmes – from housing and environmental improvement, to social care and welfare programmes.

Between 2010 and 2015, more than £100 million had been saved, without having to use up any of the council's reserves. Services were developed through informed deliberations with the citizens of Wigan, and since 2012 resident satisfaction had risen by 50% (Wigan Council,

2015). The Deal committed the council to do things differently to serve local people in response to what the public gave their commitment to support (for example, The Deal in Action), and to create conditions to help local communities do more for themselves as a result of discussions with those communities (for example, The Deal for Communities).

Effective local civic dialogue should sit at the heart of local government's approach to community engagement. This will involve both dialogue within the community and dialogue between locally elected representative and the citizens they serve. The physical development of local areas, their social and the economic wellbeing, as well as their broader renewal should all be predicated on local community dialogue and action.

The challenge of the current age is how better to connect public institutions (including local authorities) with the communities they serve. It has long been said about participatory approaches to public life that the central problem was that deliberation can get in the way of getting stuff done, or, as the US diplomat Harlan Cleveland (1985, p 51) put it, 'how to get everyone in on the act, and still get action'.

The functional focus of local government in the UK may have directed councils' attention away from community outcomes towards 'service users' and 'targeted populations'. That is perhaps unsurprising given that some 70% of the net revenue expenditure in local government is directed to just 3% of the population (through children's and adult social care). This narrowing of local authorities' civic focus has become exacerbated by the separation of the social housing delivery function from many councils. As a result, for too many people, local councils and the professionals they employ seem to have 'retreated from the street' into their civic offices.

The lesson of open dialogue is that you learn from others as much as they learn from you and that together you may discover new solutions to existing problems. With a sufficiently supportive framework for community action, most people can most of the time solve most of their own problems. When they can't, they tend to get together with other people nearby who suffer similar problems so that they try to solve their problems together. And when the problems that need solving are persistent and complex they should be able to turn to the state for help and support. When this happens, government and public institutions need to aggressively reduce their institutional and professional self-regard. They must refrain from telling or selling preconceived answers, but should concentrate instead on active listening to people's concerns and ideas.

Guiding community action with civic dialogues

The narrative of economic globalisation suggests that while nations are converging, the outcomes for regions within nations are, by contrast, diverging. The lived experience of those less educationally qualified and poorer communities outside of London and the UK's large cities may explain the disaffection and disenchantment thought to underscore the 2016 vote to leave the European Union. One analysis of the Brexit vote at the locality level across England and Wales showed that just one factor, residents' level of educational qualifications, explained 66% of the variation in the vote at local ward level. Voter age explained a further 14% of the variation; and ethnic variations came third with just a further 3% of the explained variation in the vote outcome (Rosenbaum, 2017).

The long-run deindustrialisation of the UK economy, the scaling down of the manufacturing sector and the rise of professional knowledge work and the service sector has played a crucial role in shaping people's attitudes to the communities in which they live. The critical distinction that people make is whether they see their local communities as sinking, surviving or thriving.

In cities that are characterised by cultural pluralism and substantive socioeconomic inequality it is very difficult to achieve inclusive dialogue and deliberation (Bohman, 2000). However, it is in these very cities that engaged and empowered civic dialogue is most urgently required. That is why practical civic dialogue is needed to solve local social problems. But dialogue is necessary not just to enable shared purposes and solutions to emerge but for them to be acted upon. And community action that seeks to improve the lives of a community's poorest members or which is directed at the local common good is the best affirmation for inclusive civic dialogue.

In his account of the impact of this cultural factor on the rise of populist politics, David Goodhart (2017) suggests that the growing cultural divide in the UK is between people who feel that, through education and social networks, they can connect with 'anywhere', while others feel distinctly that they are locked, trapped or simply belong 'somewhere'. Goodhart acknowledges that we each possess ascribed and acquired identities and that in consequence very many people will confound this categorisation. Moreover, he accepts that there are a number of people who exist 'in between' categories. Nonetheless, Goodhart's analysis of Anywheres versus Somewheres is useful in serving to crystallise current debates.

More generally, it may be that in the swirl, the interconnectedness and the pace of the early twenty-first century, people may be as likely to attach themselves strongly to their local community as they do to the offerings of the global world. If so, then the globalising forces of the modern world may not always be a negative force in severing people's ties to the locality in which they live, but could be developing more nuanced attachments and connections across the globe. People may be actively engaged in community action in the street where they live while they are also engaging in community action in other places across the globe – from where they originated or where they have more recently established connections. The increasing segmentation of the so-called 'broadcast' media demonstrates the complexities of modern life in Britain as TV is increasingly streamed via the web. By way of example, in 2017 the BBC's Urdu channel, Sairbeen, regularly had 5 million viewers weekly, mainly from the Pakistani diaspora in the UK and beyond.

Community action, in the UK and elsewhere, is changing dynamically alongside societal and technological changes. Of course it is important to acknowledge that misguided community action can be problematic. Like all human affairs, community action can also have its 'dark side'. Communities may possess bonds so strong that it stifles the liberties of those within them (most usually it's the liberties of women and girls that are most stifled). Community action can be energised by an impulse that protects vested interests and preserves existing advantages. This impulse promotes inaction; it may even seek to mobilise bias to stop decisions being made that would endanger existing interests. But buoyed by civic dialogues, community action can expand the public good, and increase the likelihood of its realisation.

Indeed, the very term 'community' simultaneously evokes both warmth and slipperiness. That is because it is often used in political rhetoric to summon up nostalgic images of the past or idealistic images of the future. As a word, 'community' implies membership, social integration and shared emotional connection. It is therefore a term with obvious political potential. It offers the prospect of unifying people's ambitions to a singular theme; shaping community interests, forging community purposes and marshalling community energies. It can thereby become a unifying centrepiece for action by all political parties operating at the local level.

However, through our lived experience, we know also that community life is not always unifying; it inevitably involves difference, disagreement and dispute. That may be why the most advanced approaches to civic dialogue in the UK are evident in Northern

Ireland. For if deep religiously based divides between communities are to be overcome reasonably and peacefully, sustained civic dialogue is indispensable.

Active listening leads inevitably to a nuanced, practical and pluralist approach to the public. It leads away from those all-absorbing forms of populism that project a specific form of identity politics that is anti-pluralist, and instead projects a moral claim to represent the 'people as a whole' (Muller, 2016). By empowering inclusive local community action with place-based civic dialogue, it is more likely that we can not only reimagine our democracy but rewire its very practice.

References

Bohman, J. (2000) *Public Deliberation: pluralism, complexity and democracy*, Cambridge, MA: MIT.

Cleveland, H. (1985) *The Knowledge Executive*, New York: Dutton.

Enos, R. (2017) *The Space Between Us*, Cambridge: Cambridge University Press.

Freeguard, G., Campbell, L., Cheung, A., Lilly, A. and Baker, C. (2018) *Whitehall Monitor 2018*, London: Institute for Government.

Goodhart, D. (2017) *The Road to Somewhere*, London: Hurst & Co.

Goodin, R. (2003) *Reflective Democracy*, Oxford: Oxford University Press.

Habermas, J. (1984) *The Theory of Communicative Action*, Vol. 1, Boston: Beacon Press.

Isaacs, W. (1999) *Dialogue and the Art of Thinking Together*, New York: Currency.

Ignatieff, M. (2017) *The Ordinary Virtues,* Harvard University Press.

Jefferson, T. (1816) 'Letter to Samuel Kerchavel', 12 June 1816, extracted text is inscribed on one side of The Thomas Jefferson Memorial, Washington DC.

Local Government Association (LGA) (2016) *Community Action in Local Government*. www.local.gov.uk/community-action-local-government-guide-councillors-and-strategic-leaders

Milner, H. (2002) *Civic Literacy*, Hanover: University Press of New England.

Muller, J.-W. (2016) *What is Populism?*, University Park, PA: Penn State University Press.

Nussbaum, M. (2013) *Political Emotions*, Cambridge: Belknap Harvard University Press.

Olson, M. (1971) *The Logic of Collective Action*, Cambridge, MA: Harvard University Press.

Ostrom, E. (1990) *Governing the Commons*, Cambridge: Cambridge University Press.

Quirk, B. (2007) *Making Assets Work*, London: HMSO.

Quirk, B. (2011) *Re-imagining Government*, Basingstoke: Palgrave.

Quirk, B. (2016) *The Four Forces That Make Cities Successful*, London: New Local Government Network.

Rawls, J. (1993) *The Law of Peoples*, Boston: Harvard University Press.

Runciman, D. (2014) *Politics*, London: Profile Books.

Rosenbaum, M. (2017) 'Local voting figures shed new light on EU referendum', BBC website 6 February. www.bbc.co.uk/news/uk-politics-38762034

Sandel, M. (1982) *Liberalism and the Limits of Justice*, Cambridge: Cambridge University Press.

Smith, N., Phillips, D., Simpson, P., Eiser, D, and Trickey, M. (2016) *A Time for Revolution: local government finance in the 2010s*, London: Institute for Fiscal Studies.

Wessendorf, S. (2013) 'Commonplace diversity and the "ethos of mixing": perceptions of difference in a London neighbourhood', *Identities: Global Studies of Culture and Power* 20 (4): 407–422.

Wigan Council (2015) *The Deal for the Future – Wigan Council 2020*. www.wigan.gov.uk/Docs/PDF/Council/Strategies-Plans-and-Policies/Corporate/Deal-for-future/The-plan.pdf

Young Foundation (2010) *What is an Empowering Authority?* https://youngfoundation.org/wp-content/uploads/2012/11/What-is-an-empowering-authority-Community-empowerment-and-organisational-culture-August-2010.pdf

9

Old Age and Caring Democracy

Marian Barnes

As I write this I am 65 years old. I am retired, but retain an honorary title reflecting seniority in academic life. I am in receipt of a state and occupational pension and pay income tax on the latter. My health is generally good and I live in a part of the country where as a woman I might expect to live another 22 years. If I need social care services, in the current system, I would have to pay for these. I have no children, my parents both died many years ago, but I do have other close family members who are intensive users of health and social care services. I voted Remain in the EU Referendum and have always voted Labour. I first encountered one of the other authors of *Whose Government Is It?*, David Blunkett, many years ago when I was a shop steward in Sheffield City Council and he was a local councillor.

My life as an older woman in these respects is very different from that of many others in old age. Difference and inequality over a life course impact on the experience of old age, and old age itself is a period of change over perhaps three decades. As at any other age, to assume that being old alone defines people's socioeconomic circumstances, including their identities as 'economically active' or not, their political views, their health status or personal circumstances, is both simplistic and unhelpful. Intersectionality reflects the lived reality not only of the way gender and ethnicity intersect, but also how differences such as age, disability, positioning in relation to care, constitute conflicting dimensions of advantage and disadvantage. But in spite of the differences between older people, existentially, politically and interpersonally, age *does* matter.

Age impacts on perspective – 'looking forward' to the future has different connotations at ages 20 and 70. While being old is not the same as being ill, health problems do increase for many people as they age. Age is important in the nature and significance of different interpersonal relationships. It affects how we are seen by others, not least whether we are valued or regarded as a burden. Unlike many dimensions of difference, to other older people is to other our future selves. We will, if we survive, all grow old. Age is used to determine policy, most obviously in relation to retirement and pension entitlement; though the fluidity of the precise age marker for such entitlements highlights the contested meanings attached to chronological age, as well as the political nature of decisions affecting people of different ages. Age impacts those policy or service issues that a person might recognise as relevant to themselves – had I been introducing myself at 35 I doubt I would have mentioned a potential need for social care. Age is connected to generation and to the cultural and political influences on us from an earlier age. Interviews with people currently in their 80s and 90s often reflect the significance of the Second World War in shaping their lives, but it is very nearly too late to access the lived experience of people who knew what it was like to need health services before the existence of the National Health Service in the UK. Working with students in their early 20s demonstrates how assumptions about the role of public services have shifted as a result of years of neoliberalism.

So as we consider the potential of enhanced relationships between government and citizens, we cannot ignore the significance of age. We need to consider both the contribution that old people can make to public debate, and the different contexts within which and means by which such contributions can be made. In recognising contested assumptions about 'age' conferring a particular and shared identity (Gilleard and Higgs, 2007), the contribution of old people must be promoted. Both social justice and 'participatory parity' (Fraser, 2009) demand this. There are different ideologies underpinning moves to enhance citizen participation in democratic practices and public governance and different objectives and outcomes have been claimed for this (Barnes et al, 2007). In addition to broad arguments that a healthy democracy is one that engages the diversity of citizens, and that public services will be more attuned to needs if those who use them have a say in their design, particular factors emphasise the importance of older people's involvement.

Old age is feared by some and resisted by many. Ageism endures and takes on new forms across the globe (Gullette, 2011; Lodge et al, 2016). Age has been identified as a key fault line in social relations and old people, in particular the 'boomer' generation, have been scapegoated for the failures of neoliberalism (Gibney, 2017). At the same time, a lack of historical awareness has been implicated in governmental and policy failures, in both domestic and international politics. It is well worth listening to those who know from experience why relying on private or voluntary agencies to deliver health care is not a good idea. Old people need to have confidence that they retain the respect of government and of other citizens, as well as confidence that needs associated with old age will be met to ensure justice and wellbeing. And government needs to recognise the contribution that old people make to public life, and to the interpersonal and community relations that contribute to collective wellbeing.

In this chapter I explore some of the different types of participatory spaces designed to enable old people to contribute to policies and practices that impact on their lives and those of others. I argue that we need to bring to such spaces insights not only from deliberative democracy, but also from relational ethics to understand what will make them spaces in which the benefits of participation can be experienced directly by those involved, as well as contributing to broader renewals of social and state/citizen relationships. With Tronto (2013), I argue that renewing democracy and renewing care are necessarily intertwined.

Summoning the older consumer

For many people in the UK, their most immediate encounter with the state is in the context of using services provided or commissioned by local government, the National Health Service and other public agencies. It is often in such contexts that people are motivated to have a say about policies and services. The consumerist developments of the 1990s, in particular within health and social care services, recognised old people as one group whose voices should be heard in service design and delivery. Such developments predated the influence of ideas from civil renewal on participative innovations to address public policy problems and have endured alongside them. However, concrete expression of an identity for older people as active consumers lagged behind initiatives focused on younger disabled people and those with mental health problems. A view of old age as a time of disengagement or passive dependency led to inappropriate assumptions that old people were too grateful or simply too tired to take part in 'user involvement' initiatives (Thornton and Tozer, 1995). There were examples of such involvement, such as work to involve old people in developing quality standards for home care services (Raynes et al, 2001). But such initiatives struggled to gain broad acceptance and achieve a lasting impact.

As the promotion of markets as the route to both 'empowering' customers and reducing demands on the state took hold, the emphasis on hearing old people's voices switched to asking them to make choices through various forms of 'cash for care' schemes in the UK and elsewhere (see for example Anttonen and Haikio, 2011 on Finland). In the UK the introduction of direct payments and personal budgets to enable people to choose care services reflected the success of campaigning by parts of the disability movement, not by old people themselves. Early evaluations of such schemes found that older people were less happy about them than younger disabled people (Glendinning et al, 2008) and government recognised the likely '"hassle costs" of choice' for older people of this system (Department of Health, 2010, p 16).

Among the consequences of consumerism are the individualisation of influence – impact on services is the result of the aggregation of individual choices made in private, rather than the coming together of old people to talk about the type of services that would best meet their needs; and the disruption of the state-citizen relationship. In the current system, social care services are rarely provided directly by a public authority but rather by private or voluntary agencies. Direct contact between old people and public officials may be limited to an occasional visit from a care manager and the relational aspect of service use is with private or voluntary sector employed care assistants, or volunteers. These limitations are in addition to the intrinsic problems and contradictions of 'choice' as a means to 'empowerment' that have been extensively analysed (Barnes and Prior, 1995). If we are to advocate the renewal of state–citizen relations, promoting private choice is not the way to do it. Based on her work on older people's interest organisations in Ireland, Doyle (2015) argued that the philosophy of increasing individualisation and the potential of further dismantling of the welfare state is likely to place *greater* importance on collective mobilisation of older people.

Thus, while recognising the significance of service use as a focus for engaging old people in discussions about what is necessary to renew confidence in the state and draw on the experiential knowledge of old people, we need to look beyond consumerist strategies. A key responsibility of the state is to ensure the basic needs of citizens are met. Whether it does this through direct provision of services, or through commissioner/provider arrangements, having confidence that good-quality services will be available at time of need is fundamental to a sense of security and that government cares about the people. One of the key fears about old age is becoming dependent on poor-quality services. Most people understand little about how the social care system works and can find themselves confronted with a complex system and contested rules and practices at times of greatest personal difficulty. We need old people who use services to make expert input to practices designed to improve quality and experience of service use. But we also need public debate to question fundamental policy decisions about why, for example, health conditions such as cancer entitle people to health care free at the point of delivery, but other health conditions, including dementia or acquired brain injury, result in people having to pay for the daily care they need to survive. The ill-fated 'dementia tax' proposal in the Tory manifesto in the 2017 general election in the UK was a rare example of such issues achieving a high public profile.[1]

Here I discuss two examples of projects designed to enable old people using care services to shape these in positive ways, and another that holds the potential for broadening public debate on policy issues. These illustrate some of the more general points I make about what is necessary for and what is the potential of initiatives focused specifically on older people's involvement.

Reimagining services together

In the early 1990s Age Concern Scotland, a leading NGO working with older people, developed a project to enable frail older people to talk about their experiences of growing older and using health and social care services, and to use the insights gained through discussions to influence local service delivery (Barnes and Bennett, 1998). One aim was to demonstrate that those whose physical frailty means they need regular service help retain the capability to contribute to service improvement.[2] Those who took part needed physical assistance to travel to meetings and the success of the project depended not only on project workers being able to organise transport, but also to secure appropriate

---

[1] The proposal was that the value of someone's house should be taken into consideration in the context of means testing for social care. The outcry against this included labelling the proposal a 'dementia tax'. The proposal was dropped but we cannot be confident it is entirely dead.

[2] This project did not work with people with dementia. More recently, work with people with dementia has demonstrated that they too can sustain activist identities (Bartlett, 2012). For example, in 2002 the Scottish Dementia Working Group was set up. Membership is for people with dementia and the group has established an enduring role in local and national governmental initiatives.

venues, issue reminders and retain regular contact to encourage and support continued involvement. Seven different groups met across the region. While illness, death and admission to residential care meant not all were able to take part throughout the period, the project continued over three years and involved 62 people aged 67-93 with the biggest single group aged 86-90.

Unlike consultation initiatives that invite service users to respond to issues defined by officials, this project started with participants talking about their experiences of growing older and using services. Discussions were facilitated by an Age Concern development worker. Its methodology derived from community development (see also Chapter Seven in this book). This led to the identification of common issues regarding services that provided the focus for ongoing work, including invitations to providers to listen to what older people had to say and respond to them. For some providers this was an unusual experience and one, in particular, was nonplussed at being expected to respond to concerns that panel members had already identified, rather than tell the older people why things were as they were. There are similarities with the experience of public officials and other 'experts' called to give evidence and respond to questions from citizens' juries (Barnes, 1999). But this project went beyond identifying problems and challenging service providers to do something about these. For example, having identified problematic experiences of the process of hospital discharge, the groups came up with an alternative vision of a better system. Some group members then met with local providers to plan how the proposed changes might be made. Although predating the naming of the concept, we can understand this as an example of co-production (Hunter and Ritchie, 2007).

As well as the practical arrangements necessary to enable the participation of frail older people, facilitative skills and creativity were important to make this work. Not only did this project offer opportunities for personal development, learning and genuine empowerment from working together – what one woman aged 90 called 'courage' – it also counteracted negative assumptions about the capacity of frail older people, and contributed to positive change in both services and service/user relationships.

Similar possibilities were generated in the context of residential care through work carried out by Baur and colleagues in the Netherlands (Baur, 2012). This started from recognition of the danger of enforced or encouraged passivity following admission to long-term residential care, and the need to challenge both attitudes and practices that contribute to this. It also recognised the limits of consumerist approaches that promote individual self-interest rather than building solidarity. Since 1996 there has been a statutory requirement in the Netherlands that every care organisation should create a user council. But the duty to create councils does not necessarily mean that taking part will be a positive experience. Working at the meso-level of the ways in which older residents might influence practices in residential homes, rather than the micro-level of client/professional relationship, or the macro-level of older interest groups influencing national policy, Baur and her colleagues designed a project intended to enhance residents' direct participation in processes impacting on everyday lives within the homes.

Like the Scottish project, a key starting point was that participants should define for themselves the focus for their engagement. This group focused on the quality of food within the home and the action that developed was based around improving the meals that provided a key moment at which residents came together, as well as impacting on individual satisfaction with the service. Baur describes a non-linear process during which residents got to know each other, initially downplaying negative experiences but then building confidence as they recognised that dissatisfactions were shared. Negative experiences led to what Baur (2012, p 132) describes as 'stagnation' before the group turned their discontent into creative suggestions about how meals could be improved by working in partnership between residents and staff. This process also reflects that described in relation to the issue of hospital discharge in the Scottish example. In both cases developing a generative process out of negative experiences required establishing effective relationships that continued over an extended period, and a commitment to action as well as listening.

The third example also demonstrates the potential of long-term relational practice. It concerns work that started approximately ten years ago and is ongoing. A research partnership between the University of Brighton and the local Age UK has enabled the development of a series of research projects in which older people are co-researchers as well as research 'subjects'. In common with different models of participatory research as well as community development, the aim is to move from data collection and analysis to action. Thus, following the completion of research into wellbeing in old age, a knowledge exchange was established with funding from the Economic and Social Research Council. This brought together older co-researchers and two members of a local seniors forum with social care practitioners from statutory and voluntary agencies. This group translated research findings into learning resources designed to support practice development capable of enhancing wellbeing among older people needing help from social care agencies (Ward and Barnes, 2016). Once again, success depended not only on the time available to develop and sustain long-term relationships, but an understanding of how practical and ethical sensibilities need to be brought into play to create the conditions in which effective deliberation can generate change.

As I write, some of the co-researchers who have been part of this programme of work from the start, now in their late 80s and 90s, continue to work with new recruits on a project being conducted in Brighton, Solihull and Lincolnshire exploring experiential and ethical issues associated with older people self-funding their care (www.olderpeopleselffundingcare.com/). Knowledge exchange groups have been established in the three sites from the start of the project. These bring together older co-researchers, commissioners and providers from the NHS, local government, voluntary and private sectors. These are designed to enable ongoing discussion of issues arising from the research and to facilitate a process of debate about policy and practice. This has the potential to contribute to broader public debate about a contested social policy issue as well as to impact on policy implementation.

None of these three initiatives would typically be understood as 'political', and mainstream political theory is unlikely to consider them. But the issues they engage with are political issues relating to policy, what values underpin decision making, and how we enable old people to contribute to public services. They embody the practical reality of how state–citizen relationships are enacted and recognise that the political cannot be separated from the personal. And, as I develop below, they offer insights into how an enhanced understanding of deliberation among those who are differently positioned in relation to both age and care holds potential for reducing competitive approaches to policy.

Senior citizens

Alongside developments involving older people in deliberations about health and social care services are others that have recognised that old people are also interested in and care about a range of public policy issues. Old people's councils, interest organisations and senior forums exist in many different countries and have been growing over decades (Thursz et al, 1995; Viriot Durandal, 2004; Vergeris et al, 2007; Warburton and Petriwskyj, 2007; Doyle, 2015). In common with other foci around which citizens engage to both challenge and collaborate with government and public officials, the origins of collective action lie both in autonomous action by older people (such as the Pensioners Convention in the UK and Gray Panthers in the US), and in invitations from government to take part in participatory governance. There are tensions between the implementation of official policies for older people's involvement and 'bottom-up' action led by older people themselves. We need to acknowledge such tensions but also recognise that simplistic 'insider-outsider' conceptions of the spaces in which old people (and others) can exercise power and seek influence within official policy making can be unhelpful.

Official support for older people's involvement in the UK can be traced from the 'Better Government for Older People' (BGOP) programme launched in 1998.[3] This engaged older people as citizens with an active role to play in the governance and wellbeing of their communities. The policy foci included transport, leisure, education and information technology, as well as health and social care. Mechanisms for involvement encompassed consultation; support for existing older people's groups and the establishment of new forums; participation in research and in ongoing governance processes (Hayden and Boaz, 2000).In 2008 a review of the work of BGOP led to a decision to establish a UK Advisory Forum for Older People 'to provide a stronger, clearer and louder voice for older people at national level' (DWP, 2009, p 4), which would be supported by a regional structure, in turn linking into local older people's groups. But the regional forums were not predominantly 'older people's' forums and by September 2015 the national forum had closed down, leaving no specific mechanisms through which older people's voices are heard within government.

This failure of top-down policy to promote involvement at national level reinforces the importance of understanding how local initiatives led by older people have fared. A key question asked of such initiatives is who takes part, often couched in such a way as to question the 'representativeness' of older people's forums. I have already demonstrated that 'frail' or 'vulnerable' old people can and do get involved in initiatives designed to facilitate them to do so. Here I consider how different processes contribute to the constitution of old age identities and what this might mean for the renewal of state-citizen connections with which this book is concerned.

Older people's forums enable people who have been active in trades unions, local and national politics, women's movements and community action to sustain an activist identity in old age. Commitments to issues of equality and social justice do not disappear as people grow older and time available after retirement can make it possible to devote more

---

[3]   The BGOP approach was later selected and promoted more widely as part of the UK Government's Together We Can programme throughout the 2000s.

rather than less time to activism (Barnes et al, 2012; Doyle, 2015). But such forums also offer opportunities to people who have never considered themselves 'activists' and who would be reluctant to claim such an identity. What unites both groups is resistance to the notion that old age means disengagement or passivity, a sense that old people have much to offer to policy, including issues such as environmentalism and urban regeneration that are of concern to people of all ages, and that old people continue to 'matter' both as subjects of and contributors to policy making.

Doyle (2015) identified a process of collective identity building among old people engaged in collective action in Ireland. This both referenced shared cultural pasts and social histories and called for an emancipatory vision of old age. Because of the complex processes of action and identity construction it was not possible to understand this as limited to an identity based in 'active' or 'positive' ageing paradigms, or defined by reference to entitlements as welfare recipients. But while 'members neither actively adopted nor rejected the notion of an age-based identity ... they nevertheless embraced the ageing process' (Doyle, 2015, p 87). In a study of older people's forums in Sussex, England, colleagues and I found similar complex processes in play (Barnes et al, 2012). We noted both the importance to older participants of demonstrating continuing capacity for agency and the value of contributing expert knowledge to local decision making, and a tendency for 'activists' to distance themselves from other old people who have 'given up' – reinforcing a reluctance to be identified as 'old'. The separation of what are often called 'senior citizens' forums' from the groups of frail older people considered above may reinforce such distancing and suggests the importance of encouraging linkages across different types of forum.

As well as questions about who takes part and the potential for such spaces to enable different old age identities to be constructed, we also need to understand how processes of engagement impact on contributions to a renewal of relationships between government and older people.

I have contrasted the community development ethos of the Scottish project considered above with both officially led consultative processes and forums influenced by procedures familiar to people previously active within trades unions (Barnes, 2005). Such formal methods of engagement, linked to exclusive (and potentially unenforceable) rules about membership, restrict the possibility of creative deliberation and diverse contributions. Forums constructed around 'representation' from other groups can run into difficulty in deciding which groups should be entitled to be represented, as one forum demonstrated with respect to Lesbian, Gay, Bi-Sexual and Transgender (LGBT) older people (Barnes et al, 2007, ch 7). Those seeking to work within formal procedural rules risk excluding those unfamiliar or uncomfortable with such formality. We thus need to consider not only the practical requirements for enabling and supporting older people's participation, but also what civil renewal might require in terms of the relational practices of working together.

Caring and deliberative democracy

This book is concerned with ways in which state-citizen cooperation can be enhanced and what processes of civil and democratic renewal might consist of. In drawing out key insights from experiences of working with old people I want to step back and offer theoretical perspectives, grounded in empirical experience, that can be applied not only to age-specific practices but which have broader resonance.

A number of contributors to this book base their analyses in theories of deliberative democracy. This body of work has been substantially influential on the development of innovative forms of democratic practice. I have used this in my own work and have reflected on different modes of older people's engagement from this perspective (Barnes, 2005). More recently, I have considered what additional understandings we can achieve from applying the ethics of care to participative policy making (Barnes, 2012). Care has rarely been recognised as within the remit of political science, and work on care is predominantly focused on specific policies and practices rather than issues that might be understood to be relevant to an interest in state-citizen relationships. But feminist scholarship on care ethics (Tronto, 1993, 2013) has been changing awareness of the importance of thinking about care and politics together. Care ethicists have been expanding the significance of care thinking beyond policy domains traditionally thought of as related to care – see for example Robinson (1999) on care ethics in international relations. And more activist-oriented responses to recent fractures within politics and social relations have argued for 'care and caretaking' as a key value focus for progressive political alliances (Klein, 2017, p 240).

We can think of this both at the level of the micro-relational processes necessary to enable effective involvement and at the macro-level of the type of democracy and social relations that we seek to achieve through enhanced state-citizen cooperation. Elsewhere I have argued that 'deliberating with care' is necessary to ensure that conversations between citizens and public officials enable diverse ways of speaking and making contributions to be respected and valued (Barnes, 2012).

My argument here takes Young's (2000) critique of deliberation as requiring solely rational argumentation and extends this by applying Tronto's (1993) analysis of the phases of care – attentiveness, responsibility, competence and responsiveness – to the process of deliberation. We can see this in practice in instances such as that described in the Scottish user panels project. The role of the facilitator involved taking responsibility for ensuring that attentiveness to the circumstances of panel members led to a competent approach to engaging them in conversations, and awareness of their responses to such involvement fed back into an overall process reflecting the 'integrity of care' in the way in which participation was enabled. A more self-conscious approach to applying care ethics to engaging old people was adopted in the participatory research on wellbeing in Brighton and in the knowledge exchange that followed on from the research (Ward and Barnes, 2016).

The centrality of relationality is both intrinsic to effective practice and an outcome of it. It encompasses relationships among the older people who take part, and those initiating and/or facilitating such processes, including researchers, voluntary sector facilitators and public officials. It does not preclude difference or even conflict among participants, but does require respect, openness to change and to recognising the multiplicity of identities we carry in addition to that related to our age. It also both requires and enables discussion of the very different experiences of old age, with the potential to counteract the fears and resistances often associated with being old. One positive indication of that is a growing understanding of and preparedness to advocate for old people who are unable to take part directly (Barnes et al, 2012). Petriwskyj and her colleagues in Australia (2011) have highlighted the significance of respect for diversity in the preparedness among older people to get involved in participatory governance.

Newman, Sullivan and I have argued elsewhere that we should understand participatory spaces as spaces in which identities are constituted rather than represented or expressed (Barnes et al, 2006). That includes the identities of people whose role may be that of public official, service provider or researcher, but who are also people who are growing older, who may have older relatives experiencing the impact of ageist attitudes, poor health or frailty. In the Brighton knowledge exchange we felt a breakthrough was achieved when a social worker recognised the likely impact of starting visits to her elderly father by saying 'Can't stop long!' She made this comment during a conversation about the importance of time to care. In doing so she was both stepping outside her formal practitioner role to recognise the impact of her personal behaviour, but also recognising the constraints imposed by policy decisions that fail to understand what is necessary to achieve care, in this instance by limiting 'care' visits to 15 minutes.

Tronto (2013) extended her analysis of the four phases of care to add a fifth: 'caring with', a phase associated with the value of solidarity. Collective action involving older people is valued not least because of the experience of being with others who share similar experiences and the opportunities for social contact and friendships this brings. But there is a more obviously political dimension evident in the responses of older people involved in the examples discussed in this chapter.

Collective action enables old people to demonstrate that they care about issues impacting on the lives of other old people, but also people of all ages. And it enables conversations about the importance of being cared for and the consequences of an absence of care for personal wellbeing and collective justice. Both are important for building solidarity not only within but also across generations. Such conversations demonstrate the centrality of care to living well together. As Tronto (2013, p x) argues: 'what it means to be a citizen in a democracy is to care for citizens and to care for democracy itself'. This implicates people of all ages. Without explicitly enabling old people to be part of this conversation we run the risk of outcomes such as the citizens' jury hosted to engage teenagers in debate about how to design a city suitable for an ageing population (Barnes, 1999). A key design feature that emerged from discussions was that of age segregation, justified by a claim that old people would not want to be disturbed by the noise made by young people. What might have been the outcome of a discussion facilitated to enable conversation between old and young about this issue?

Conclusion

The examples of older people's participation considered here have resulted in specific outcomes such as the production of learning resources, better systems for hospital discharge and better quality food in residential homes. But we cannot separate consideration of innovative practice in collaboration between government and citizens with the broader outcomes they can achieve – what kind of society do we want and who has responsibility to enable this? This means attention to the values that should underpin policies as well as how public debate can be enabled. The ethics of care rejects a separation between ethics and politics. Deliberation on matters of public policy must involve moral deliberation as well as enabling contribution from those affected by policy and who have experiential knowledge to contribute. Conflict between old and young people is being exacerbated by policies of austerity. Rather than accept the inevitability of a conflict of interests, our task is to build solidarity through engaging with the reality of being old and to develop creative ideas about how government can fulfil its responsibilities to ensure old age is a good time now and for future generations.

References

Anttonen, A. and Haikio, L. (2011) 'From social citizenship to active citizenship? Tensions between policies and practices in Finnish elderly care', in Newman, J. and Tonkens, E. (eds) *Particiaption, Responsibility and Choice. Summoning the active citizen in Western European welfare states*, Amsterdam: Amsterdam University Press, 45–66.

Barnes, M. (1999) *Building a Deliberative Democracy: an evaluation of two citizens' juries*, London: Institute for Public Policy Research.

Barnes, M. (2005). 'Same old process? Older people, participation and deliberation', *Ageing and Society* 25 (2): 245–259.

Barnes, M. (2012) *Care in Everyday Life: an ethic of care in practice.* Bristol: Policy Press.

Barnes, M. and Prior, D. (1995) 'Spoilt for choice? How consumerism can disempower public service users', *Public Money and Management* 15 (3): 53–58.

Barnes, M. and Bennett, G. (1998). 'Frail bodies, courageous voices: Older people influencing community care', *Health and Social Care in the Community*, 6 (2), 102–111.

Barnes, M., Harrison, E. and Murray, L. (2012) 'Ageing activists: who gets involved in older people's forums?', *Ageing and Society* 32: 261–280.

Barnes, M., Newman, J. and Sullivan, H. (2006) 'Discursive arenas: deliberation and the constitution of identity in public participation at a local level', *Social Movement Studies* 5 (3): 193–207.

Barnes, M., Newman, J. and Sullivan, H. (2007) *Power, Participation and Political Renewal: case studies in public participation*, Bristol: Policy Press.

Bartlett, R. (2012) 'The emergent modes of dementia activism', *Ageing and Society*. doi:10.1017/S0144686X12001158

Baur, V. (2012) *Participation and Partnership. Developing the influence of older people in residential care homes*, 's-Hertogenbosch: Uitgeverij BOXPress.

Department of Health (2010) *A Vision for Adult Social Care: capable communities and active citizens*, London: Department of Health.

Department for Work and Pensions (DWP) (2009) *Empowering Engagement: a stronger voice for older people*, London: Department for Work and Pensions.

Doyle, M. (2015). *The Politics of Old Age. Older people's interest organisations and collective action in Ireland*, Manchester: Manchester University Press.

Fraser, N. (2009) *Scales of Justice. Reimagining political space in a globalizing world*, New York: Columbia University Press.

Gibney, B. C. (2017). *A Generation of Sociopaths: how the baby boomers betrayed America*, New York: Hachette Books.

Gilleard, C. and Higgs, P. (2007) 'The power of silver: age identity politics in the 21st century', *Journal of Aging and Social Policy* 21 (3): 227–295.

Glendinning, C., Challis, D., Fernez, J., Jacobs, S., Jones, K., Knapp, M., Manthorpe, J., Moran, N., Netten, A., Stevens, M. and Wilberforce, M. (2008) *Evaluation of the Individual Budgets Pilot Programme. Final Report*, York: Social Policy Research Unit, University of York.

Gullette, M. M. (2011). *Agewise: fighting the new ageism in America*, Chicago: Chicago University Press.

Hayden, C. and Boaz, A. (2000) *Making a Difference. Better Government for Older People Evaluation Report*. Warwick: Local Government Centre, University of Warwick.

Hunter, S. and Ritchie, P. (eds) (2007) *Co-Production and Personalisation in Social Care*, London: Jessica Kingsley.

Klein, N. (2017) *NO is Not Enough. Defeating the new shock politics*, London: Allen Lane/Penguin.

Lodge, C., Carnell, E. and Coleman, M. (2016) *The New Age of Ageing: how society needs to change*, Bristol: Policy Press.

Petriwskj, A., Warburton, J., Everingham, J. and Cuthill, M. (2011) 'Diversity and inclusion in local governance: an Australian study of seniors' participation', *Journal of Aging Studies*. doi:10.1016/j.jaging.2011.12.003.

Raynes, N. V., Temply, B., Glenister, C. and Coulthard, L. (2001) *Quality at Home for Older People: involving service users in defining home care specifications*, Bristol: Policy Press.

Robinson, F. (1999) *Globalizing Care: ethics, feminist theory and international relations*, Boulder, CO: Westview Press.

Thornton, P. and Tozer, R. (1995) *Having a Say in Change. Older people and community care*. York, Joseph Rowntree Foundation.

Thursz, D., Nusberg, C. and Prather, J. (eds) (1995) *Empowering Older People. An international approach*, London: Cassell.

Tronto, J. (1993) *Moral Boundaries. A political argument for an ethic of care*, London and New York: Routledge.

Tronto, J. (2013) *Caring Democracy: markets, equality and justice*, New York and London: New York University Press.

Vergeris, S., Barnes, H., Campbell-Barr, V., Mackinnon, K. and Taylor, R. (2007) *Beyond the Tick Box. Older citizen engagement in UK local government*, London: Policy Studies Institute/BGOP.

Viriot Durandal, J.-P. (ed) (2004) *Grey Power? Volume 2: Economic and social influences*, Paris: Les Cahiers de la FIAPA; Action Research on Ageing.

Warburton, J. and Petriwskyj, A. (2007) 'Who speaks for Australia's seniors? Policy partnerships and older Australians', *Just Policy* 45: 38–43.

Ward, L. and Barnes, M. (2016) 'Transforming practice with older people through an ethic of care', *British Journal of Social Work* 46 (4): 906–922.

Young, I. M. (2000) *Inclusion and Democracy*, Oxford: Oxford University Press.

10

Young People and Everyday Democracy

James Sloam

The 2017 general election provided a major shock to the British political establishment. The surge in youth turnout – from 40% of 18 to 24 year olds in 2015 to over 60% among the same age group only two years later – and in support for the Labour Party, deprived the Conservative Government of its parliamentary majority (Sloam and Henn, 2018). This so-called 'youthquake' marked the dramatic reversal of a 25-year slump in electoral participation. Yet we should not be too quick to celebrate this turn of events. Young Labour Party supporters (and young Remainers in the EU Referendum) were actually less trusting of politicians and political parties than the average young person. Indeed, the appeal of Jeremy Corbyn (much like that of Bernie Sanders in the United States) was founded on his anti-establishment credentials. The truth is that, while young people in the UK are interested in politics per se, their participation in electoral politics remains very low in comparison to their peers in other established democracies.

The critical question is not only how politicians and public officials can get young people to vote, but also whether democratic engagement can be sustained between elections. This chapter focuses on the latter question. It argues that participation in everyday democracy at a local level can stimulate contact between younger citizens and policy makers and counter the exclusion of young people from formal politics and governance. Such engagement – particularly at local community level – has the potential to rejuvenate democracy by strengthening 'civic agency' (Boyte, 2011): building trust in the political system and a sense of efficacy among those young people who become involved.

But it requires sustained support from a range of actors, including local councillors, youth services and youth councils; relevant non-governmental organisations that promote youth civic engagement and civic literacy; schools and universities to make sure that *all* young people are afforded with opportunities for engagement. The work of these different actors needs to be coordinated by 'local democracy hubs'. The three case studies at the end of the chapter illustrate how hard-to-reach young people can be mobilised around issues that hold meaning for their everyday lives, and identify the resources (economic, social and cognitive) that are required for such participation.

Young people, political participation and contact

Academics and policy makers have become concerned about the apparent decline in youth participation in democracy. Public involvement in traditional political institutions has declined significantly over the past few decades, leading to what some have described as a crisis in citizenship (Putnam, 2000; Stoker, 2016). In Europe, we have witnessed a large decline in voter turnout (Franklin, 2004; Fieldhouse et al, 2007; Wattenberg, 2008) and a dramatic fall in the membership of political parties (Van Biezen et al, 2012). These trends are most striking among young people, who have become alienated from mainstream electoral politics. In the UK, the decline in youth electoral participation has been particularly sharp. The turnout of 18 to 24 year olds in general elections fell from over 60% in 1992 to an average of around 40% in the four elections between 2002 and 2015 (Sloam and Henn, 2018).

Young people have also become disillusioned with public policy, which – in the aftermath of the recent financial crisis – has placed a disproportionate burden on younger generations: from worsening levels of child poverty, to *precarious jobs* and youth unemployment, to cuts in youth services and education budgets. In the UK, this was vividly illustrated by the abolition of the Education Maintenance Allowance and trebling of university tuition fees (despite the Liberal Democrat election pledge not to increase them) under the 2010–2015 Coalition Government.

Pippa Norris (2002) and others have shown that citizens have increasingly turned their attention *from politics to policy*: away from institutionalised forms of politics to issue-based modes of engagement. And young people's repertoires of participation have become more diverse. For instance, issues such as climate change, global poverty and free higher education might be more easily pursued through pressure group membership (such as joining Greenpeace), consumer action (including, buying fair trade products) or joining a demonstration (for example, the British anti-tuition fees rallies of 2010 and 2011), rather than through long-term membership of a traditional political organisation.

Young people in the UK are as interested in 'politics' as their peers elsewhere in Europe but are put off by political actors that have neglected both their voice and their interests. The surge in youth participation in 2017 showed that it is possible to engage young Millennials when politicians address key issues of concern. The Labour Party successfully appealed to 18 to 24 year olds through its commitments to scrap university tuition fees and provide extra investment in social housing. And the campaign group Momentum provided a machine for engaging with young people on the ground and through various social media (Pickard, 2018). However, national 'youthquakes' are the exception rather than the rule. National political parties have a limited capacity to appeal to the issues and concerns that affect citizens' everyday lives. What is really missing from the picture is the grassroots engagement of young people in local democracy (politics *and* governance) between elections.

Support for grassroots participation in political decision making is inherent in civic republican notions of citizenship, which are deeply embedded in United States political culture (Barber, 2003). Indeed, the idea of participation in civic life and 'town hall democracy' are intrinsically tied up in ideas about what it means to be American (de Tocqueville, 1969).[1] US-based scholars have also highlighted the role played by local democratic practices, from town hall meetings (Mansbridge, 1983) to workers' cooperatives (Pateman, 1970), in building trust, developing democratic skills and establishing a sense of efficacy among those who choose to participate (Fung, 2004). However, it is important that such engagement – if it is to last – is a two-way process between citizens and policy makers. This resonates with Boyte's (2011, p 632) concept of 'public work', which involves 'co-operative, egalitarian, practical labors "across ranks" on public projects'.

Civic engagement in the US has increased over recent decades despite falling levels of trust in Congress and state legislatures. According to Dalton (2017, pp 6–7), the proportion of Americans contacting local

---

[1]   The traditional focus in the US on civic activism is even reflected in the language used in academic studies in which the term 'civic engagement' is preferred to 'political participation' (the latter is more common in the UK).

government over a policy matter has increased by around 50% since 1967. Pattie, Seyd and Whiteley (2004) have shown that, in the UK context, everyday democracy offers promising pathways into political engagement. They show, for example, that citizens are more willing to intervene in matters regarding their local hospital or school than to actively engage in politics more generally.

Yet the academic literature also tells us that these forms of democratic participation are relatively demanding of an individual's cognitive, economic and social resources (Dalton, 2017). As a result, engagement with politicians is overwhelmingly the preserve of 'expert citizens' (Bang, 2003) who are predominantly middle-aged, college-educated and financially well-off. Archon Fung (2004, p 5) tell us that: the 'voices of minority, less educated, diffident or culturally subordinate participants are often drowned out by those who are wealthy, confident, accustomed to management or otherwise privileged'.

These social inequalities of civic and political engagement are illustrated by the varying levels of contact between different groups of citizens and policy makers within a particular country. European Social Survey figures show that the rate of contact between young people and politicians or public officials in the UK is the lowest in Western Europe (Sloam, 2016): only 6% of young Britons (16 to 25 year olds) had contacted a politician or government official over the past 12 months, compared to 9% of young people in 14 other European Union democracies and 18% of all adults in the UK. The British Social Attitudes Survey reported, in 2011, that only 5% of 18 to 29 year olds had contacted their MP and just 2% had contacted a government department compared to 20% and 7%, respectively, of citizens over 60 years of age (Park et al, 2013).

The existing literature on political campaigning and voter mobilisation (Gerber and Green, 2000; Johnston et al, 2012) and citizen-to-citizen engagement through new social movements (Castells, 2012; Bennett and Segerberg, 2013) suggests that contact may be an answer to reducing the distance between younger citizens and the political system. Barack Obama's 2008 presidential campaign was famously successful in using new communication media to encourage young people to engage other young people within their social networks. However, national surges in youth participation are few and far between and relate to elections that might take place only once every four or five years. In fact, trust is more easily built at the local level through participation in 'everyday democracy' (Boyte, 2005).

This chapter argues that it is critical to intensify interactions between elections, to build trust and develop democratic skills among younger citizens. It also emphasises the role played by mediating organisations, such as local councils and youth services, schools and universities, in scaffolding the participation of traditionally marginalised groups in local democracy (Flanagan and Levine, 2010).

Democracy and civic participation in the UK

One of the greatest challenges in contemporary democratic politics is the mismatch between politics and policy (Hay and Stoker, 2009). In recent decades, public policy has been outsourced away from political control to expert bodies (such as the Bank of England and the Low Pay Commission),[2] international organisations (particularly the European Union) and financial markets,[3] while national politics has remained dominant. As a result, policy makers at the national level have become increasingly unable to meet citizens' demands, which has led to further dissatisfaction with politicians and political parties. And 'the managerial approach shared by most politicians does not offer young people ideals and values with which to identify' (Spannring et al, 2008, p 73).

This disruption in the chain of political accountability has, in the civic republican spirit, made it more necessary than ever to encourage citizen participation in subnational layers of governance. The situation is particularly challenging in the UK, where policy making is considerably more centralised than in comparable liberal democracies. In this regard, the devolution and localisation agenda pursued by the last Labour Governments (1997–2010) attempted to make politics and governance less remote.

Constitutional reforms led to the establishment of a Scottish Parliament, a Welsh Assembly, and a London Mayor. While regional devolution has undoubtedly had some positive effects, the powers of the devolved bodies vary greatly and large swathes of the country have remained untouched by the changes. This led to the delivery of a rather 'haphazard and idiosyncratic' system of governance (Hay and Stoker, 2009, p 237). These devolved authorities also suffer from a lack of formal representation in the national legislature. In Germany,

---

[2]   Political actors have often driven the outsourcing or 'depoliticisation' of policy. For example, Lord Falconer, Secretary of State for Constitutional Affairs in 2003, argued quite explicitly that the 'depoliticising of key decision-making is a vital element in bringing power closer to the people' (cited in Flinders and Buller, 2006, p 312).

[3]   Ironically, Britain's exit from the European Union has dramatically reduced the prospects of recapturing parts of the policy-making process from the unpredictable forces of economic globalisation.

by contrast, state governments are formally represented in the upper chamber of parliament.

The 'Together We Can' civil renewal programme (2003–2010), initiated by Hazel Blears and David Blunkett (and discussed in Chapter Five), sought to strengthen state–citizen cooperation in local communities with the awareness that civic activism was dominated by older and better-off participants (DCLG, 2008). But the implementation of these reforms focused on a mix of priority areas with high deprivation, and forward thinking local partners willing to engage in democratic innovations. In other parts of the country, the reach was limited. For example, local officials in many areas only paid lip-service to the planned expansion in the role of youth councils. And many local authorities also allowed these youth councils to be dominated by young people from middle-class backgrounds – many of whom were already politically engaged (Wyness, 2009). These well-intended efforts to rebalance the relationship between local and central government were also undermined by 'the restriction of policymaking powers within councils and the greater mechanisms of monitoring and centralised regulation available to central government' (Chandler, 2001, p 14).

Furthermore, the reforms enacted through Together We Can were vulnerable to political and economic change. Their fragility became more obvious in the aftermath of the financial crisis, under the Coalition Government. Although the rhetoric of localisation and citizen participation remained – Prime Minister Cameron's Big Society project aspired to provide greater autonomy to local councils and foster community action – efforts to promote local engagement were critically undermined by huge cuts in local government funding.[4]

The cuts fell particularly heavily on youth services, and also led to a major withdrawal of funding from charities and community groups. The dramatic impact of austerity was illustrated by a Unison (2016) report, which found that £387 million had been cut from local youth services budgets in England and Wales between 2010 and 2016. And, 'the overwhelming majority (91%) said the cuts were having a particular impact on young people from poorer backgrounds' (Unison,

---

[4] For example, Liverpool City Council withdrew from the Big Society pilot scheme on learning that it would lose £100m in specialist grants from the government, many of which were allocated to charities and community groups tackling welfare issues. Council Leader Joe Anderson asked: 'How can the City Council support the Big Society and its aim to help communities do more for themselves when we will have to cut the lifeline to hundreds of these vital and worthwhile groups?' (Guardian, 2011).

2016, p 6). According to the research, conducted through a freedom of information survey, 603 youth centres were closed in England and Wales and 3,652 youth services jobs were lost between 2012 and 2016 alone.

To complement the Big Society project, the Coalition Government developed a National Citizen Service (NCS) for 15 to 17 year olds, which was strongly advocated by David Cameron himself.[5] The NCS was launched in 2011, and £1.5 billion was allocated to the scheme up until 2020. In principle, the NCS was designed to solve many of the problems regarding a lack of youth engagement in local democracy discussed in this chapter, but the remit from the government tilted the scheme towards life skills and team building, and away from elements involving 'planning and delivering social action' (Mills and Waite, 2017).

The following case studies provide examples of where local political and social actors have managed to overcome the many obstacles to engaging younger citizens in local democracy.

Everyday democracy in action

This chapter examines three positive examples of local youth civic engagement. The case studies were investigated through discussions with the key participants, analysis of the Local Government Association's evaluations, and local council documentation regarding the initiatives in London, Wiltshire and Oldham.

The first case study took place in Lewisham, South East London, and emphasises the role that resources and facilitating institutions play in youth civic engagement. Lewisham is a relatively young and poor London borough, has one of the highest proportions of black and minority ethnic citizens in the country, and suffers from relatively high levels of poverty, social exclusion and crime.

In 2009, a small group of young men (aged 11 to 16) formed a Skate Park Action Group (SPAG). The group was established in response to plans to close the local skateboarding facilities in Telegraph Hill Park following complaints about the noise from residents. To support its case, the SPAG launched a petition that managed to gather 800 signatures from other young people and adults within the wider community. But unlike most petitions, that was not the end of their involvement.

---

[5]   After the end of his prime ministership, David Cameron's first appointment was as chair of the trustees to the NCS, which illustrated his close personal interest in the scheme.

After submitting their petition, the group attended the council's Local Assembly meetings, where they made their case to officials. At one of these meetings, they found out about the existence of a locality fund. The SPAG applied for funding and were awarded money to carry out a wider public consultation about the feasibility of building a permanent skate park in the area. Support from various local actors – from the group members' parents to local assembly members – and contact with local officials thus provided them with further resources to pursue their goal.

The SPAG faced opposition from a Save the Upper Park group of residents and some of the local assembly members. But the persistence and determination of its members led to the completion of the consultation exercise, assisted in their work by the local youth service and assembly coordinator. The young people's efforts, and their willingness to compromise with the Upper Park group over the exact location of the facility, were ultimately rewarded when the local ward assembly agreed to their proposal for the construction of a new skate park in Lower Park. Its design and construction were made possible through the SPAG's successful application to the local Youth Opportunities Fund. The skate park was built and finally opened in 2011.

The SPAG, in addition to its considerable success in gaining support for their proposal and getting the skate park agreed and built, had many positive effects on its participants. According to one member of the group: "My favourite thing was us all coming together and work hard non-stop and the feeling of victory when we got the skate park". The campaign not only increased the participants' understanding of local processes, democratic skills and sense of efficacy, but also had a positive bearing on community relations and civic engagement in the area. SPAG participants also told their stories to their peers and encouraged them to become more active. Nevertheless, the experiences were not all positive.

Participants had to overcome several hurdles, including the scheduling of local meetings in school hours, and adapting to alien situations where they were scrutinised and stereotyped by older adults. In this respect, the campaign was also a learning process for the local authorities and officials regarding how to better facilitate youth engagement in their area. The scheduling of local meetings at inconvenient times is a poignant illustration of how young people can become excluded from the policy process through a seemingly innocuous scheduling issue.

The second case study of youth civic engagement took place in rural Wiltshire in 2005 (before the financial crisis). In contrast to

Lewisham, Wiltshire has a significantly older, less ethnically diverse and better-off population than the national average. However, it is not uncommon within these rural settings for pockets of poverty to exist. And their relative isolation can often lead to a geographical sense of social exclusion for young people that is not as relevant in urban settings (Shucksmith, 2004). In this regard, young people in Wiltshire were unhappy with the provision of transport in the area: the fact that 16 to 18 year olds were expected to pay full fares to and from their places of full-time education; and the lack of regular and direct buses routes between villages and isolated areas and local towns.

These concerns with local transport were raised vociferously, unlike in the Lewisham case, through the council's existing youth-related structures. Children and Young People's Issue Groups, supported by the county council's Youth Development Service and the Wiltshire Youth Assembly, organised a transport conference to deal with these issues. This allowed the Wiltshire youth groups to expand contacts between young people and local officials and draw in the private providers of bus services: two national companies, First Group and Stagecoach; and a local company, the Wiltshire and Dorset Bus Company.

Over 100 young people aged 13 to 19 attended the conference and were asked to vote on their top two priorities. The young people then worked in community area groups with transport representatives to try to find solutions to the problems they had identified. The conference, therefore, acted as a deliberative and problem-solving forum, educating young people about economic and logistical workings of public transport (in relation to this everyday issue), and how to address their concerns in a public forum. The conference achieved some concrete goals: the adult fare for the Wiltshire and Dorset Bus Company would only be paid by those over 18 years of age; and the allocation of £100,000 by local area boards to respond to youth concerns with public transport. The initiative also resulted in the establishment of a countywide transport development steering group, including 20 young participants, to take the work forward. Through these interactions, lines of contact between young people, local government and the bus companies were maintained, even if the achievements from their work were rather modest.

However, participants in the conference reflected on the need for better preparation – in particular, regarding the business cases for their proposals – before the conference. It should also be emphasised that the exercise exposed the council's lack of control over the bus companies, which relates to the process of depoliticisation through the outsourcing of public services discussed above.

The final case study relates to the role that schools can play as mediating institutions, connecting young people in a meaningful way to their local communities through citizenship education (as discussed in detail by Weinberg and Flinders in Chapter Eleven). The initiatives took place at Royton and Crompton School in Oldham. Oldham is recorded as one of the most deprived areas in England. It is ranked in the bottom 10% of local authorities for income, employment and health.

Royton and Crompton school, recognising the need to develop stronger ties with the local community in its provision of citizenship education, embarked on a number of initiatives after 2010. The school focused on experiential learning through engagement in youth conferences and the invitation of speakers to discuss political issues. Emphasis was placed on turning these events into deliberative exercises through interactions with other young people, politicians and local officials.

The most significant of the events was their participation in a Young Voices Conference, organised by the local council, which provided the opportunity for young people from different schools to think about how their areas could be made safer and how leisure facilities could be improved. The conference provided a space for them to discuss these issues with pupils from other schools, and introduced them to the decision-making procedures through which councils allocate money in local government. This knowledge-based approach is important given the strong relationship that exists between civic and political knowledge and participation, and given the fact that as a topic government is largely absent from politics teaching in schools and universities.

Clearly this conference was helpful in developing young people's knowledge about how to influence policy making as well as confidence in their own democratic skills. For example, one pupil spoke of having "gained confidence from having to speak to people from different schools". The importance of peer-to-peer learning in these initiatives should not be forgotten. Another student remarked that "the people who were holding it seemed really interested in what we had to say, so that also made it easy for us to put our views out". For yet another student, this event showed them that "it was important to get involved in your community".

A second feature of these efforts to strengthen the practical dimension of citizenship education was providing opportunities for pupils to meet politicians through visits by members of parliament. On one occasion students interacted with the then local MP for Oldham West and Royton, Michael Meacher, who held a 'day in the life' workshop about what it was like to be an MP. According to the school's citizenship co-ordinator: "It's better than a lesson just trying to teach about MPs ... it's real life, talking from experience". And there is no doubt that students benefited from their personal contacts with their MP, which helped to 'humanise' the politicians by exposing pupils to what they did in their everyday lives.[6]

Although the MP visits provided a valuable opportunity to connect young people with politicians, there were also problems with regard to the lack of a policy agenda: the discussions focused on procedure – what an MP does – more than the issues that the young people cared about (which was a successful element of the schools' conference). A particularly disappointing aspect of the MP's workshop was that it was conducted only with 'gifted and talented students' (who were more likely to be predisposed towards civic and political engagement) as opposed to a broader selection of the student body. In other words, although all contact between young people and politicians is likely to hold some value, there is an obvious need to consider how these interactions can be optimised: in this case, which pupils they talk to and what they talk about.

The Youth Voices Conference also suffered (though to a lesser extent) from the lack of clear policy agenda – not much effort was made to connect the discussions with actual change in the community. The truth was that, in the school's attempt to better incorporate a practical dimension into its citizenship education, there was no real focus on tangible policy outcomes. This resulted in suboptimal benefits for the young people, despite all of the hard work that had been invested in these outreach activities.

Conclusion

The Lewisham and Wiltshire case studies each illustrate how young people's participation in focused, local policy-making processes can help to tackle exclusion, build trust in the political system (otherwise known as 'external efficacy') and develop young people's confidence in being able to make a difference to the policy-making process ('internal efficacy'). The young people's experiences of assessing the feasibility of rival options, and the economic realities of turning appealing ideas into deliverable schemes, carried with it substantial developmental

---

[6] Another opportunity for Royton and Compton students to meet local politicians came with the visit of Phil Woolas, former MP Oldham East and Saddleworth, to meet and chat to students at a school fête.

benefits for equipping young citizens with the know-how for shaping public policy.

Although the pupils involved in the Oldham case study undoubtedly gained benefits, in terms of their knowledge about the policy-making process and their sense of efficacy in expressing and debating their views in public, through their interactions with other young people and politicians, the quality of these interactions must also be considered. The Oldham experience reminds us that these initiatives must – as far as possible – be supported by older adults and institutions, but led by young people themselves. This relates to Boyte's (2011, p 630) emphasis on 'citizens as co-creators ... not simply deliberators and decision-makers'.

These examples offer us a glimpse of what might be possible. However, they also show how existing examples of best practice are very dependent upon the endeavours of key individuals, whose interventions scaffolded the civic engagement of young people in each of these communities. This chapter also found, in the case studies, that this highly motivated core of professionals, local officials and parents was required to support the engagement of young people and enable them to achieve positive outcomes.

They also demonstrate the diverse pathways that young people might take to participation in political governance. These pathways depend upon the issue that is involved, how widespread the problem is – that is, how many people are affected – the existence of competing interests within a community, as well as the financial implications of any decision and the capacity of a local authority to implement the requested changes (especially if the issue involves the actions of private companies).

If we are to promote young people's engagement with everyday democracy more widely, we should be aware of its main drawback – namely, the social inequalities of participation that are amplified by the lack of civic resources available in poorer communities. This relates to justified concerns, in the context of austerity in public spending, that the necessary financial support for relevant organisations – ranging from local youth services, to NGOs promoting youth engagement – has dried up. It also emphasises the need to develop the cognitive resources of our young people – for example, through more specialist training for teachers and more funding for schools to improve the provision of citizenship education. Higher education institutions should also be required to play a much more central role in providing young people with the skills they need for civic engagement, and ensuring outreach for this training to young people into deprived communities (Kisby and Sloam, 2014).

Even within the current climate of austerity, public resources can be made available if policy makers take youth civic engagement seriously. The establishment of the widely criticised National Citizen Service shows that this is true. NCS resources could be more effectively used if they were channelled into self-sustaining 'local democracy hubs'.

Another obstacle to the rejuvenation of everyday democracy is the lack of coordination of existing institutions and work in the area of youth civic engagement. Here, the idea of local democracy hubs could also play a pivotal role. Schools and universities could act as permanent centres of youth civic engagement, alongside local authority youth services and youth councils and relevant NGOs. We could achieve so much more through the creation of these hubs within our local communities.[7]

Finally, the pivotal role of contact – between young people, politicians and public officials – should be emphasised. These contacts provide an interface between formal political and governmental structures and individual citizens, whereby citizens can be inspired to co-create democracy in relation to issues that affect their everyday lives.

References

Bang, H. (ed) (2003) *Governance as Social and Political Communication*, Manchester: Manchester University Press.

Barber, B. (2003) *Strong Democracy: Participatory politics for a new age*, Berkeley: University of California Press.

Bennett, W. L. and Segerberg, A. (2013) *The Logic of Connective Action: digital media and the personalization of contentious politics*, New York. Cambridge University Press.

Boyte, H. C. (2005). 'Reframing democracy: Governance, civic agency, and politics', *Public Administration Review*, 65(5), 536-546.

Boyte, H. C. (2011) 'Constructive politics as public work: organizing the literature', *Political Theory* 39 (5): 630-660.

Castells, M. (2012) *Networks of Outrage and Hope*, Cambridge: Polity.

Chandler, D. (2001) 'Active citizens and the therapeutic state: the role of democratic participation in local government reform', *Policy and Politics* 29 (1): 3-14.

---

[7] Compare this with the 'Take Part' hubs as discussed in Chapter Thirteen in this book.

Department for Communities and Local Government (DCLG) (2008) *Communities in Control*. www.gov.uk/government/uploads/system/uploads/attachment_data/file/228678/7427.pdf

Flanagan, C. and Levine, P. (2010) 'Civic engagement and the transition to adulthood', *The Future of Children* 20 (1): 159-179.

Flinders, M. and Buller, J. (2006) 'Depoliticisation: principles, tactics and tools', *British Politics* 1 (3): 293-318.

Dalton, R. J. (2017) *The Participation Gap: social status and political inequality*, Oxford: Oxford University Press.

De Tocqueville, A. (1969 [1875]) *Democracy in America*, Garden City, NY: Doubleday.

Fieldhouse, E., Tranmer, M. and Russell, A. (2007) 'Something about young people or something about elections? Electoral participation of young people in Europe: Evidence from a multilevel analysis of the European Social Survey', *European Journal of Political Research* 46 (6): 797-822.

Franklin, M. (2004) *Voter Turnout and the Dynamics of Electoral Competition in Established Democracies since 1945*, Cambridge, MA: Cambridge University Press.

Fung, A. (2004) *Empowered Participation: reinventing urban democracy*, Princeton, NJ: Princeton University Press.

Gerber, A. S. and Green, D. P. (2000) 'The effects of canvassing, telephone calls, and direct mail on voter turnout: a field experiment', *American Political Science Review*, 94(3), 653-663.

The Guardian (2011). '"Big Society" Suffers Setback in its Showcase Liverpool', 3 February. www.theguardian.com/society/2011/feb/03/liverpool-big-society

Hay, C. and Stoker, G. (2009) 'Revitalising politics: have we lost the plot?', *Representation* 45 (3): 225-236.

Johnston, R., Cutts, D., Pattie, C. and Fisher, J. (2012) 'We've got them on the list: contacting, canvassing and voting in a British general election campaign', *Electoral Studies* 31 (2): 317-329.

Kisby, B. and Sloam, J. (2014) 'Promoting youth participation in democracy: the role of higher education', in Mycock, A. and Tonge, J (eds) *Beyond the Youth Citizenship Commission: young people and politics*, London: Political Studies Association, 52–56.

Mansbridge, J. J. (1983) *Beyond Adversary Democracy*, Chicago: University of Chicago Press.

Mills, S. and Waite, C. (2017) 'Brands of youth citizenship and the politics of scale: national citizen service in the United Kingdom', *Political Geography* 56: 66-76.

Norris, P. (2002) *Democratic Phoenix: Reinventing political activism*, Cambridge: Cambridge University Press.

Park, A., Bryson, C., Clery, E., Curtice, J. and Phillips, M. (2013) *British Social Attitudes 30*, London: NatCen.

Pateman, C. (1970) *Participation and Democratic Theory*, Cambridge: Cambridge University Press.

Pattie, C., Seyd, P. and Whiteley, P. (2004) *Citizenship in Britain: values, participation and democracy*, Cambridge: Cambridge University Press.

Pickard, S. (2018) 'Momentum and the movementist "Corbynistas"', in Pickard, S. and Bessant, J. (eds) *Young People Re-Generating Politics in Times of Crisis*, Basingstoke: Palgrave, 115–137.

Putnam, R. D. (2000) *Bowling Alone: the collapse and revival of American community*, New York: Simon and Schuster.

Shucksmith, M. (2004) 'Young people and social exclusion in rural areas', *Sociologia Ruralis* 44 (1): 43–59.

Sloam, J. (2016) 'Diversity and voice: the political participation of young people in the European Union', *The British Journal of Politics and International Relations* 18 (3): 521–537.

Sloam, J., and Henn, M. (2018) *Youthquake 2017: the rise of young cosmopolitans in Britain*, Basingstoke: Palgrave.

Spannring, R., Ogris, G. and Gaiser, W. (2008) *Youth and Political Participation in Europe: results of the comparative study EUYOPART*, Opladen: Barbara Budrich.

Stoker, G. (2016) *Why politics matters: Making democracy work*. Basingtoke: Palgrave.

Unison. (2016) *A Future at Risk: Cuts in Youth Services*. www.unison.org.uk/content/uploads/2016/08/23996.pdf

Van Biezen, I., Mair, P. and Poguntke, T. (2012) 'Going, going,... gone? The decline of party membership in contemporary Europe', *European Journal of Political Research* 51 (1): 24–56.

Wattenberg, M. P. (2008) *Is Voting for Young People? With a postscript on citizen engagement*, New York: Pearson.

Wyness, M. (2009) 'Children representing children: participation and the problem of diversity in UK youth councils', *Childhood* 16 (4): 535–552.

PART THREE

How To Expand Our Civic Capability

11

Improving Citizenship Education

James Weinberg and Matthew Flinders

The very premise of this book seeks to identify positive and progressive manifestos for democratic renewal and, in their commitment to that mission statement, the chapters thus far have made clear the crisis of contemporary democracy. In this context, political science has arguably been preoccupied with supply-side theories of democratic design and demand-side studies of populism or extra-statal politics, but there has been only nascent consideration given to the role of schools in both promoting political engagement and cultivating deeper understandings of democratic politics. Twenty years since the publication of the final report of the Advisory Group on Citizenship (AGC; 'Crick Report'), which led to the introduction of citizenship education as a statutory feature of the UK national curriculum, this chapter makes three interrelated arguments:

1. Citizenship education can play a major role in promoting political understanding and state-citizen cooperation.
2. Citizenship education as it has been implemented in the UK has generally not lived up to this potential.
3. This raises distinctive questions about the existence of blockages, barriers and the 'politics of' citizenship education more broadly.

In order to substantiate and tease apart these arguments, this chapter is divided into four main sections. The first section introduces citizenship education as a normatively contested concept and describes its introduction as a statutory feature of education in the UK. The second section reviews the existing research and data on the impact of citizenship education globally in order to reveal the existence of particular correlations with sociopolitical outcomes (Schulz et al, 2016). The third, most substantive section identifies a gap between the 'Crick vision' laid out 20 years ago (AGC et al, 1998) and the delivered reality of citizenship education in the UK. The fourth and final section offers a number of solutions that seek to realign citizenship education with the principles of shared governance and democratic citizenship. These suggestions incorporate practical recommendations for teacher training and school-based delivery of citizenship education as well as more abstract proposals for reconceiving policy and public discourse in a way that supports globalised, communitarian and critically active conceptions of the subject.

Citizenship education in theory and practice

As David Kerr (2000, pp 74-5) highlighted almost 20 years ago – yet the sentiment seems no less applicable today – worries abound regarding the 'seemingly pervasive erosion of the social, political, economic and moral fabric of society in England, in the face of rapid economic and social change'. To some extent, concerns regarding the rise of political alienation, distrust and representative inequalities – the end of Almond and Verba's so-called *Civic Culture* (1963) – are not new and in this sense the Trilateral Commission's report of 1974, *The Crisis of Democracy*, provides a critical reference point. It was these sentiments that underpinned the Crick Report's focus on 'worrying levels of apathy, ignorance and cynicism about public life', which 'could and should be remedied' (AGC et al, 1998, pp 8, 16). The policy response placed citizenship education (CE) onto the National Curriculum in England for all secondary-level students (aged 11-16), as effective from September 2002.

Although increasingly in vogue in policy circles in recent years, there remains contestation about what CE means, how it should be taught and what it should aim to achieve. Citizenship and accordingly CE have, historically, been incredibly fluid terms. From the city-state visions of classical writers such as Plato and Aristotle to the 'mirror of princes' literature in the early modern period, the nation-state era of the industrial revolution to the postcolonial, postmaterial decades of the later twentieth and early twenty-first centuries, the requirements and envisioned outcomes of CE have been bound to the ebbs and flows of philosophical and governing thought. The challenges now facing the UK, and indeed much of Europe, are as unique as at any time in our history, and as such they require careful consideration of how CE might, in a contemporary, postmodern setting, facilitate sustained democratisation.

In sum, we argue that CE should support the ideals of democracy as an outcome, where that term is understood as both a type of government and a set of practices; that, subsequently, CE must incorporate some balance of knowledge, skills and values; and that these three components of CE should encourage students to develop a range of democratic competences (see Hoskins et al, 2015). While the labelling of these competences is contested in the academic literature, a number of national and international policy documents have attempted to collate them. In particular, the Council of Europe has conceived four categories of competences, which it claims 'enable an individual to participate effectively and appropriately in a culture of democracy' (Council of Europe, 2016, p 12; Table 11.1).

Table 11.1: Citizenship competences

Interacting effectively and constructively with others	Thinking critically	Acting in a socially responsible manner	Acting democratically
Self-confidence Responsibility Autonomy (personal initiative) Respect for different opinions or beliefs Cooperation Conflict resolution Empathy Self-awareness Communicating and listening Emotional awareness Flexibility or adaptability Inter-cultural skills	Multi-perspectivity Reasoning and analysis skills Data interpretation Knowledge discovery and use of sources Media literacy Creativity Exercising judgement Understanding the present world Questioning	Respect for justice Solidarity Respect for other human beings Respect for human rights Sense of belonging Sustainable development Environmental protection Cultural heritage protection Knowing about or respecting other cultures Knowing about or respecting religions Non-discrimination	Respect for democracy Knowledge of political institutions Knowledge of political processes (e.g. elections) Knowledge of international organisations, treaties and declarations Interacting with political authorities Knowledge of fundamental political and social concepts Respect for rules Participating Knowledge of or participation in civil society

Source: European Commission/EACEA/Eurydice (2017, p 48).

How these competences may be utilised, understood and operationalised in national settings relies, as Kerr (1999) argues, upon contextual and structural factors. While cultural factors refer to the traditions, geography, economic ideologies and sociopolitical history of a country, structural factors incorporate the organisation of its education system, including funding and targets. Combined, these conditions spurn a spectrum of conceptions and applications of democratic competences in CE that reproduce McLaughlin's (1992) distinction between 'minimal' and 'maximal' citizenship. The autarchic, minimal citizen is taught to be law–abiding and public-spirited; the maximal or autonomous citizen is encouraged to be highly active and ultimately commands a 'distanced critical perspective on all important matters' (McLaughlin, 1992, p 242). The difference, when it comes to education for democratic citizenship, is between 'Education ABOUT citizenship ... Education THROUGH citizenship ... Education FOR citizenship' (Kerr, 2000, p 210). At one end of this continuum, liberal and neoliberal models of CE promote individual rights and responsibilities alongside a small but strong state (Keating, 2014). At the other end is a communitarian vision of citizenship and CE, in which citizens are organic parts of a polity comprised of diverse interests. Westheimer and Kahne (2004) characterise the citizens 'produced' along this spectrum, identifying the critically equipped justice-oriented citizen as the ideal type (Table 11.2).

Table 11.2: Three types of citizen

The individualised citizen	The participatory citizen	The justice-oriented citizen
Understands democratic governance and remains obedient and law abiding; makes personal contributions to collective endeavours like recycling and fundraising; focuses on the moral compass of being a 'good citizen'; understands citizenship in terms of personal responsibilities.	Active volunteer in the community; contributes to/leads on local issue-oriented projects; works within and according to established hierarchies of political power to help others; understands citizenship in terms of local involvement and collective endeavour.	Critical capacity to affect systemic change; challenges established structures of power through understanding of democratic processes and the social, economic or cultural inequalities that exist in local or national communities; campaigns on root causes of political problems; understands citizenship in terms of questioning, debating and changing established systems.

Source: Adapted from Westheimer and Kahne (2004, p 240).

For Sir Bernard Crick – who chaired the AGC in England – the act of politics and democratic citizenship pivoted upon the active contestation of public policy by the public, and in turn the peaceful reconciliation of that process through meaningful debate. Steeped in civic republican theory and supported by the then Education Secretary David Blunkett (see also Chapter Five in this book), who recognised that a new model of CE needed to go beyond teaching the formalities of government and governance (Pollard, 2004), Crick directed a vision for CE in England that conceived of citizenship as not simply a state of membership but as an activity. The final report defined CE in three strands:

1. Social and moral responsibility – learning from the very beginning self-confidence and socially and morally responsible behaviour both in and beyond the classroom, both towards those in authority and towards each other;
2. Community involvement – learning and becoming helpfully involved in the life and concerns of their communities, including learning through community involvement and service to the community;
3. Political literacy – learning about and how to make themselves effective in public life though knowledge, skills and values. (AGC et al, 1998, pp 11-13)

The introduction of CE as a statutory subject in England took place against a backdrop of immense constitutional reform in the UK. It was, as Anthony Giddens (2000, pp 23-4) commented, 'extraordinarily important ... [as part of New Labour's] programmes of political change'. Underpinned by principles of experiential learning, the Crick Report offered a deeper, more collective and engaged vision of justice-oriented CE.

The impact of citizenship education

The previous section briefly outlined the theoretical debate surrounding CE and its introduction in England. It argued that different ideas about what democracy is or what 'learning for democracy' actually is or should be translate directly into varying commitments to national education policies as well as more specific forms of pedagogy, curriculum and assessment. This section now engages with the extant research on the impact of CE in England and abroad to argue that CE, effectively and consistently delivered, has the potential to (a) improve young people's political outcomes, and (b) mitigate socioeconomic inequalities in political participation. Taken together, this evidence is used to argue for the radical capacity of CE to overcome barriers to impactful state-citizen cooperation.

In England, the most robust and detailed body of evidence on CE was collected by the Citizenship Education Longitudinal Study (CELS), which was commissioned by the Department for Children, Schools and Families (DCSF) to investigate the impact of compulsory CE on school students between 2001 and 2010. The final report noted:

> [T]he CELS cohort [i.e. a group of pupils who were tracked and regularly surveyed during their period of full-time education] was more likely to have positive attitudes and intentions towards civic and political participation (both in the present and in the future) if they had high levels of 'received citizenship' (i.e. if they reported having received 'a lot' of citizenship education). (Keating et al, 2010, p vi)

As the Crick Report stipulated, effective CE would be identifiable where pupils developed a sense of political efficacy, improved their formal political literacy, and became helpfully involved in their local communities (AGC et al, 1998, pp 11-13). Using CELS data, Paul Whiteley (2014, p 16) shows that – controlling for both civic voluntarism (which links resources to enhanced political involvement) and social capital (which suggests that obligations and expectations in communities can enhance their mutual activity) – levels of exposure to CE across secondary school significantly predicted participants' civic engagement in terms of efficacy, current and anticipated participation, and political knowledge. In Crick's terms, CE had started to achieve success in less than a decade.

Avril Keating and Jan Germen Janmaat (2016) have conducted path analysis on CELS data to show that those participants who experienced maximum exposure to citizenship education in school were 14.9% more likely to vote at age 18 than those who received minimum delivery in school; similarly, expressive political participation in adulthood increased by 13.1% between the two groups, even after controlling for sociodemographic variables. Focusing specifically on disadvantaged youth in England – where the intergenerational transmission of political disaffection and inequality is strongest (Brady et al, 2015) – Hoskins and colleagues (2017) utilise CELS data in latent curve analysis to reveal a strong interaction effect between CE and socioeconomic variables in determining participants' intention to vote. This research suggests that CE can have a 'compensatory effect' (Campbell, 2008) on students from disadvantaged backgrounds who do not receive positive political stimuli at home or in their local communities.

The IEA International Civic and Citizenship Education Study (ICCS) has provided a similar body of data on the effects of CE worldwide. Working with 24 countries around the globe, the latest iteration of this study concludes:

The links that the ICCS 2016 findings suggest between civic knowledge, school-based experiences with civic engagement, and expectations to vote and participate in other civic activities in adulthood indicate that promotion of civic and citizenship education, in both formal and informal ways, should be considered as an essential means of helping young people become more conscious of their political roles and the importance of being participating citizens. (Schulz et al, 2016, p 209)

The ICCS also revealed diversity in both the content and style of CE programmes (Schulz et al, 2016). In many parts of the world, the dichotomy between democratic knowledge and skills, minimal and maximal CE, is striking and reflects 'political choices that have political consequences' (Westheimer and Kahne, 2004, p 237). In East Asia, for example, a knowledge-heavy curriculum promotes patriotism and 'personally responsible' liberal citizenship over internationalism and justice-oriented active citizenship. Lai and Byram (2012, p 210) note '[t]he discourse on national and patriotic sentiment [in China] polarises people into the liberal or patriotic camp', stymieing discussion and understanding of democratic politics. This might be contrasted with the skills-focused, participatory programme of CE in Mexico, with its 'strong emphasis on group work, solidarity and the collective good' (Levinson and Elizarrarás, 2017, p 412), or the depoliticised model of service learning preferred in the US (Ransom, 2009). When these different political agendas and conceptions of CE are placed along the spectrums discussed in the first section above, it is not surprising – but nevertheless worrying – that only 35% of ICCS participants attained the highest level in the study (Level A), which we would associate here with a range of knowledge, skills and attitudes required of justice-oriented citizenship.[1]

---

[1] 'Students working at the highest level (Level A, called Level 3 in ICCS 2009) are able to make connections between the processes of social and political organisation and influence, and the legal and institutional mechanisms used to control them. They generate accurate hypotheses on the benefits, motivations and likely outcomes of institutional policies and citizens' actions. They integrate, justify and evaluate given positions, policies or laws according to the principles that underpin them. Students also demonstrate familiarity with broad international economic forces and the strategic nature of active participation' (Schulz et al, 2016, p 200).

Barriers and blockages

In the last section, this chapter engaged with a range of research on CE to demonstrate that the transmission of civic knowledge about formal political systems and the experience of democratic school environments can underpin engaged citizenship (for example, Torney-Purta et al, 2001). It also highlighted the role of government policy in enabling CE to act as a lightning rod for greater state-citizen cooperation. In this section, we identify a number of blockages and barriers to effective CE in the UK. These reduce to what we call an 'implementation gap' under New Labour and a 'vision shift' under the subsequent Coalition and Conservative governments.

The 'implementation gap'

Although the CELS revealed a number of positive trends among those who received consistent CE, the participant population represented a small percentage of all secondary school students in England. In 2006 the Office for Standards in Education (Ofsted) discovered that 'only a few schools … have created a coherent programme which pupils can recognise as an entity' (Ofsted, 2006, para 69); the final report of the CELS itself echoed these and similar worries that 'CE is delivered by staff with little experience of, expertise in, or enthusiasm for CE' (Keating et al, 2010, p 47). While the initial momentum behind CE was fast-paced and well-resourced, this was a highly symbolic policy that did not ultimately embed within school curricula or the broader governance of education.

CELS reports found that citizenship was only delivered in a discrete timetable slot, separate from PSHE ('personal, social and health education'), in just under a third of schools (Kerr et al, 2007); where these subjects were combined, the final CELS report concluded that it had 'a negative effect on received citizenship and citizenship outcomes' (Keating et al, 2010, p 5). Although citizenship is a statutory foundation subject with examinable components and recognised as a Progress 8 accountability measure (DfE, 2016), it remains marginalised by comparison to established subjects that have traditionally carried weight in league tables. Crick (2002, p 499) admitted that '[n]o other curriculum subject was stated so briefly', and in many ways it was this light-touch approach that led to the fractured delivery of the subject.

In hindsight, the Crick Report overshot the practicalities of delivering a statutory curriculum subject in its adherence to a theoretical vision of CE. The Report's essential recommendations only stipulated that schools should spend up to and no more than 5% of curriculum time on achieving CE outcomes (ACG et al, 1998, pp 23-4). The potential for 'lossiness' (Trowler, 2003) was immense insofar as official documents were quickly forgotten, summarised and reinterpreted as they progressed through the education system. The first of the CELS interim reports revealed:

> limited familiarity [among school personnel] with the key citizenship curriculum documents, such as the Curriculum Order and Qualifications and Curriculum Authority (QCA) schemes of work, and little or no familiarity with the key policy texts, notably the Crick report and Post-16 report. (Kerr et al, 2003, p viii)

Subject to renewed research in this area, it is likely that structural reforms in recent years (academisation, the rise of free schools, and subsequent autonomy from the National Curriculum in particular) have hollowed out the potential of CE in England even further.

If curriculum documents in 2002 were unprecedented in their brevity, then New Labour and subsequent governments have also not done enough to train teachers in the content and associated pedagogy of CE. Although the UK (England) was the first nation in Europe to offer initial teacher training (ITT) in CE, the momentum for this initiative was not sustained. Only 284 newly qualified teachers (NQTs) practised the subject in 2006 (against a target of 540); in 2010 only 220 CE teacher training places were available; and by 2017 the number of trainee CE teachers reportedly dropped to fewer than 50.[2] The result is that non-specialists, with no formal training and a plethora of competing obligations, must deliver CE. In a recent study with non-specialist teachers delivering CE alongside their main subject in more than 60 schools around England, Weinberg and Flinders (2018) found that (a) teachers do not have a shared understanding of citizenship and the purpose of CE; (b) there is a distinct gap between academic work on good pedagogy for CE and classroom practice due to an absence of initial teacher training and/or continued professional development

---

[2]   This figure was cited by Liz Moorse, CEO of the Association for Citizenship Teaching, in a recent evidence session for the 2017/18 House of Lords Select Committee on Citizenship and Civic Engagement. A full transcript can be obtained at: http://data.parliament.uk/writtenevidence/committeeevidence.svc/evidencedocument/citizenship-and-civic-engagement-committee/citizenship-and-civic-engagement/oral/72120.html

(CPD) opportunities; (c) CE continues to be sorely neglected and/or ignored in state secondary school curricula; and (d) where citizenship is taught, it is delivered with individualistic and inward-looking liberal conceptions of 'good' rather than 'active' citizenship. The last of these findings suggests a worrying link between recent macro-level policy rhetoric and frontline provision. It is to this shift in the politics of CE that we now turn.

The 'vision shift'

Following the 2010 General Election and the formation of the Liberal Democrat–Conservative Coalition Government, the policy discourse around CE shifted to the right in ideological terms. We argue that this 'vision shift', characterised by the promotion of a more individualised character education (revolving around minimal citizenship) at the expense of collective active citizenship, is particularly significant for understanding why CE in England is not fulfilling its potential.

The Jubilee Centre at Birmingham University is the foremost centre for character education studies in the UK and takes a broad and unambiguously Aristotelian approach to 'character' as a set of educational outcomes: 'a set of personal traits or dispositions that produce specific moral emotions, inform motivation, and guide conduct' (Jubilee Centre, 2017). The concept of 'character' has been operationalised in English education policy – in particular by former Education Secretary Nicky Morgan – as a narrower, more instrumental set of 'traits, attributes and behaviours that underpin success in education and work' (DfE, 2015a). The government's slimmed down, character-heavy CE curriculum now diverges substantially from the three strands set out by the Crick Report in 1998. Instead of a model seeking to promote civic and political participation at the meso- and macro-levels (locally, nationally, internationally), the new guidance to schools focuses on promoting 'a sound knowledge and understanding of the role of law ... volunteering as well as other forms of responsible activity ... [and] enabl[ing] them (students) to manage their money on a day-to-day basis, and plan for future financial needs' (DfE, 2013, p 214). While there is evident cross-fertilisation between the moral base of character education and the CE competences put forward by the Council of Europe, the character agenda developed in the UK since 2010 downplays, in particular, the democratic competences of criticality, active participation and political literacy. Put differently, character education is imbued with a neoliberal market logic that aims to deliver a highly knowledgeable, obedient and employable workforce (see Leach, 2018).

At the same time, character education has become a vehicle for the Coalition and Conservative Governments of 2010 to the present to address concerns about multiculturalism and national unity. Following the London riots in August 2011, Prime Minister David Cameron told the nation that this was 'not about poverty ... No, this was about behaviour ... people showing indifference to right and wrong ... people with a twisted moral code ... people with a complete absence of self-restraint' (Cameron, 2011). This rhetoric is indicative of a 'vision shift' away from communitarian ideals of justice-oriented citizenship and CE, and towards a staunchly individualised, depoliticised and 'personally responsible' model (Table 11.2; see also Kisby, 2017). There was, for example, no recognition that those young people who rioted in 2011 were doing so out of anger at structural inequalities, inaccessible public services and an austerity agenda that was hitting them the hardest. In its latest iterations – specifically the Essential Life Skills package presented by the government in 2017 (DfE, 2017) – character education is an increasingly econocentric strategy that aims to anticipate post-Brexit market volatility. If the UK's departure from the European Union does 'hit hard', it is possible that young people will, as with the riots in 2011, face *personal* blame for the failures of a closed political process conducted in elite circles.

The 'vision shift' identified here also characterises related CE policies in the UK such as spiritual, moral, social and cultural education (SMSC), the Prevent Programme and 'fundamental British values'. These policies carry more resource and incentive than discrete CE lessons and at the same time reinforce minimalist conceptions of citizenship. For example, the Counter Terrorism and Security Act 2015 obliges schools and universities to 'prevent radicalisation' and delineates democracy as a 'British value' (DfE, 2015b). As Suke Wolton (2017, p 2) argues, this legislation directly contradicts centuries of thought in which democracy, where it is meaningful, entails a constant churn of ideas about how society should be governed. Tied to the underlying assumptions of the character agenda, Prevent not only portrays citizens as passive recipients of politics – removing their involvement as Tocquevillian 'associates' in a democratic process – but reduces the democratic space for disaffected youth to question, debate and interrogate ideas openly.

Reimagining citizenship education in the UK

We argue that young people in the England are no less interested in 'the political' than their counterparts in Europe but their comparative disengagement with formal politics (see also Chapter Ten in this book) is an alarming indictment of a system that has ill-equipped them with the skills and knowledge to feel empowered as citizens. To correct this, this section makes a bold case for a minimum guaranteed offer of CE for every young person in the country. Underpinning this change there will need to be:

- Policy reorientation away from the nationalistic and individualised introspection promoted by character education and embodied in Brexit rhetoric.
- Changes to initial teacher training and CPD that prepare our frontline educators in the art of critical pedagogy.
- New curriculum designs that reconceptualise the horizons of sovereignty (and thus democratic citizenship) for young people.

At the theoretical level, our minimum offer revolves around CE as a participatory endeavour that is 'lived' as much as it is 'learnt'. We take inspiration from the philosophical work of Hannah Arendt and, in particular, her conception of action (Arendt, 1958). We are only free, according to Arendt, where we appear and act in the public realm and thus our freedom is interwoven with the freedom of others. This is a highly political understanding of freedom and one akin to civic republican notions of democratic citizenship: '[t]he raison d'être of politics is freedom and its field of experience is action' (Arendt, 1977, p 146). To harness Arendt's concept of action to CE is not simply to acknowledge the need for a more reciprocal model of learning for democracy but also to view young people as citizens of now, not just the future (see also Biesta and Lawy, 2006).

At a practical level, the implementation of this vision for CE requires regular opportunities for young people to participate in the political communities of their classroom, school or society. To facilitate such learning, we find a pedagogic link in the practice of critical pedagogy (McLaren, 2003). The word 'critical' has been a favoured buzzword for repeated curriculum documents in the UK but it is important here to distinguish between critical *thinking* – based on the application of logic but lacking moralistic or ideological content – and critical *pedagogy* – a context-specific pedagogical approach centred on dialogue, synergistic reflection and action, and a critical consciousness of social injustice.

Laura Johnson and Paul Morris (2010, p 80) identify four distinguishing features of critical pedagogy that can be incorporated into CE: the ideological/moral; the collective/social; the subjective/context driven; and praxis (reflection action) (Table 11.3). In its focus on providing the conditions for social change and stimulating democratic citizenship through knowledge and skills, we argue that critical pedagogy not only encompasses all four competences set forward by the Council of Europe but also harnesses these to a justice-oriented, maximal model of CE. As such, CE as critical pedagogy goes back to and beyond the ambitions of the Crick Report, which itself was criticised for overlooking antiracism and parallel structural inequalities (Osler and Starkey, 2006).

Table 11.3 Citizenship education through critical pedagogy

	The Ideological	The Collective	The Subjective	The Practical
Knowledge	Of macro-structural relationships and their expression through history.	Of the synergy between culture and power, as well as non-dominant discourses from other social groups.	Of one's own identity and culture in context.	Of how collective and individual action can best affect systemic change.
Skills	Of structural analysis and the ability to politicise power as a concept.	Of critical debate in the sense of being able to interrogate others' viewpoints and empathise.	Of independent reflection and the capacity to think and speak for oneself; to give informed yet original opinions.	Of critical thinking in action-oriented scenarios to achieve a socially-just goal.
Values	Of justice, equality and anti-oppression.	Of dialogical understanding of others' cultures and values.	Of carefully considered self-worth in relation to others.	Of responsible and ethical action followed up by reflection.
Dispositions	Of active involvement in society and a genuine desire to seek out and question injustice.	Of social awareness and cooperation, as well as a willingness to collaborate.	Of informed yet autonomous thoughts, action and emotion.	Of civic courage in order to commit to enacting change.

Source: Johnson and Morris (2010, p 90).

To implement a new CE curriculum underpinned by critical pedagogy, which makes manifest Arendt's concept of action and thus learning for democracy in UK schools, will require three clear commitments from policy makers. Firstly, we recommend that the government not only recommits to training specialist CE teachers but also introduces modules in critical pedagogy and CE as a feature of all ITT schemes. In doing so, it would be following developments in the Czech Republic, Estonia, Latvia, Lithuania, Austria, Poland and Slovakia, where all prospective teachers are now trained during ITE to become semi-specialists of CE (European Commission et al, 2017, pp 133–7).

Secondly, the Government must issue effective guidance materials and exemplar resources to all schools. At the moment, England is one of only nine education systems in Europe (out of 42 assessed by the Eurydice network) where top-level authorities do not issue guidance documents on CE to teachers (European Commission et al, 2017, p 81). By contrast, the *Loi 2013 pour la refondation de l'école de la République* in France introduced a new academic pathway for students' 'Citizenship Journey' (*Parcours Citoyen*), which is supported by online and printed resources for all schools and teachers.

Finally, the UK Government must introduce a more globalised National Curriculum in general, and for CE in particular. The global financial crash of 2007/2008, increasing concerns about the sustainability of human development and climate change, mass migration across continents and conflict resolution, as well as the spread of instant worldwide communication technologies, are just a few recent changes that are directly pertinent to critical citizenship education and, in turn, truly global in nature. To tackle these and similar issues will, increasingly, require a global community of democratic, justice-oriented citizens. In fact, we argue that Brexit should provide the trigger for a full-fledged review of the state of CE in the UK. Two decades on from the original Crick Report, Brexit has recast a spotlight on a range of sociopolitical challenges that point to an increasingly frail and worn social fabric as well as the need to emphasise what unites individuals and communities rather than what pulls us apart. Though not a panacea, the need for a communitarian model of active CE has arguably never been greater.

References

Advisory Group on Citizenship (AGC)/Department for Education (DfEE)/Qualifications and Curriculum Authority (QCA) (1998) *Education for Citizenship and the Teaching of Democracy in Schools*, London: HMSO.

Almond, G. and Verba, S. (1963) *The Civic Culture* (1st edn), Princeton, NJ: Princeton University Press.

Arendt, H. (1958) *The Human Condition*, Chicago: The University of Chicago Press.

Arendt, H. (1977) *Between Past and Future: eight exercises in political thought*, Harmondsworth: Penguin Books.

Biesta, G. and Lawy, R. (2006) 'From teaching citizenship to learning democracy: overcoming individualism in research, policy and practice', *Cambridge Journal of Education* 36 (1): 63-79.

Brady, H. E., Schlozman, K. L. and Verba, S. (2015) 'Political mobility and political reproduction from generation to generation', *The ANNALS of the American Academy of Political and Social Science* 657 (1): 149-173.

Campbell, D. E. (2008) 'Voice in the classroom: how an open classroom climate fosters political engagement among adolescents', *Political Behaviour* 30 (4): 437-454.

Cameron, D. (2011) *PM's Speech on the Fightback after the Riots.* www.gov.uk/government/speeches/pms-speech-on-the-fightback-after-the-riots

Council of Europe (2016) *Competences for Democratic Culture – living together as equals in culturally diverse democratic societies*, Strasbourg: Council of Europe.

Crick, B. (2002) 'Education for citizenship: the citizenship order', *Parliamentary Affairs* 55: 488–504.

Department for Education (DfE) (2013) *The National Curriculum in England: framework document, September*, London: DfE.

Department for Education (DfE) (2015a) *Character Education: apply for 2015 grant funding, 12 January.* https://www.gov.uk/government/news/character-education-apply-for-2015-grant-funding

Department for Education (DfE) (2015b) *Protecting Children from Radicalisation: the prevent duty.* https://www.gov.uk/government/publications/protecting-children-from-radicalisation-the-prevent-duty

Department for Education (DfE) (2016) *Progress 8: How Progress 8 and Attainment 8 measures are calculated.* www.gov.uk/government/uploads/system/uploads/attachment_data/file/561021/Progress_8_and_Attainment_8_how_measures_are_calculated.pdf

Department for Education (2017). *Plans Launched to Drive Social Mobility in Opportunity Areas.* www.gov.uk/government/news/plans-launched-to-drive-social-mobility-in-opportunity-areas

European Commission/EACEA/Eurydice (2017) *Citizenship Education at School in Europe – 2017. Eurydice Report*, Luxembourg: Publications Office of the European Union.

Giddens, A. (2000) 'Citizenship education in the global era', in Pearce, N. and Hallgarten, J. (eds) *Tomorrow's Citizens: Critical Debates in Citizenship and Education*, London: IPPR, 23–24.

Hoskins, B., Saisana, M. and Villalba, C. (2015) 'Civic competence of youth in Europe: measuring cross national variation through the creation of a composite indicator', *Social Indicators Research*, 123 (2): 431–457.

Hoskins, B., Germen Janmaat, J. and Melis, G. (2017) 'Tackling inequalities in political socialisation: A systematic analysis of access to and mitigation effects of learning citizenship at school', *Social Science Research* 68: 88-101. www.sciencedirect.com/science/article/pii/S0049089X16304458

Johnson, L. and Morris, P. (2010) 'Towards a framework for critical citizenship education', *The Curriculum Journal* 21 (1): 77-96.

Jubilee Centre for Character and Virtues (2017) *A Framework for Character Education in Schools.* www.jubileecentre.ac.uk/userfiles/jubileecentre/pdf/character-education/Framework%20for%20Character%20Education.pdf

Keating, A. (2014) *Education for Citizenship in Europe. European policies, national adaptations and young people's attitudes*, Basingstoke: Palgrave-Macmillan.

Keating, A., Kerr, D., Benton, T., Mundy, E. and Lopes, J. (2010) *Citizenship Education in England 2001–2010: young people's practices and prospects for the future: the eighth and final report from the Citizenship Education Longitudinal Study (CELS). Research Report DFE-RR059*, London: DfE.

Keating, A. and Janmaat, J. G. (2016) 'Education through citizenship at school: do school activities have a lasting impact on youth political engagement?', *Parliamentary Affairs*, 69: 409–429.

Kerr, D. (1999) 'Citizenship education in the curriculum: an international review', *The School Field* 10n(3/4): 5-32.

Kerr, D. (2000) 'Citizenship education: an international comparison', in Lawton, D., Cairns, J. and Gardner, R. (eds) *Education for Citizenship*, London: Continuum, 200-227.

Kerr, D., Cleaver, E., Ireland, E. and Blenkinsop, S. (2003) *Citizenship Education Longitudinal Study: First Cross-sectional Survey. 2001–2002*, London: DfES.

Kerr, D., Lopes, J., Nelson, J., White, K., Cleaver, E. and Benton, T. (2007) *Vision versus Pragmatism: citizenship in the secondary school curriculum in England*, London: DfES.

Kisby, B. (2017) '"Politics is ethics done in public": Exploring linkages and disjunctions between citizenship education and character education in England', *Journal of Social Science Education*, 16(3): 8-21.

Lai, P. and Byram, M. (2012) *Re-shaping Education for Citizenship: democratic national citizenship in Hong Kong*, Newcastle-upon-Tyne: Cambridge Scholars Publishing.

Leach, T. (2018) 'Democracy in the classroom', *Power and Education* 10 (2): 181-194. http://ray.yorksj.ac.uk/id/eprint/2404/

Levinson, B. A. and Elizarrarás, M. E. L. (2017) 'Stealth diversity and the indigenous question: the challenges of citizenship in Mexican civic education', in Banks, J. A. (ed) *Citizenship Education and Global Migration: implications for theory, research and teaching*, Washington, DC: AERA, 403-429.

McLaren, P. (2003) 'Critical pedagogy: a look at the major concepts', in Darder, A., Baltodano, M. and Torres, R. D. (eds) *The Critical Pedagogy Reader*, New York and London: RoutledgeFalmer, 69–97.

McLaughlin, T. H. (1992) 'Citizenship, diversity and education: a philosophical perspective', *Journal of Moral Education* 21 (3): 235–250.

Ofsted (2006) *Towards Consensus? Citizenship in secondary schools*, London: HMI.

Osler, A. and Starkey, H. (2006) 'Education for democratic citizenship: a review of research, policy and practice 1995–2005', *Research Papers in Education* 21 (4): 433–466.

Pollard, S. (2004) *David Blunkett*, London: Hodder & Stoughton.

Ransom, L. S. (2009) 'Sowing the seeds of citizenship and social justice: service-learning in a public speaking course', *Education, Citizenship and Social Justice* 4 (3): 211–224.

Schulz, W., Ainley, J., Fraillon, J., Losito, B., Agrusti, G. and Friedman, T. (2016) *Becoming Citizens in a Changing World: IEA International Civic and Citizenship Education Study 2016 International Report*, Amsterdam: Springer Open.

Torney-Purta, J., Lehmann, R., Oswald, H. and Schulz, W. (2001) *Citizenship and Education in Twenty-eight Countries: civic knowledge and engagement at age fourteen*, Amsterdam: International Association for the Evaluation of Educational Achievement.

The Trilateral Commission (1974) *The Crisis of Democracy: on the governability of democracies*, New York: New York University Press.

Trowler, P. (2003) *Education Policy*, London: Routledge Falmer.

Weinberg, J. and Flinders, M. (2018) 'Learning for democracy: the practice and politics of citizenship education in the United Kingdom', *British Educational Research Journal*, 44(4): 573-592.

Westheimer, J. and Kahne, J. (2004) 'What kind of citizen? The politics of educating for democracy', *American Educational Research Journal* 41 (2): 237-269.

Whiteley, P. (2014) 'Does citizenship education work? Evidence from a decade of citizenship education in secondary schools in England', *Parliamentary Affairs* 67: 513–535.

Wolton, S. (2017) 'The contradiction in the Prevent Duty: democracy vs "British values"', *Education, Citizenship and Social Justice* 12(2): 123–142.

12

Rethinking Civic Roles

Jane Roberts

The preceding chapters have painted a vivid picture of the growing gap between elected representatives and citizens that contributes to 'the disenchantment, disengagement and, at times, mutual incomprehension that exists now between the citizen and the state' (DCLG, 2007). Our systems of governance may seem bewildering: Who is accountable to whom? How? Promoting understanding about how our democracy works is a key element in addressing this issue, but alone it will not suffice. Political engagement depends not only on what people know but on how they feel, not least about politicians (Coleman, 2005) and here the omens are not good. People have lost confidence in elected representatives. Politicians are no longer seen as part of the solution to the profound changes of our time but instead as part of the problem – despite the UK having, by international standards, competent, hard-working and honest politicians at all levels of governance.

Politicians and citizens seem a world apart, each looking, talking and behaving very differently from one another. Fairly or not, politicians are perceived to be a separate 'political class' far removed from the lives of ordinary people (for example, Riddell, 1995, Coleman, 2005; DCLG, 2007; Mair, 2013; Wright, 2013). The term 'political class' is often used loosely but Allen and Cairney (2017) distinguish three elements: a political elite; the professionalisation of politics (with politicians able to make a living from politics alone); and political careerism (with politicians having worked in the political sphere prior to being elected). Of course some sort of political elite is inevitable in any complex society but access to it will be influenced by the degree to which politics has become professionalised and the extent of political careerism, both of which tend to separate the experiences of elected representatives from those whom they represent. With the rise in the number of career politicians comes 'the tendency of politicians … to develop a private language, private quarrels, their own interests, priorities and preoccupations' (King, 1981, p 278). The expenses scandal[1] in Westminster in 2009 only heightened a sense that different rules applied to parliamentarians from ordinary people and led to politicians in general being tarred with the same brush. We know that the behaviour of politicians plays a significant role in fuelling political discontent (Jennings et al, 2016).

Against this background, this chapter considers two aspects of how the divide between elected representative and citizen might be tackled: (i) how the relationship between the two could be improved and (ii) how there could be more fluidity across the two, with a less restrictive and problematic path into and out of elected office.

Improving relationships

The role of an elected politician at whatever level of governance is to link the communities that they represent to the formal decision-making process, and thus 'Representative politics needs to be understood as a more active exchange between citizen and representative' (Stoker, 2006, p 15). In other words, representative politics is about a relationship between politician and citizen and both will have responsibilities within such a relationship. While the responsibilities of each will vary depending on the nature of the decisions being taken – and here language and prepositions matter, whether a government is conducting its business *to, for, by* or *with* its people (Mulgan, 2017) – elected representatives and citizen are necessarily, even if unwillingly, mutually involved.

An effective link to the decision-making process is important not just because decisions taken in a democratic society should reflect the range of different views held by people in that society but because such a link is likely to promote a sense of agency or 'political efficacy' among citizens: that is, the belief that if individuals engage in the political process, they can bring about change (DCLG, 2007). At the very least, people need to feel that their views will be listened to and taken into account. As Anna Coote has argued, a well-functioning sustainable democracy needs its citizens to feel that they can have

---

[1] In 2009, *The Daily Telegraph* newspaper leaked details of alleged over-claiming of expenses and manipulation of rules on property by members of both Houses of Parliament, leading to a public furore.

some control over what goes on around them (Chapter Three in this book). We have seen in the referendum debate in 2016 on the UK's membership of the European Union how resonant was the phrase 'Take Back Control'.

With its smaller scale within a wider single system of governance (Lyons, 2007) and intimate knowledge of its people and place, local government offers powerful opportunities to enhance political efficacy and to improve the relationship between citizen and state (Clarke et al, 2018). Echoing Burall, its potential contribution should be far more widely recognised (Chapter Four in this book). After all, more people believe that voting influences decision makers in a local authority than that it influences those in the House of Commons (Pattie et al, 2004). Taking a cue from George Jones (1997), who argues that it is the task of local government to foster the habit of citizenship, the Councillors Commission strongly recommended that local authorities should be charged with a statutory duty to facilitate local democratic engagement (DCLG, 2007). The recommendation was taken forward by the government of the day but later scuppered by the incoming Coalition Government after 2010.

In order to improve the relationship with citizens, elected representatives could usefully follow the principles set out below in terms of both *what* they do and, equally importantly, *how* they act. These may seem blindingly obvious and straightforward – but they are not always adhered to. How many elected representatives could affirm, with hand on heart, that they and the political institution of which they are a part truly embrace such ways of working? Those who are elected to serve should:

- Be responsive and ensure their organisation puts great store on responsiveness. Coleman (2014, p 233) is clear, 'political representation ... depends on a two-way communicative relationship characterised by responsiveness'. Nothing is more guaranteed to leave citizens feeling enraged, disempowered and disrespected as a lack of response or, almost as bad, one that appears wilfully not to address what had been raised – diminishing further attempts by citizens to engage (Sjoberg et al, 2017). Yet, inexcusably, it happens.
- Take on board the key elements that enhance mutual respect between elected representative and citizen (as in any relationship): authenticity; the willingness to listen respectfully and attentively; reciprocity; curiosity; and humility. Admit to and hold uncertainty when necessary, sometimes a deeply uncomfortable experience. More uncomfortable still, recognise that they may at times have to

deal with unsettling emotions that may be unconsciously projected into them (Hoggett and Thompson, 2012).

- Honestly present the challenges facing the place and people represented. Hope and optimism are a necessary and persuasive part of any political mix, but an essential task of leadership is to tackle tough problems and, at times, uncomfortable truths need to be acknowledged (Heifetz, 1994). It may feel easier to avoid such discomfort in the short term but it wins no respect.

- Welcome accountability for decisions taken with proactive explanation of how and why any decision was arrived at and especially to those who may disagree. Decisions rarely please everyone – consensus may not be possible – but the reason that they were taken should at least make sense. If a mistake was made, admit it.

- Demonstrate a genuine openness and give encouragement to bring participative elements into representative democracy where such participation will make a difference to the decision made. Representative and participatory democracies are complementary (DCLG, 2007). It should be openly acknowledged however that a participatory approach is not useful in every decision.

- Encourage opportunities where elected representatives and citizens can engage, learn more about the circumstances of the other and recognise mutual constraints. Deliberative fora such as citizen juries and citizens panels (Stewart, 2000; Chapter Six in this book) can be especially powerful in deepening considerations of complex issues. Breaking down preconceptions of the other can be powerful particularly when people's perceptions of politicians are largely formed now through media events and professionalised, often slick campaigning (Clarke et al, 2018).

- Promote opportunities to enhance citizens' sense of political efficacy, whether through information giving, explanation, (genuine) consultation, involving citizens in the design or provision of services. It may require some letting go of authority. The art for an elected representative is to balance letting go with keeping a watchful stewardship eye over the patch.

- Nurture continuing relationships. Good elected representatives know their patch well: they are part of a dynamic, fluid network, knowing who is involved in what, where and how and they can facilitate new, perhaps synergistic, connections. At times of crisis especially, those established relationships will be crucial.

- Embrace digital communication for its unparalleled opportunities to engage widely with people for a range of purposes – to inform, to consult, to encourage debate, to facilitate reporting of problems

– but bear in mind a significant minority of the UK population, predominantly those who are already marginalised, rarely or never use the internet (Rumbul, 2017). Conversational digital mechanisms – email or online messaging – especially can enhance responsiveness.

• Bear in mind that even in the digital age, face-to-face interaction remains powerful for its capacity for authentic conversation. Elected representatives at local level are best placed for such interaction, and conversations at this level may promote confidence in representative democracy more generally, local government thereby acting as a crucial link in the chain of governance.

Let us turn to a few practical examples of the principles described above. While examples are drawn from local government, the underlying principles apply to any level of governance.

The first examples were part of a package of measures to make local democracy and council business in the London Borough of Camden more accessible in the early 2000s (when I was leader of the council). Aware that a number of citizens, including some who were relatively new to the country, did not know anything about the process of voting, we set up polling booths at each citizenship ceremony – with the short, stubby pencil with which to make a (counterintuitive) X on the ballot paper against the name of (usually) one preferred candidate – in order to demonstrate how to vote. Here too was the opportunity to ask wider questions to a friendly face without risk of embarrassment about who is responsible for what in the local area. In a fragmented and often confusing governance landscape, the importance of accessible information and explanation that may be taken for granted by many can be underestimated. Why could polling booths similarly not be routinely be set up in schools, perhaps for the sixth form (while the voting age remains 18) on the first day of the Year 12/13 school year, marking students' imminent transition to adulthood and as part of wider ongoing discussions about democracy?

At the same time, Camden Council's Cabinet instituted a series called 'Executive Question Time' in community settings in different parts of the borough. The idea was to hold meetings at which more informal conversations could take place regularly with people in the borough and councillors in the Cabinet (then called 'Executive') about what the council was doing and why. They were widely advertised and anyone could turn up. For those who were less confident or who wanted very detailed specific information, questions could be written and/or handed in before but otherwise people simply raised their hands on the night on any matter that they wished. There was no attempt to stage-manage the meetings. The constraints of local politicians were discussed as well as citizens' experiences of the council. Like the nursery rhyme, when Executive Question Times worked, they worked very well: citizens and senior councillors exchanged views candidly and respectfully, each learning more about each other's situation and their respective views. On the other hand, the few that were targeted by fringe political groups were unsurprisingly less useful – 'horrid' indeed – but taking the rough with the smooth is an intrinsic part of political representation. A change of control sadly put paid to this initiative.

In a similar vein, Kirklees Council set up a quarterly Kirklees Question Time, the first having taken place during Democracy Week in 2017 in response to a recommendation from the Kirklees Democracy Commission that same year. The cross-party Democracy Commission was instigated by Kirklees Council to gather evidence about democracy locally from which then to make recommendations to bring about a step change in the relationship between the council and citizens by 2020. The commission has an independent chair from the University of Huddersfield and active participation from Kirklees Youth Council. The Question Times are held with the four party group leaders represented on Kirklees Council and a youth councillor. Local residents had urged more face-to-face contact with their councillors and had suggested the format of the Question Time that was subsequently adopted. The Commission's report (Kirklees Democracy Commission, 2017) makes clear that, 'Our citizens want to be part of an on-going conversation, not stop start consultation': Kirklees Council has committed itself to facilitating precisely this but it knows that it will require a sustained effort to embed such thinking into its narrative and culture.

Public meetings may now be thought to be redundant given the plethora of digital communication mechanisms, but they offer an opportunity to connect that is not possible in more impersonal arenas. Smaller meetings enable a frank but measured and respectful exchange of views, and, where emotions are running high, the possibility of containing those emotions – a concept drawn from psychoanalytic thinking (Bion, 1962) – more effectively than would otherwise be the case. As Coleman (2005) highlights, the public seek authentic conversations with their elected representatives and it is the communicative, affective dimension of representation that is so important and it is this that is most easily addressed in face-to-face interaction.

My next example illustrates how elected representatives can help to sow the seeds of political efficacy from the earliest years. It draws on a powerfully engaging real (note, not mock) election at Eleanor Palmer Primary School in Camden in 2014, the year of local government elections in London and not long before the 2015 General Election. The school needed new flooring but what should it be? Working with staff and pupils, Camden Council Electoral Services set up a polling station in the school, complete with polling booths, genuine signage, a ballot box, presiding officer, clerks and tellers at the culmination of a week-long campaign to decide which floor covering the school should have. Candidates for each of the three options were selected, political parties formed and hustings held, all passionately advocating 'Pebbles', 'Meadow' or 'Autumn Leaves' for the floor. Councillors came in to talk about their role as community representatives but pupils owned the process and they were highly engaged. Four year olds were indignant that they could not vote before their fifth birthday, thus learning about voting age. Final turnout was 99.7%, with staff having consciously stood back from urging pupils to vote. Crucially, the school acted on the result, subsequently laying down 'Pebbles' flooring, the clear election winner. What a resonant example of what can be done to engage even very young children in how they can influence what goes on around them! Notably, the children shared their excitement and enthusiasm for the electoral process with their parents, urging them to vote in the forthcoming local elections.

A powerful illustration of the importance of the manner in which elected representatives deal with events is provided by the respective leaders of Kensington and Chelsea and Camden councils in the highly fraught aftermath of the tragic fire at Grenfell Tower in 2017. It would have undoubtedly been very difficult for any leader of Kensington and Chelsea Council following the death of 72 people in a burning tower block when almost immediately serious concerns were raised about the quality of the building's refurbishment and maintenance. But the then leader compounded the ire of local people by his apparent coolness and defensiveness in media interviews and his reluctance to meet directly with local residents. People were understandably distraught and angry that they seemed unable to have meaningful contact with any senior politician in the authority.

In contrast, around the same time the leader of Camden Council dealt very differently with residents following Camden's decision to evacuate residents from its tower blocks at The Chalcots at very short notice because of concerns about the nature of the cladding of the towers, similar to that used at Grenfell. The Camden leader, Councillor Georgia Gould, herself knocked on doors through the night in order to urge residents to leave and to explain why they should. She was unquestionably bringing unwelcome news that profoundly disrupted people's lives. Understandably she encountered distress, bewilderment and anger. But she knew it was her role as council leader not only to be accountable for the decision to evacuate but to be seen to be accountable, to explain and to acknowledge residents' distress. Despite initial hostility from some, Councillor Gould's demeanour and willingness to engage were recognised by residents and enabled their distress to be more effectively contained. Be in no doubt that this is no easy task – but this example demonstrates the importance of the affective component of the relationship between elected representative and citizen.

Promoting political fluidity

Elected representatives *are* different from those whom they represent. In the UK, while there has been a modest increase in the number of women and people from a black and minority ethnic background (BME) elected to Westminster and to local government (DCLG, 2007; Durose et al, 2013; Roberts, 2017), after the 2017 General Election still only 32% of MPs are women (www.bbc.co.uk/news/election-2017-40192060) and 8% are from a BME background (www.bbc.co.uk/news/election-2017-40232272), compared with 14% of the population in England and Wales from a BME background in the 2011 Census; 33% of local councillors (IPPR, 2017) are women and 4% (Kettlewell and Phillips, 2014) are from a BME background. Notably, all seven 'metro mayors' elected to lead mayoral Combined Authorities in England in 2017 and 2018 were white men.

Just as importantly but less discussed, there remains a wide disparity between citizens and those who represent them in terms of socioeconomic class, with access to political office having narrowed in recent years predominantly to those from the urban, professional and middle classes (Rush and Cromwell, 2004; Cairney, 2007; Durose et al, 2013; Cairney et al, 2016; Lamprinakou, 2017). In 1964, 37% of Labour MPs came from a working class background, many through experience in trade unions, contrasted with under 10% in 2010 (Heath, 2015). But even within middle class occupations, Westminster MPs have increasingly been drawn from 'instrumental politics-facilitating' occupations such as journalism and lobbying, where political skills can be honed and networks expanded (Cairney, 2007; Henn, 2014). MPs coming from such occupations are younger and promoted faster to higher positions than those who worked elsewhere prior to their election (Allen, 2012).

With political seniority tends to come a higher media profile and it is these career politicians with less experience of a 'proper job' that are most visible to the public, fuelling the perception of difference. While there have always been career politicians in Parliament, it is the change in the balance between them and those with wider experience that is at issue here (Riddell, 1995). The class and educational background of Members of the Scottish Parliament (MSPs), Welsh Assembly Members (AMs) and councillors are not dissimilar from their Westminster counterparts (DCLG, 2007; Cairney et al, 2016; Roberts, 2017). There is a similar picture in other Western democracies with long-established political systems: in Europe, women's parliamentary representation was 26% in 2016 (IPU, 2016).

While it is not necessary for elected representatives to match those whom they represent in terms of background, if the balance between their backgrounds and life experiences and that of citizens is significantly out of kilter, it can affect the relationship between the two and compound the perception of distance between them (Wright, 2013; Heath, 2015). And if access into political office is narrowly restricted, fewer people, even those who are very motivated, will share the fullest experience of political citizenship in an elected role.

How can more citizens be encouraged to stand for and gain political office, and more from a wider range of backgrounds? We know that those with more faith in politicians are more likely to express an interest in running for political office (Allen and Cutts, 2017). But what if there were more interchange between roles in elected office and ordinary citizens so that more people had the opportunity to experience at closer hand the demands and the rewards of political decision making? What if the model of holding political office facilitated those who sought political office for a limited period in their lives, thus enabling more people to serve in elected office, and bring to elected office broader experiences other than the political as well as take back the experience of political office to other fields?

These questions are hardly new. The notion of 'democratic rotation' – that there should be an obligation on an office holder to leave office after a defined period and others to serve in turn – is an idea with deep roots in classical republican political thought (for example, Aristotle, 1992; Petracca, 1992). The principle of rotation was key to Aristotle's understanding of the relationship between citizens and rulers and the importance of both ruling and being ruled in turn. The idea was later taken up in the Renaissance city states of Venice and Florence and in England by Harrington and other intellectuals.

In the twenty-first century, incumbency has a significant impact: the higher turnover of parliamentary seats at the 2010 UK General Election contributed to a more representative House of Commons during the next Parliament (Keep, 2010); and of those councillors serving 20 years or more, three in four are men. Incumbents win 80% of council seats at each election and as around 70% of incumbents are white males, it is a challenge for women and BME groups to advance (Fawcett Society, 2017).

Of course, in larger societies it is always a minority of people who will seek to experience political office. While holding political office is not for the faint hearted and inevitably something of a risky business, it is the fullest experience of political citizenship on which our democracy depends.

If there were more 'fluidity' into and out of elected office – that is, that citizens should have a reasonable chance of moving into and out of positions of elected political leadership should they be able and motivated to do so, and not be precluded either from seeking office or leaving it by disproportionate risks that might be encountered – the benefits and challenges of political office could be shared among a wider group of people and our democracy would be enhanced. Access into and exit from elected office are therefore the focus of exploration here.

The principle of political fluidity applies at all levels of governance. Although fluidity into and out of political office may be more obviously applied at local government level where councillors can more easily combine council duties with paid employment and/or caring responsibilities, there is little reason not to explore means by which access into and out of office in any national or devolved legislature could become more fluid.

Seeking political office as a legislator is a fraught business. Unless they are very well connected, aspiring candidates must dedicate enormous amounts of time and often money to the endeavour, both to get selected and once they have been selected. Many jobs and domestic commitments preclude such an investment. Selection is often the most difficult hurdle, especially for women and minority groups (Riddell, 2003; DCLG, 2007). Most who are subsequently elected will relinquish prior jobs, with disfavour cast upon those who attempt to keep up their professional skills, potentially burning their boats in terms of pre-election income (journalists are one curious exception to this). Worryingly, similar considerations increasingly now pertain to council leaders, with more undertaking their role full-time after the changes in political management structures imposed by the Local Government Act 2000. The tag of 'career politician' may increasingly apply within local government, not least with the advent of directly elected mayors of both local authorities and combined authorities in England.

Although selection at a local government level may be less competitive, many potential candidates are deterred by factors such as an insistence by political parties on long experience in campaigning and a lack of support in the role of councillor (DCLG, 2007). Yet what happens at the local level has wider impact: councillors may later seek political office at other levels of governance and hence opening access into local government can usefully broaden political candidature more generally. Furthermore, while some councillors are motivated to stand because of a longstanding interest in politics, others may not have considered running for elected office before, instead having become involved in a local issue in the community or perhaps simply having been asked to consider standing (DCLG, 2007). The affirmation of being asked to stand may be particularly important to those who feel less confident and who are likely to be from more excluded groups.

Despite the (often similar) recommendations of a number of inquiries set up to address the difficulties of access into political office (for example, Riddell, 2003; DCLG, 2007; House of Commons, 2010; Communities and Local Government Committee, 2012; Fawcett Society, 2017), the pace of change remains stubbornly slow. Why? Is it so very difficult to implement the practical suggestions that have been put forward?

Inevitably, for some to gain political office for the first time, others must leave. That is the rub. The tendency of those in power to remain in power should never be underestimated (Keane, 2011). Power is seductive. Letting go of it is a complicated affair. Despite the challenges, holding political office is often an intoxicating brew: being in the know; having influence to bring about change; having high status still; and constantly being in demand – in short, simply mattering. Leaving all of this behind – either voluntarily or by electoral defeat – is no easy task, especially for career politicians who have little to fall back upon (Roberts, 2017). Politicians' identity is often deeply entwined with their elected office and the transition from office may well be a discombobulating time. Positions of influence, social networks, income, status, busyness, media interest all rapidly disappear. Council leaders and directly elected mayors immediately lose their income, with not even the statutory redundancy pay or any pension despite many having worked full-time in the role. There is little in the way of practical support for politicians leaving office that is now taken for granted after redundancy or retirement in other sectors. Given the risks, some may be deterred from standing for political office in the first place (Roberts, 2017).

Of political office, Thomas Jefferson wrote in 1811 that, 'there is a fullness of time when men should go, and not occupy too long the ground to which others have a right to advance' (quoted in Keane, 2011, p 280). Yet over 200 years later, it may be harder than ever to go (King, 1981; Riddell, 1995; Roberts, 2017; Roberts, 2018). Writing in 1995, Riddell observed the determination of 'the new breed of full-time politicians ... to cling on to both office and seats in the Commons' (Riddell, 1995, p 189).

Yet since then, the professionalisation of politics and the proportion of career politicians have continued apace at all levels of governance (Durose et al, 2013; Lamprinakou, 2017) with significant implications for the relationship between citizen and elected representative. The trend towards ever more specialisation is now seen in most professional jobs and it is hard to imagine politics not being similarly drawn. But the nature of political representation is different from a profession: it requires knowledge, skills and experience certainly, but at the same time it requires a deep understanding of how the world appears from the perspective of a citizen. It is a tricky balance – best captured by the memorable line, 'the challenge for democratic politicians is to be seen as ordinary enough to be representative, while extraordinary enough to be representatives' (Coleman, 2005, p 15).

How can more 'ordinariness' be harnessed into our representative democracy without losing a necessary 'extraordinariness'? There are a plethora of recommendations from assorted reports (Riddell, 2003; DCLG, 2007; House of Commons, 2010; Childs, 2016; Fawcett Society, 2017) on how best to open up access to elected office in the UK. Few have been implemented. With political will they could be – albeit to the probable disgruntlement of those currently in office. There are practical steps that could be taken to mitigate some of the risks associated with leaving political office but few can even bear to contemplate the subject of political mortality (Roberts, 2017). Enhancing fluidity into and out of political office is a tough nut to crack in the face of forces pushing in the opposite direction.

Would term limits help? Generous term limits were recommended in local government by two commissions (DCLG, 2007; Fawcett Society, 2017) and were predictably greeted with howls of outrage by established local politicians. A suggestion made by Trevor Phillips, head of the Equality and Human Rights Commission, in 2009 that MPs should serve a maximum of four years in order to improve representation by women, BME groups and those with disabilities similarly got the thumbs down. Term limits are a crude mechanism for sure but, as Phillips observed:

> Four-fifths of MPs stand for election again. If you've only got a fifth of the seats to play with each time, the parties would have to put a humongous number of women or ethnic minorities or disabled people in to make a difference to the Commons as a whole. The only way would be to impose term limits. (Aitkenhead and Watt, 2009)

More recently, the Five Star Movement in Italy has called for term limits in order to reduce political careerism. Evidence from the US suggests that term limits have disadvantages, including possible loss of expertise, 'shirking' and accountability in the final term (Alt et al, 2007) but that they also increase turnover, representation by women and the perception of truthfulness on the part of politicians by citizens (Moncrief et al, 2004; Smart and Sturm, 2013). In the UK Parliament, with an executive drawn from the legislature, term limits are less straightforward, with the possibility of a serving Cabinet Minister, for example, having to stand down. There may however be advantages in local authorities where one political party tends to remain in control for many years. And term limits could be easily brought in for directly elected mayors where there is a separation of the executive from the legislature, and for appointments to the (overfull) House of Lords. The use of term limits here would at least reintroduce the idea of democratic rotation into our political culture. At a more local level, why could parish and town councils not experiment with appointing some councillors randomly by lottery? After all, many parish council seats are currently uncontested. If more people were to take their turn in elected office, there could be more understanding of the nature of political office and those who had taken their turn could disseminate their knowledge and experience more widely in society.

This chapter has focused on how the quality of the complex and dynamic relationship between elected representatives and citizens could be improved, and how fluidity across the two could be increased. The former may seem obvious and the latter too difficult. But building better relationships is harder than it appears: it requires emotional intelligence, humility and empathy, not always in plentiful supply. And measures to increase political fluidity and oil the wheels between the role of ordinary citizen and elected representative could be introduced without undue difficulty were they not likely to encounter stiff opposition from those reluctant to leave political office. However, we cannot blithely assume that our democracy will survive the levels of political distrust we see currently without radical steps being taken.

References

Aitkenhead, D. and Watt, N. (2009) 'Limit MPs to four terms, says equalities chief', *The Guardian*. https://www.theguardian.com/politics/2009/feb/23/mps-divesity-women-parliament

Allen, P. (2012) 'Linking pre-parliamentary political experience and the career trajectories of the 1997 general election cohort', *Parliamentary Affairs* 68 (1): 1–23.

Allen, P. and Cairney, P. (2017) 'What do we mean when we talk about the "political class"', *Political Studies Review* 15 (1): 18–27.

Allen, P. and Cutts, D. (2017) 'An analysis of political ambition in Britain', *The Political Quarterly*. http://journals.sagepub.com/doi/abs/10.1177/2053168017691444

Alt, J. E., Bueno de Mesquita, E. and Rose, S. (2007) 'Accountability, selection, and experience: theory and evidence from U.S. term limits'. http://bcep.haas.berkeley.edu/conferences/docs/alt_20071104.pdf

Aristotle (1992) *The Politics,* London: Penguin.

Bion, W. R. (1962) *Second Thoughts*, New York: Jason Aronson.

Cairney, P. (2007) 'The professionalisation of MPs: refining the "politics-facilitating" explanation', *Parliamentary Affairs* 60 (2): 212–233.

Cairney, P., Keating, M. and Wilson, A. (2016) 'Solving the problem of social background in the UK 'political class: do parties do things differently in Westminster, devolved and European elections?', *British Politics* 11 (2): 142–163.

Childs, S. (2016) *The Good Parliament*, Bristol: University of Bristol.

Clarke, N., Jennings, W., Moss, J. and Stoker, G. (2018) *The Good Politician*, Cambridge: Cambridge University Press.

Coleman, S. (2005) *Direct Representation: towards a conversational democracy*, London: IPPR Exchange.

Coleman, S. (2014) *How Voters Feel*, New York: Cambridge University Press.

Communities and Local Government Committee (2012) Councillors on the frontline: Sixth Report of Session 2012–13. https://publications.parliament.uk/pa/cm201213/cmselect/cmcomloc/432/432.pdf

Department of Communities and Local Government (DCLG) (2007) *Representing the Future: report of the Councillors Commission*, London: Communities and Local Government Publications.

Durose, C., Richardson, L., Combs, R., Eason, C. and Gains, F. (2013) '"Acceptable Difference"': diversity, representation and pathways to UK politics', *Parliamentary Affairs* 66 (2): 246-267.

Fawcett Society (2017) *Does Local Government Work for Women? Final report of the Local Government Commission,* London: The Fawcett Society.

Heath, O. (2015) 'Has the rise of middle class politicians led to the decline of class voting in Britain?' http://blogs.lse.ac.uk/politicsandpolicy/the-rise-of-middle-class-politicians-and-the-decline-of-class-voting-in-britain/

Henn, S. J. (2014) 'The further rise of the career politician – and its consequences'. https://scholar.harvard.edu/soeren-jannik-henn/publications

Heifetz, R. A. (1994) *Leadership Without Easy Answers,* Cambridge, MA: Harvard University Press.

Hoggett, P. and Thompson, S. (2012) 'Introduction', in Thompson, S. and Hoggett, P. (eds) *Politics and the Emotions,* New York: Continuum.

House of Commons (2010) *Speaker's Conference (on Parliamentary Representation). Final report,* London: The Stationery Office.

IPPR (2017) 'Gender balance of power: women's representation in regional and local government in the UK and Germany'. www.ippr.org/research/publications/gender-balance-of-power

IPU (2016) 'More ambitious measures needed to enhance women's representation in parliament'. www.ipu.org/news/press-releases/2017-03/more-ambitious-measures-needed-enhance-womens-representation-in-parliament

Jennings, W., Stoker, G. and Twyman, J. (2016) 'The dimensions and impact of political discontent in Britain', *Parliamentary Affairs* 69: 876-900.

Jones, G. (1997) *New Local Government Agenda,* London: ICSA Publishing Ltd.

Keane, J. (2011) 'Life after political death', in Kane, J., Patapan, H. and 't Hart, P. (eds) *Dispersed Democratic Leadership,* Oxford: Oxford University Press.

Keep, M. (2010) 'Characteristics of the new House of Commons'. www.parliament.uk/documents/commons/lib/research/key_issues/Key-Issues-Characteristics-of-the-new-House-of-Commons.pdf

Kettlewell, K. and Phillips, L. (2014) *Census of Local Authority Councillors 2013 (LGA Research Report,* Slough: NFER.

King, A. (1981) 'The rise of the career politician in Britain – and its consequences', *British Journal of Political Science* 11: 249-285.

Kirklees Democracy Commission (2017) *Growing a stronger local democracy, from the ground up*, http://www.democracycommission. org.uk/growing-a-stronger-local-democracy-from-the-ground-up/

Lamprinakou, C., Morucci, M., Campbell, R. and van Heerde-Hudson, J. (2017) 'All change in the House? The profile of candidates and MPs in the 2015 British general election', *Parliamentary Affairs* 70 (2): 207-232.

Lyons. M. (2007) *Place-shaping: a shared ambition for the future of local government. Final Report of the Lyons Inquiry into Local Government*, London: The Stationery Office.

Mair, P. (2013) *Ruling the Void: The Hollowing of Western Democracy*, London: Verso.

Moncrief, G. F., Niemi, R. G. and Powell, L. W. (2004) 'Time, term limits and turnover: trends in membership stability in US state legislatures', *Legislative Studies* 29 (3): 357-381.

Mulgan, G. (2017) 'The grammar of good government – or why prepositions matter'. https://www.nesta.org.uk/blog/grammar-good-government-or-why-prepositions-matter

Pattie, C., Seyd, P. and Whiteley, P. (2004) *Citizenship in Britain. Values, participation and democracy*, Cambridge: Cambridge University Press.

Petracca, M. (1992) 'Rotation in office: the history of an idea', in G. Benjamin and M. J. Malbin (eds) *Limiting Legislative Terms*, Washington, DC: Congressional Quarterly Press, pp 15-51.

Riddell, P. (1995) 'The impact of the rise of the career politician', *The Journal of Legislative Studies* 1 (2): 186-191.

Riddell, P. (2003) *Candidate Selection: the Report of the Commission on Candidate Selection*, London: Electoral Reform Society.

Roberts, J. (2017) *Losing Political Office*, London: Palgrave Macmillan.

Roberts, J. (2018) 'Exiting the political stage: exploring the impact on representative democracy', *British Politics* https://doi.org/10.1057/s41293-018-00091-3

Rumbul, R. (2017) *Citizenship and civic engagement*, http://research. mysociety.org/publications/citizenship-civic-engagement [Accessed 4 January 2018]

Rush, M. and Cornwall, V. (2004) 'Continuity and change: legislative recruitment in the United Kingdom 1868-1999', in Best, H. and Cotta, M. (eds) *Parliamentary Representatives in Europe 1848–2000. Legislative recruitment and careers in eleven European countries*, New York: Oxford University Press.

Sjoberg, F. M., Mellon, J. and Peixoto, T. (2017) 'The effect of bureaucratic responsiveness on citizen participation', *Public Administration Review* 77 (3): 340-351.

Smart, M. and Sturm, D. M. (2013) 'Term limits and electoral accountability', *Journal of Public Economics* 107: 93–102.

Stewart, J. (2000) *The Nature of British Local Government*, Basingstoke: Macmillan Press.

Stoker, G. (2006) *Why Politics Matters. Making democracy work*, Basingstoke: Palgrave Macmillan.

Wright, T. (2013) 'What is it about politicians?', *Political Quarterly* 84 (4): 448–453.

13

Promoting the 'Take Part' Approach

*Marjorie Mayo, Zoraida Mendiwelso-Bendek
and Carol Packham*

As previous chapters have demonstrated, state-citizen relationships would seem to present particular challenges in the current context. While there are examples of people of all ages taking an interest in the development and promotion of fairer public policies, there are, conversely, a growing number of cases of people participating in anti-Semitic and Islamophobic campaigns, white supremacist rallies and xenophobic attacks on migrants and refugees. Such activities have been associated with the increasing levels of alienation and the erosion of trust between many citizens and their governments, processes of erosion that have been exacerbated by scandals both financial and more personal.

This chapter explores the ways in which the Take Part approach has been contributing to the promotion of active citizenship and community engagement, based on the values of social justice, equality and respect for diversity, emphasising mutuality, cooperation and social solidarity. The Take Part approach was developed through a series of initiatives under the UK Government's Together We Can programme (2003-2010), facilitating active learning for active citizenship. The aim was to empower individual citizens and their communities to acquire the confidence and competence to set out their concerns, while encouraging the relevant structures of governance to learn to listen and to respond more effectively, working both sides of the equation 'to build a more active and engaged civil society and a more responsive and effective state that can deliver needed public services' (Gaventa, 2004, p 27), as an early report summarised these objectives (ALAC, 2006). Through these initiatives, delivered via community-university partnerships, based in regional hubs, involving voluntary and community-based organisations, faith-based organisations and learning providers, the 'Take Part' approach developed strategies for addressing the barriers to learning for active citizenship and community engagement.

While Take Part was developed in Britain, the approach drew upon the theoretical contributions of the Brazilian Paulo Freire (1972, 1992), the Colombian Orlando Fals-Borda (Fals-Borda and Rahman, 1991) and other international pioneers of learning for social transformation, linking theory and practice as ongoing processes of praxis. This was experiential learning, starting from people's own experiences and interests, critically reflecting upon these as the basis for developing strategies for change.

The Take Part approach encompassed a variety of delivery mechanisms, ranging from one-off workshops and teach-ins through to more structured sessions, over a period of time, depending upon the needs and interests of the communities in question, and the barriers to be overcome in order to address them. We will look at the learning from these before moving on to consider the wider implications.

Although Take Part no longer has government funding, the approach continues to be applied both in Britain and internationally. Our chapter concludes by reflecting upon experiences of applying the approach in USA, as universities and libraries have been developing responses to the growth of far right populism, along with experiences in Colombia, where universities have been building upon the legacies of Orlando Fals-Borda and others in developing strategies for working with communities to support the peace process.

The theoretical basis for Take Part

As Henry Tam explained, reflecting upon the Take Part programme (which began under the name 'Active Learning for Active Citizenship', or ALAC) that he helped to initiate:

> By its very nature, no government can enable citizens to have a real sense of greater political efficacy by handing to them a ready-made package of solutions. The solutions must be generated with the involvement of citizens, not merely as service users, taxpayers or even once-every-four-years voters, but as civic decision-makers in their own right. (Tam, 2010, p 13)

This was the starting point for the developing concept of 'citizenship' that was operationalised in the programme.

Bernard Crick's (2001) civic republican approach to the concept of citizenship was an important influence here. Rather than adopting a narrow exclusionary view, focusing upon citizenship in terms of formal status, with rights before the law, including the right to vote, the civic republican approach that he advocated added a wider emphasis upon the group, with both rights and responsibilities to engage as active, politically literate citizens (see Chapter Eleven of this book). Drawing upon Westheimer and Kahne's (2004) categorisation, Take Part distinguished between:

- The citizen as voter and volunteer (the most limited, 'liberal' approach).
- The citizen as participant in existing structures of decision making and governance, including structures for participation in the planning and delivery of services.
- The citizen who participates in existing structures and who also participates within group(s) actively challenging unequal relations of power, promoting agendas for social solidarity and social justice, both locally and beyond.

There are parallels here with Cornwall's view of the spaces for participation as being far from neutral, being 'permeated with relations of power' (Cornwall, 2004, p 79). Rather than confining themselves to engaging in such formal spaces of participation and power, she argued, active citizens would also need the capacity to challenge exclusionary structures, widening existing agendas to take account of their communities' needs.

This type of approach had significant implications for learning for active citizenship. This was to be learning for political literacy, according to Crick, active learning through the practice of active citizenship. As the political sociologist Ralph Miliband explained, in a similar vein, education for citizenship 'means above all nurturing the capacity and willingness to question, to probe, to ask awkward questions, to see through obfuscation and lies' (particularly relevant, it would seem, in the context of debates about 'fake news'), and it would require 'the cultivation of an awareness that the request for individual fulfilment needs to be combined with the larger demands of solidarity and concern for the public good' (Miliband, 1994, p 56).

There were significant implications here for the approaches to learning that were to underpin the Take Part programme. Before moving on, though, one further point about theories of active citizenship needs to be emphasised. As has already been suggested, the Take Part approach was developed as a work in progress. Drawing upon their experiences in practice, project participants argued for a more nuanced approach. Citizens could – and did – become active as volunteers, experiences which could lead them to engage more fully as active citizen, or not. It was unhelpful to draw rigid distinctions between different models of active citizenship, the projects argued, rather than recognising the fluidity of people's aims and experiences in practice.

As Recknagel and Holland's (2013) reflections on their subsequent experiences illustrated, individuals and groups could – and did – make their own decisions about the nature and extent of their participation as active citizens. Just to take one example here for illustration: taster sessions to encourage citizens to take on civic roles (such as becoming magistrates and school governors) were oversubscribed in one area. But not all learners were interested in taking up these roles. Rather, many wanted to use their new knowledge subsequently, as active citizens, advocating/campaigning from *outside*. As Recknagel and Holland (2013, p 31) concluded from these experiences: 'attempts by governments to prescribe particular forms of active citizenship involvement were overwhelmingly rejected'. It was for learners to 'set their own priorities in terms of how they chose to engage as active citizens', in any case, according to tutors, reflecting their commitment to learner-centred approaches.

Take Part was explicit about this commitment to active learning to build a deliberative democratic culture. This was to be a process of learning and reflection, drawing upon models of participatory action research, as developed by Orlando Fals-Borda (Fals Borda and Rahman, 1991), Paulo Freire (1972), Miles Horton (Bell et al, 1990), John Gaventa and others (Bell et al, 1990) from a range of international contexts, including, as we will see below, Colombia and the USA. The emphasis was upon learning together, taking the notion of transformative learning further, beyond shifting individuals' frames of reference (Mezirow, 1991), to focus upon groups and communities more fully, working together for democratic social change.

In summary, then, the learning was to start from people's own experiences, promoting processes of critical dialogue between learners and learning providers. These processes were to be 'firmly rooted within civil society, rather than being simply provided for citizens as public policy should deem fit' (Mayo, 2010, p 53). But the learning processes were not to be confined within civil society. On the contrary, the processes were to promote more effective dialogues between civil society and the state. There were illustrations of interventions to facilitate learning to listen, for service providers, for instance, as well as interventions to enable service users to make their voices heard more effectively, as with the 'Speak Up' initiatives with people with disabilities and their carers in the South West (Mangan et al, 2010).

While there was broad agreement on the overall approach to learning as a participative process, there was a wide range of learning provision in practice. The content varied flexibly according to local interests and needs – and so did the delivery mechanisms. For example, there were formal courses tailored to provide women with the information that they needed in order to engage with health service providers; informal courses based on the schools of participation approach, with participant-determined themes leading to 'actions' for change (Packham, 2008, pp 74-5), and there were one-off workshops to share strategies for addressing common problems. There were informal learning events and group visits, to learn from people's experiences elsewhere. There were also examples of learning via mentoring, and e-learning (as geographically dispersed refugee communities learned to communicate with each other more effectively via the internet). Summing up the learning from these initial programmes, it was concluded that the pilot projects 'saw the set curriculum as being controlling, failing to respond to particular requirements and settings' (Packham, 2008, p 109). For this reason, the stakeholders developed a learning framework instead, to reflect this flexibility, rather than attempting to produce a more specific curriculum for learning for active citizenship.

Active citizenship learning is a transdisciplinary area of research that implies greater understanding of the mutual constitution between the individual and social structures, but also the need to produce evidence on how effective participation requires the formation and facilitation of self-organisation for a collective action promoting civil society values. A fair distribution of power in the self-organisation of local communities cannot be taken for granted (Mendiwelso-Bendek, 2015).

Participatory action research methodologies in theory and practice

Take Part's approach to research was correspondingly participative. Here too there was broad agreement on the relevance of participatory action research, monitoring and evaluation, drawing upon the work of Fals Borda (Fals Borda and Rahman, 1991), Tandon (2005), Freire (1972), Gaventa and others (Bell et al, 1990, Estrella, 2000).

But here too, in parallel, research and evaluation processes have involved different methodologies in practice. Quantitative methods have included the use of surveys, as well as the analysis of official statistics as applied to particular communities, for example. And subsequent programmes have developed innovative approaches to the measurement of impact (Dinham, 2013; Jones et al, 2013). Meanwhile qualitative methods have included the use of community arts (Rooke, 2013; Tiller, 2013). Overall, these have been mixed methodologies, then, tailoring the choice of research tools to the issues and experiences in question.

For example, following the arrival of a new Manchester Metropolitan University (MMU) campus within a particular neighbourhood, local older residents asked for some support in identifying the impact of the campus and a large influx of students on older people living in the area. As a result, MMU, working with the GAP Unit,[2] and a local resident as co-trainer, trained a team of local older residents in participatory research approaches, particularly focus groups. This enabled them to explore the issues for their community, themselves.

The team carried out a series of semi-structured focus groups across a range of older people's groups and organisations in the area. Their findings and recommendations were presented to the university and other service providers. Their research confirmed that although the new university campus had brought life to the area, it had coincided with cuts to many services and closure of pubs and community centres. One focus group drew attention to the disappearance of community pubs. For many older people, the increase in the number of younger residents had increased their sense of isolation and social exclusion.

Recommendations from the research team suggested that there should be an older persons' panel in Hulme to ensure that voices are heard and that community groups and MMU should maintain the opportunity to work together in partnership. There are ways in which the community and the university could learn from one another. For example, the community could play a role in supporting MMU to carry out ethical and sensitive research in the area and ensuring that research benefits local people. The collaborative research contributed to MMU's successful bid to deliver some of the elements of the 'Greater Manchester Ambition for Ageing' programme. Several of the residents on the research team subsequently joined a local partnership board for the programme, where they have had joint responsibility for identifying

---

[2]   A team that specialises in Freirean approaches to working with marginalised groups, focusing upon the 'gap' between the opportunities open to women and men.

and responding to local issues through ongoing local research and the allocation of small grants to older people's groups and activities.

In some cases it was easier for participants to relate to issues of an immediate and personal nature rather than to more abstract and distanced concepts. A research project carried out by the University of Lincoln about sports volunteering, community engagement and cohesion illustrates ways in which such relationships between theory and practice could be explored, together with the relationships between individuals' issues and wider social concerns. A review of the Lincoln project found that since participants were given an opportunity to view their sports organisation and their own activities from an external perspective, they could more readily look at their organisational structures and how their roles related to wider discussions about volunteering and building a more just and equal society (Wright et al, 2013).

Also, as Watts (2013) illustrated, learning approaches to developing solidarity between generations made visible a key aspect – that merely by the group members being offered the opportunity and agreeing to set aside the time from their busy lives to participate, the space was opened up for identifying evidence and entering into dialogue and discussion across the community. It is clear that family learning and resultant intergenerational activities had also enabled there to be greater intergenerational solidarity in the neighbourhood. As the head of the community learning service wrote:

> For the families in [the neighbourhood], it hasn't been a choice of 'state' or 'society'. This pilot project has demonstrated how committed and expert local government professionals can work alongside local residents to empower them to bring about positive community change ... Through the research, we found that the link between intergenerational, or rather multigenerational, learning and active citizenship needs to be made explicit and the support workers and other intermediaries, as well as the group, need to be very determined to succeed and ensure that it reflects the needs, wishes and capacity of the community. (Quoted in Watts, 2013, p 127)

The university's contributions were thus centrally important in enabling communities and service providers to draw out the wider implications of their initiatives.

Similar conclusions can be drawn from other aspects of Lincoln University's research role. There was a focus on encouraging the articulation of local knowledge; engaging people in shaping agendas that concern them, helping local authorities to develop new forms of knowledge sharing, and promoting collective reflection on issues of importance to local people (Herron and Mendiwelso-Bendek, 2017). For example, there was the case where Lincoln City Council, local residents and the university have been developing active learning spaces with community groups (including newly arrived communities) to help contribute to shaping local community plans. In the urban context the city has also seen rapid changes to its population demographics with inward migration that has brought international students, European and international workers and other new residents in a relatively short space of time. The City Council has repeatedly sought to create mechanisms to engage local residents in ongoing conversations to help shape agendas and impact on the creation of the formal local plans and has worked with researchers as part of this wider activity (Herron and Mendiwelso-Bendek, 2017).

Impact of Take Part

From 2004 Manchester Metropolitan University was asked to take on the coordination of the Take Part programme across Greater Manchester. Initially with Groundwork (an environmental organisation working in the most deprived areas) as its partner, and then with Community Pride (part of Church Action on Poverty), the university worked with a total of 17 projects, across 6 different local authorities, building links and increasing partnership working within the region and nationally. This brought together groups of people who wanted to work to challenge and change, focusing on themes of their choice.

The team built on already existing relationships between the Voluntary and Community Sector (VCS) and MMU, particularly through its Youth and Community Work Courses, and through the Community Audit and Evaluation Centre. A series of short courses had developed responding to the needs and interests of VCS and statutory services, initially training community teams in participatory research, working with groups to identify their own responses to local concerns (Packham, 2000). For example, they worked with a team of volunteers from the VCS groups in Tameside, who researched what was required to enable effective volunteering. They then developed a range of short courses, particularly utilising the Freirean framework of 'schools of participation'. These schools developed critical dialogues to raise the participants' levels of awareness, followed by an 'action' phase where participants identified areas where they aimed to influence change.

One such school of participation was run with 12 members of the deaf community in Greater Manchester, for example. Together with their interpreters, members of the deaf community had been meeting with a deaf facilitator and school facilitator funded by the Take Part programme, using the medium of sign language. They identified that their shared concern was access to employment and Job Centres. So the group decided they would like to make an educational video to be used as a training tool for Job Centre staff, to improve communication with them and so to improve opportunities for deaf people. The video that they produced – 'The World Changed Upside Down' – was used for training staff. It was launched at a seminar for Department of Work and Pensions staff and others in November, 2006, challenging stereotypes of deaf people and 'exposing the barriers to communication within the hearing world' (Anne Stewart, quoted in Packham (2008) pp 75-76).

Although the initial participatory researcher training drew on an existing MMU Youth and Community Work course module, in this particular instance the short courses that were developed in partnership with VCS groups increasingly had new foci. This informed the development of new MMU course content. For example, courses in asset-based approaches, developed with the Public Health Department and Voluntary Action Oldham, became accredited modules at undergraduate and postgraduate levels at MMU. In these ways, links between the university and local communities were being developed for the future.

In addition to the development of short courses, citizen involvement was also evident through developing work exploring gender and participation. The project was established as part of the Women's Network of the Community Network for Manchester. Through the Take Part programme, the GEM (Gender Engagement in Manchester) initiative trained teams of people with an interest in how decisions were made from local to city levels. The teams carried out city-wide participatory evaluations into exclusion from decision-making bodies, and subsequently carried out gender awareness training with community groups and local authority officers in Manchester, Rochdale and Oldham, developing an 'Engagement' toolkit to support this work.

With MMU providing quality assurance and coordination, Take Part in Greater Manchester was able to develop organisational partnerships and engage people in educational programmes that were co-designed and delivered by community partners, based on the needs and interests that had been identified locally. And the further aim was always to bring about some sort of improvement in people's lives and in the services to be provided to meet their needs more appropriately.

The team was able to work with a range of small, often neighbourhood or thematically based groups to plan and deliver these short courses. All the course participants were registered as guest MMU students and received MMU certification. Some of the courses were delivered on campus, and for those further afield they had at least one session at the university, where an induction to the university and the potential for partnerships and for educational opportunities were discussed – to facilitate access and break down barriers between universities and communities more generally. So all of those who registered with MMU became part of an email community too, through the establishment of the North West Citizenship Network. This continues to provide updates of courses, conferences, resourcing and opportunities from MMU as well as sharing information between members.

The legacy of the Take Part programme was carried forward through the 'Taking Part?' Economic and Social Research Council (ESRC) research cluster, where several of those who had been involved in the Manchester short courses developed their work through research. For example, the Chair of Manchester Refugee Support Network (MRSN), carried out participatory research and community leadership training, and helped engage others in the city to develop a Refugee Charter for Manchester covering basic rights, healthcare, housing, education and employment. He went on to become one of the ESRC Case Students to complete a PhD, exploring ways to 'Give voice to the voiceless' within MRSN and the wider refugee and asylum seeker communities. One of the facilitators of 'schools of participation' through the GEM initiative also became a PhD student, exploring 'Practices of Alliance and Solidarity with Asylum Seeking and Refugee Women'.

A third PhD student was the regional coordinator of North West Together We Can. She had identified the financial struggles that many small VCS groups were having. Through the ESRC research programme, she carried out surveys, workshops and telephone interviews with small VCS groups to build an evidence base on how the economic climate and public spending cuts were impacting on communities and the groups that support them in the North West, with a focus on promoting resilience and sustainability. This focus was subsequently followed up with partnership working on 'Sustainable Livelihoods' analysis, resulting in the redesign of new Sustainable Livelihoods analysis tools. These were then produced as on online resource book to enable groups to 'identify their organisational assets and are then able to build strategy which will enable them to develop as a group' (Goldstraw et al, 2017).

The move to asset-based working has led to MMU being able to respond to requests from local authorities, VCS infrastructure organisations and public health bodies to work with local groups to train people in using asset-based approaches. The team started by working with Community and Voluntary Action Oldham, and with the public health authority to carry out training with local groups, and managers in how to apply asset-based approaches. The wide range of participants from across different sectors resulted in asset-based and community-focused approaches being established in a range of settings including aural health, domestic violence services to Asian women, and work with the police. The asset-based approach focuses on strengths and the potential for change within communities, as opposed to focusing upon what they lack. This means that 'patients' and participants are seen as actively involved in making decisions about how they can bring about change in their lives.

Asset-based working is, like Freirean approaches to informal education more generally, seeing renewed interest in its potential to 'problem pose' and enable groups of citizens to engage in action. There are potentially massive implications for the relationship between the citizen and the state, moving from a disempowering 'deficit model' to one in which citizens have the potential for working together for developments and improvements.

However, critics of asset-based approaches have, conversely, seen them as providing justifications for austerity policies, arguing that asset-based approaches serve to shift the responsibility of the state for inequality onto to the citizen (Garven et al, 2017). In addition, asset-based approaches, in contrast to Freirean popular education models, may fail to carry out political analyses or to encourage people to see themselves as part of social movements for political change, through 'unity in diversity' (Freire, 1992, p 51).

At the time of writing, such criticisms have particular relevance. The legacy of the Manchester Take Part programme has become increasingly threatened by the university's failure to appreciate the mutual benefits of community engagement in general, and short informal education courses in particular. Research and Knowledge Exchange initiatives have become increasing focused on narrower approaches to students' employability and to partnerships geared towards income generation, in this period of continuing austerity. This is, of course, part of wider shifts in public policy, as will be discussed in the following section.

Take Part approaches in contemporary contexts internationally

Following the General Elections of 2010, British government priorities shifted, with funding directed towards training for community organisers as part of the then Coalition Government's 'Big Society' programme. This initiative aimed to work with people who felt disillusioned with government, and not listened to (Pearce et al, 2011), aiming to ensure that local people would define the issues to be addressed (Taylor and Wilson, 2016). But the focus was to be upon one-to-one listening, rather than group learning and engagement. As Taylor and Wilson and others have pointed out, this was a very different approach.

While the Take Part model per se ran out of funding, subsequent programmes continued, as the previous section has already indicated. These subsequent initiatives have included a Third Sector Research Capacity Building programme, which continued to develop participatory action research approaches through community-university partnerships, and Connecting Communities, community-university partnerships with a community arts focus. Meanwhile, similar approaches have been developing in other contexts internationally, including programmes in the USA and in Colombia. These locations were, of course, the original bases for the work of Fals Borda and Miles Horton and others, respectively.

The US and UK network, Community-Library Inter-Action (CLIA: http://librariesforpeace.org/projects/clia/about/) emerged from a 2017 symposium at the Mortenson Center for International Library Programmes, based at the University of Illinois at Urbana-Champaign, organised with Take Part partners from the UK. This brought a range of library-based community educators and academics together to share their experiences, reflecting upon the most effective ways of promoting learning for active citizenship – learning that was seen as particularly crucial given the context, with widespread interest in addressing the problems of alienation along with the accompanying problems of 'fake news' and 'alternative facts', following the election of Donald Trump as president the previous year.

Libraries emerged as potentially valuable bases for community-based education for active citizenship in the US context. They could be – and were – seen as relatively safe places, where people could engage in debates on topics of current concern. Citizens did not need to label themselves, or risk being labelled or even stigmatised as 'the other', if they participated in debates in such spaces, a particularly significant factor in the rapidly polarising context of the US.

In June 2017, the Take Part approach was considered at another symposium, this time organised with the University of Los Andes, focusing on the challenges of community-based research and peace building in Cartagena, Colombia. Here the Take Part approach was welcomed as the basis for creating a sustainable co-laboratory, as a community-based learning network, supporting the design and development of local peacebuilding processes, using participatory community-based research methodologies. At the time of writing, this network of university–community partnerships is in the process of becoming more fully established. This builds upon previous experiences of developing participatory action research approaches to community development, drawing upon the thinking of Orlando Fals Borda and others. Examples have included community–university initiatives to tackle very practical issues such as local energy systems, access to clean water and sanitation, for instance, as well as initiatives to support those who have been displaced as a result of violence and human rights abuses.

There are plans to develop a number of pilot projects, promoting inclusive community-based learning and research to tackle such development issues and to support peace-building processes in areas that have been ravaged by civil conflict over so many years. These plans are anticipated to have an impact at many different levels: at the level of individuals, identified groups (such as young Afro-descendants, ex-combatants and their communities and women in poor rural areas), municipalities and the academic community. Along with the research led by Colombian partners, this would leave the legacy of a Co-Lab Paz (a network of regional universities working in community based research and implementing the peace process agreement in Colombia) and the accompanying development of research capacity in both countries.

Since then CLIA has been carrying out three key phases of work. The first has been to co-develop the CLIA Guide in the United States; the second to refine the guide in Colombia to support and draw on the experiences of libraries in the Colombian peace process; and third, to engage in a process of global implementation and learning through community dialogues and community-based learning. So far, CLIA has also been engaged in Peru, Costa Rica and Spain.

In summary, then, CLIA's approach has proved to be urgently needed. This has been about recognising and valuing local community voices and knowledge, building on the role of libraries as community anchors. And, as in the Colombian case, this has been about supporting communities themselves as they engage in developing alternatives to violence.

Conclusion

The Take Part approach has been developed through a series of initiatives in Britain, promoting community-based learning and participatory action research, bringing communities together to address the issues that most concern them. Through such partnerships, at both local and regional levels, citizens can develop the knowledge, the confidence, skills and critical understandings that they need in order to identify the causes, as well as the symptoms, of their problems, exploring ways of addressing these more effectively as active citizens. This represents an approach that can be tailored to the requirements of varying contexts, both in Britain and internationally, as the examples from the USA and Colombia illustrate.

The Take Part approach needs to be appropriately adapted, though, if this is to have relevance in wider contexts too. As the original participants in the programme argued so forcefully, they should be developing a flexible framework for community-based learning and participatory action research, starting from people's own views and experiences, rather than attempting to impose any particular methodology, let alone devising a national curriculum for learning for active citizenship. The Take Part approach was not to be presented as any type of panacea, to tackle the democratic deficit in a sceptical age, but rather as a more modest contribution to developing more inclusive and more deliberative ways of engaging citizens in the promotion of social solidarity and social justice for all.

As Henry Tam (2013) noted, Take Part's research findings have shown that:

> Researchers should be given scope to tailor their study to help community groups learn more about their own strengths and weaknesses as a constructive exercise, rather than simply to churn out data to respond to measures drawn up by funders. The former approach would actually often lead to more improvements than the all too frequent use of the latter.

References

ALAC (2006) *Active Learning for Active Citizenship*, London: Department for Communities and Local Government.

Bell, B., Gaventa, J. and Peters, J. (eds) (1990) *We Make the Road by Walking: conversations on education and social change, Myles Horton and Paulo Freire*, Philadelphia: Temple University Press.

Cornwall, A. (2004) 'Spaces for transformation', in Hickey, S. and Mohan, G. (eds) *Participation: from tyranny to transformation?*, London: Zed Books, pp 75-91.

Crick, B. (2001) 'Introduction', in B. Crick (ed) *Citizens: towards a citizenship culture*, London: Blackwells.

Dinham, A. (2013) 'Measurement as reflection in faith-based social action', in Mayo, M., Mendiwelso-Bendek, Z. and Packham, C. (eds.) *Community Research for Community Development*, Basingstoke: Palgrave Macmillan, 92-110.

Estrella, M. (ed) (2000) *Learning from Change*, London: Intermediate Technology.

Fals Borda, O. and Rahman, M. A. (1991) *Action and Knowledge*, London: Intermediate Technology.

Freire, P. (1972) *Pedagogy of the Oppressed*, Harmondsworth: Penguin.

Friere, P. (1992) *Pedagogy of Hope*, New York: Continuum.

Garven, F., McLean, J. and Pattoni, L. (2017) *Asset based approaches: their rise and reality*, London: Dunedin Academic Press.

Gaventa, J. (2004) 'Towards participatory governance: assessing the transformative possibilities' in S. Hickey. and G. Mohan (eds), *Participation: from tyranny to transformation*, London: Zed, 25-41.

Goldstraw, K., Davidson, E. and Packham, C. (2017) 'Sustainable livelihoods analysis as a response to the crisis in the community and voluntary sector', *Illness, Crisis and Loss*. http://journals.sagepub.com/doi/abs/10.1177/1054137317715000

Jones, H., Jones, V. and Cock, J. C. (2013) 'Impact measurement or agenda-setting?', in M. Mayo, Z. Mendiwelso-Bendek and C. Packham (eds) *Community research for community development*, Basingstoke: Palgrave Macmillan, pp 43-64.

Mangan, P., Recknagel, G. and Pooley, L. (2010) 'Enabling people with disabilities and other service users to "speak up"; enabling public service providers to listen', in Mayo, M. and Annette, J. (eds) *Taking Part?*, Leicester: NIACE, 211-225.

Mayo, M. (2010) 'Competing perspectives, definitions and approaches', in Mayo, M. and Annette, J. (eds) *Taking Part?*, Leicester: NIACE, 41-60.

Mendiwelso-Bendek, Z. (2015) 'Community-based research: enabling civil society's self-organisation', *Kybernetes* 44 (6/7): 903-912.

Mezirow, J. (1991) *Transformative Dimensions of Adult Learning*, San Francisco: Jossey-Bass.

Miliband, R. (1994) *Socialism for a Sceptical Age*, Cambridge: Polity Press.

Packham, C. (2008) *Active Citizenship and Community Learning*, Exeter: Learning Matters.

Pearce, J., Taylor, M. and Zipfel, T. (2011) 'Interview transcripts to inform theory of change', Unpublished paper quoted in Taylor and Wilson (2016).

Recknagel, G. with Holland, D. (2013) 'How inclusive and how empowering? Two case studies researching the impact of active citizenship learning in a social policy context', in Mayo, M., Mendiwelso-Bendek, Z. and Packham, C. (eds.) *Community Research for Community Development*, Basingstoke: Palgrave Macmillan, 19-39.

Rooke, A. (2013) 'Contradictions, collaboration and criticality; researching empowerment and citizenship in community-based arts', in Mayo, M., Mendiwelso-Bendek, Z. and Packham, C. (eds) *Community Research for Community Development*, Basingstoke: Palgrave Macmillan, 150-169.

Tam, H. (2010) 'The importance of being a citizen', in Mayo, M. and Annette, J. (eds) *Taking Part?*, Leicester: NIACE, 7-15.

Tam, H. (2013) 'The art of nurturing communities', *Question the Powerful*. http://henry-tam.blogspot.co.uk/2013/12/the-art-of-nurturing-communities.html

Tandon, R. (ed) (2005) *Participatory Research*, New Delhi: Mosaic Books.

Taylor, M. and Wilson, M. (2016) 'Community organising for social change', in Shaw, M. and Mayo, M. (eds.) *Class, Inequality and Community Development*, Bristol: Policy Press, 219-234.

Tiller, C. (2013) 'Participatory arts and community development: taking part', in Mayo, M., Mendiwelso-Bendek, Z. and Packham, C. (eds) *Community Research for Community Development*, Basingstoke: Palgrave Macmillan, jm133-149.

Watts, J. (2013) 'Community learning approaches to solidarity between the generations', in Mayo, M., Mendiwelso-Bendek, Z. and Packham, C. (eds) *Community Research for Community Development*, Basingstoke: Palgrave Macmillan, 111-130.

Westheimer, J. and Kahne, J. (2004) 'What kind of citizen? The politics of educating for democracy', *American Educational Research Journal*, 41 (2): 237-269.

Wright, R., Mendiwelso-Bendek, Z. and Herron, R. (2013) 'Sports volunteering and community engagement and cohesion', in Mayo, M., Mendiwelso-Bendek, Z. and Packham, C. (eds) *Community Research as Community Development*, London: Palgrave Macmillan, 170-194.

14

Developing Public–Cooperative Partnerships

Pat Conaty

The era of curtailing state power by passing more and more of it to private corporations could be coming to an end. In the UK, the country that has championed privatisation in all forms since the 1980s, contractors of public services have increasingly been found to be totally unreliable. The collapse of Carillion, for example, not only revealed a balance sheet overwhelmed with £900 million of liabilities and a company pension scheme deficit of £590 million, but has called into question the future of PFI (private finance initiative). Along with other failures, it is leading to growing policy work on alternatives to relying on the private sector to meet public objectives (Press Association, 2018). Innovative public policy action has indeed been emerging in the UK, the US and cities from Barcelona and Bologna to Cardiff and Montreal. And they all share a strategic focus on the development of public–cooperative partnerships to meet basic needs, create better employment and improve public services.

The vocabulary varies. In the US the term 'pluralist commonwealth' is used, while in regions of Italy, Spain, Portugal and France 'solidarity economy' and 'commons' are deployed (Alperovitz, 2013; Bollier, 2017). What these approaches have in common is the goal of creating forms of democratic ownership that provide agency and control to the partners and those involved in the development and provision of services. Public–cooperative partnerships were first proposed and experimented with in the UK during the 1920s, and then revived but again curtailed in the 1980s. This chapter explores the past and recent history of public–cooperative partnerships and draws out the lessons to be learned for informing a new social contract between the state and the public – both to improve public services but also more fundamentally to meet basic needs where deregulated markets are failing in respect to housing, social care, health services, energy, finance and decent work.

Public services that 'take back control' for democratic stakeholders

Since the early 1990s the promise of outsourcing has rested on the policy argument that the corporate sector is more efficient and would deliver cheaper public services. A National Audit Office report released three days after Carillion went bust revealed that Whitehall still has no means of measuring if PFI contracts are value for money. In its appraisal of 719 current contracts the report concludes there is little evidence of financial benefits from PFI (NAO, 2018). Indeed projects appraised were found to be up to 40% more costly than if government had used its own borrowing to do the work.

PFI contracts are always structured to prioritise shareholder returns. This has led to absurd outcomes. Studies of hospitals have found routine maintenance work trumping clinical services, where a contract for the tending of the grounds is so contractually inflexible that nurses get laid off (Monbiot, 2018). Thus for investors risks are socialised, with staff, patients and communities all lower down the totem pole to shareholders.

Carillion is just the latest in a growing list of failed public outsourcing contracts including Capita for GP back office services and the courts translation service; G4S for security services at the Olympics; the fining of G4S and Serco for dishonesty in their handling of electronic tagging of offenders; and the liquidation of Southern Cross, the largest corporate provider of residential care homes (Pratley, 2017; Toynbee, 2018).

In response to these failures, there is a discernible policy shift. In-sourcing of public services is now on the increase among local authorities.[1] After a privatisation failure, Welsh Water was successfully converted into a mutual in 2001. Mutual Energy in Northern Ireland

---

[1] Newcastle-upon-Tyne curtailed the private sector running of its Metro system. By taking the work in-house the Council has improved the service and is replacing older trains (Toynbee, 2018). Redbridge in London and Blackpool will take waste collection services in-house next year. Thurrock Council has had to pay £9.9 million to buy out its Serco contract for office services but the annual profit of £3.6 million being made by the private operator is repaying the outlay. Birmingham, North Tyneside, Slough, West Sussex and a growing group of local authorities are following suit – including Conservative councils.

has replicated this model (Conaty, 2011). Both mutuals have had no difficulty raising capital for investing to improve infrastructure and services.

The Coalition Government supported public service mutuals and there are 110 of these public sector spinouts in England (OCS, 2017). The Labour Party has announced that a change in governance is core to their pledge to renationalise the National Grid (for electricity), water companies, the Royal Mail and the train network (Merrick, 2018). Unlike nationalised industries in the past, John McDonnell has proposed a stakeholder model with workers and service users on the governing boards. Labour's plan is that future public services will be of two types: in-house public services partly run by workers and users, and other services provided by cooperatives.

The Labour plan echoes the public mood, with polls showing 80% support for renationalising rail and utilities. To tackle fuel poverty and to offer better services, several local authorities have set up energy supply companies, including Robin Hood Energy in Nottingham, White Rose Energy in Leeds and others in Bristol, Liverpool and Reading.

So how might public-cooperative partnerships be implemented for a wide range of provisioning services, and what can we learn from history and international best practice?

The historical roots of public–cooperative partnerships

The social insurance model of public services across the developed world, from adult education to health care, have had their roots in social struggles and grew out of innovations made by working class self-help and mutual aid organisations. Polanyi (1944) documented this historical development in nineteenth century Europe as a countermovement resisting land enclosure, child labour, the factory system and dispossession by the unregulated free market. Mutual aid models predated municipal socialism by decades (Claeys, 1987).

From the eighteenth century friendly societies pioneered sickness insurance, primary health care and maternity grants. They also developed funeral plans and small pensions. Building societies developed lower cost solutions to housing provision, with the early terminating societies making interest free loans from 1775 until the late nineteenth century. They were a significant developer of entire streets in many cities and towns (Hopkins, 1995). Friendly societies and building societies were founded and held their meetings in pubs. Adult education was advanced by mutual improvement societies. Before they were legalised in the 1820s, trade unions operated covertly as friendly societies. They remained close partners in providing benefit-based services for workers until the NHS was founded.

By 1914 cooperative membership had risen to 3 million in Britain (Birchall, 1997). Working class people had multiple membership, and increasingly in trade unions. A deep-rooted working class culture of mutual aid and self-help was strong and democracy was experienced first-hand in these organisations long before the suffrage was won by men and women.

The success of friendly societies in delivering a wide range of sickness and medical aid benefits inspired both Lloyd George and the Labour Party. The 1911 National Insurance Act provided an enhanced sickness benefit and health scheme through a three-way contributory partnership by workers, employers and the government. The legislation also introduced a retirement pension and the administration of the scheme was awarded to approved friendly societies and mutual insurance companies. The Tredegar Mutual Aid Society in South Wales expanded the friendly society to include a cottage hospital and provided the Labour Party a prototype for the NHS.

The design for a public-cooperative plan emerged out of debates in the weekly *New Age* magazine from 1907. Contributors and participants included G. D. H. Cole, R. H. Tawney, George Bernard Shaw, Bertrand Russell, Hilaire Belloc, George Lansbury and many others. Unlike private property, mutual aid organisations (co-ops, friendly societies and trade unions) used their funds to secure a social purpose. Four guiding principles informed the vision of public-cooperative partnership: economic diversity, economic democracy, economic wealth distribution and economic decentralisation.

The public-cooperative case made by Cole and Tawney (Cole, 1920; Tawney, 1918), including national guilds for larger industries like railways, shipping, mining and steel, persuaded Sidney Webb to amend his draft of Clause IV in the Labour Party constitution. The use of the term 'common ownership' was inserted in 1918 to recognise a diversity of democratic ways to transfer property and ownership to achieve social justice.

Cole (1920) advanced a theory of civic co-sovereignty with a Guild Congress becoming a 'functional democracy' whose purpose was to decentralise power and to coordinate the efforts of diverse public-cooperative partnerships to meet citizen needs. Within the Congress there were four broad types of guild groups: producer guilds, consumer councils and cooperatives, civic services (municipal) and citizen's organisations (voluntary sector). The Guild Congress was designed to complement the local authority and parliamentary political system.

In 1921 100 local building guilds were established and consolidated under the National Building Guilds (Ostergaard, 1997). Finance was arranged with the Co-operative Bank. Housing constructed was paid for on a cost of production basis and this worked well for 18 months. However, during the economic slump in 1923, the private building industry's success in lobbying Whitehall led to a change in procurement rules requiring the guilds to wait much longer for payment and additionally to local authority subsidy reductions from central government that forced prices below cost (Blewitt, 2017). At the end of 1923, with their credit facilities exhausted, the National Building Guilds were forced to wind up.

The mineworkers were advised and supported by Cole, but after seven years of discussion with the government, their plan for the joint control of the coal industry was rejected in 1926. The plan by Beveridge to include friendly societies in managing health services as co-partners within the NHS was rejected in 1946 (Hirst, 1994).

One key legacy of public–cooperative partnership was the land reform innovation of the Garden City movement. Letchworth Garden City developed from 1903 and was also championed by Cole. All 5,500 acres of land for the new city was bought at near agricultural prices and the city developed to its target of 33,000 residents just after World War II. The land was held in the common ownership of the Garden City company for the residents. The joint ground rent-rate system was a revenue innovation co-developed with the local authority (Conaty and Large, 2013). By 1948 Letchworth was self-financing from revenues earned on commercial property and from municipally owned utilities. New Towns adopted the capturing rent system. Harlow was so successful in self-financing through capturing commercial rents that during the 1970s its huge surpluses were expropriated by the Treasury (Hall and Ward, 2014). And public policy has since by and large ignored the self-financing success of both Letchworth and Harlow, and how common ownership of land could be redeployed for housing and urban regeneration today.[2]

Public–cooperative partnership – lessons for public policy and legislation

There are 2.6 million cooperatives internationally with 1 billion members. In G20 countries they account for 12% of employment

---

[2]   In 2018, the Conservative Government programme and the first new Garden City at Ebbsfleet rely on private land development methods.

(ICA, 2014). If we can establish enabling conditions and supportive public policies, the potential today for public-cooperative partnerships is greater than ever.

Housing and energy

In Europe, the UK was a pioneer in cooperative housing in the early twentieth century. Tenant co-partnership societies were developed from 1900 – first in London and then in other cities. Their aim was to attract capital from the cooperative movement and other social investors to build good quality housing co-owned by tenants who could secure up to 25% equity. By 1914, 7,000 homes had been built by 14 societies in 40 suburban developments including Ealing and Hampstead in London, at Letchworth Garden City and in southern England (Birchall, 1988). The housing developed was popular but the governance poorly designed. As a consequence, unscrupulous investors in the 1930s found ways to block tenant votes, demutualise and asset strip many schemes.

But the UK model came to be adapted and redesigned in the 1920s by Swedish and Danish cooperatives. The Swedish model was called Tenant Ownership Cooperatives. The major design improvement was that Tenant Savings Banks were set up by the cooperative sector to provide the finance and a resilient three-way partnership was developed. The building trade unions formed a company, Riksbyggen, to develop the homes. The consumer co-op HSB set up the Tenant Savings Bank to finance construction. Then the completed homes were handed over to local housing co-ops set up by tenant savers who took collective responsibility for the mortgage repayment to HSB.

In Denmark the capital was provided by the Workmen's Cooperative Building Society and the Danish Cooperative Bank. In each country and in Norway after 1951, strong partnerships were developed with local government and planners in cities and towns. In the Norwegian model, public housing tenants were offered democratic control for managing and owning a share of their housing through co-ops. Today 16% to 19% of housing nationally in these countries is in the cooperative sector. Like Norway, Swedish housing co-ops have developed partnerships with the state to regenerate public housing through cooperative tenure. Germany also has over 2,000 housing co-ops with 3 million members and regional cooperative banks providing finance.

As it is common for the housing stock in suburban areas to be managed by local co-ops, cooperative energy services have emerged in Scandinavia. A public-cooperative partnership will typically involve the urban management of the combined heat and power grid by the municipality with district or neighbourhood energy co-ops managing the local generators, heating and lighting systems – both for the housing co-ops and also for other residents. Copenhagen has 21 district energy co-ops in its networks and other cities have a smaller network (King, 2013).

There are ongoing programmes to upgrade and green the local grid in Scandinavian countries through a switch to renewable sources of energy. A weakness in the Scandinavian co-op model is that the land has not been taken out of the market in the ways the Garden City movement demonstrated. Therefore, Tenant Ownership Co-op homes have become more expensive at resale as land values have risen (Birchall, 1997). By contrast, with the community land trust approach of the original Garden Cities, housing costs could be reduced by 30% to 60%. This was the approach adopted by the Burlington Community Land Trust (CLT) in Vermont with the backing in 1984 of the city's mayor, Bernie Sanders, and $1 million investment from the city pension fund. It became the pathfinder for 250 CLTs in the USA, and an inspiration for the growing CLT movement in the UK.

Workplace innovations

In Spain, the Mondragon co-ops grew in the Basque country after they set up in 1959 their own cooperative savings bank, the Caja Laboral Popular. This was co-owned and controlled by the worker co-ops and led to the renowned success of the Mondragon Corporation with its diverse network of more than 120 manufacturing, food, retail, housing and social service co-ops with over 60,000 worker owners and an annual turnover of more than €12 billion. The co-op bank established a research and development arm that has since the 1990s become the Mondragon University. Unlike the UK cooperative movement, worker cooperatives are at the heart of the success of Mondragon.

Instead of being locked in a dichotomy of either the state must take on the role of an employer itself or leave it to private employers, the experience of Mondragon suggested that government institutions could promote more sustainable employment by backing the development of worker cooperatives. In the UK, from 1979 on, almost 60 Cooperative Development Agencies (CDAs) were set up with the support of local authorities (Cockerton and Whyatt, 1984).

In 1981, the Greater London Council (GLC) recruited Mike Cooley, who had been a leading exponent of worker involvement in the development and delivery of socially useful goods. Cooley had been sacked by Lucas Aerospace for setting out ideas for saving jobs in the company by switching from armaments to products that would be in high demand to improve society, such as solar heating equipment, artificial kidneys and innovative transport systems (Cooley, 1982). The GLC brought him to work on the London Industrial Strategy, based on popular planning with workers and service users in 20 local economy sectors. The strategy drew on key lessons then emerging from Emilia Romagna in Italy (GLC, 1985). Working with the CDAs, the GLC and other councils supported the development of over 2,000 worker cooperatives during the 1980s. The closure of GLC and metropolitan authorities by the Thatcher Government in 1986 curtailed the development of public-cooperative partnerships in the UK. One of the final acts of the GLC was to endow land at discounted values to establish Coin Street Builders in 1986, the pioneering Community Land Trust in London for cooperative housing.

Business development and social care

In the region of Emilia Romagna in Italy, there are over 8,000 cooperatives (by comparison, in the whole of the UK there are only 7,000). This is the highest density of cooperative ownership in Europe and accounts for 40% of the area's GDP (Mayo, 2015). Emilia Romagna also has one of the lowest levels of inequality in Europe along with the Basque country where the Mondragon cooperatives are located. Public-cooperative partnerships, innovative financing and democratic governance have been key success factors in Italy as well as in Scandinavia.

In the 1970s northern Italy experienced the same problems of stagflation as other parts of Europe. Emilia Romagna launched a 'solidarity economy' experiment that spread to other parts of northern Italy to become renowned as the Third Italy. Echoing the ideas of G. D. H. Cole, a diversity of democratic ownership innovation was pursued. The major breakthrough was the co-development of a supportive local ecosystem of policies and practices to design and proactively support public-cooperative partnerships.

Local authority leaders championed research partnerships between city officials, local universities, the co-op movement and local businesses (Restakis, 2010). Research teams investigated in each local district the types of small and medium enterprises and how they could be expanded by co-developing new products and services. Mutual societies to provide cooperative insurance were developed to pool the risk for borrowing and to negotiate very low-cost financing from regional cooperative banks. The researchers worked with the banks to develop cooperative capital products. After a decade, the success was dramatic, with a huge diversity of small firms expanding in farming, manufacturing, food processing, knitwear and clothing, specialised engineering and also in social services.

The national Marcora law was passed in 1985 to enable companies to sell their business to their workforce. Through the law the state co-developed a public–cooperative financing system to increase the number of worker cooperative buy-outs. The law has been highly successful. In 1991 a second Social Cooperative law was passed to expand cooperatives in the fields of social care, public health, advice/education and to create decent jobs for the disabled, vulnerable and ex-offenders (Conaty, 2014). In recognition of their success in advancing the common good, this law provided social cooperatives with a lower rate of VAT and corporation tax and an exemption from national insurance contributions for disadvantaged people they employed.[3]

The impact of public–cooperative partnerships has been remarkable. Italy now has 23,858 worker and social cooperatives with an annual turnover of €41.3 billion (Co-operatives Europe, 2015). Employment among social cooperatives is over 360,000 with a turnover of €9 billion and 5 million service users (Conaty, 2015). They can include in their ownership and governance workers, volunteers and service users. They have forged co-production partnerships with local authorities. The public sector commonly will build a facility such as a community centre or day care centre and the social cooperative will provide the services. In the early 1990s the social cooperative movement negotiated an ongoing national trade union agreement for creating decent work.

The social cooperative model has been replicated in Quebec with support from a 1997 law and in Japan without legislation. Similar enabling legislation has been passed in Portugal (1998), Spain (1999), France (2001) and Greece (2011) (Conaty, 2014).

---

[3] Within the cooperative sector historically, the main ownership models have been single stakeholder including consumer co-ops (for food, retail and financial services), producer co-ops (workers and farmers), housing co-ops (tenants) and community benefit societies (for a defined community). Multiple stakeholder governance is complex and difficult to implement. Northern Italian co-ops in the mid-1960s developed a radical new model, the social cooperative.

Social Solidarity Economy

Inspired by the success of the Italian model, Social Solidarity Economy (SSE) ideas, practices and policies have been growing and becoming influential globally. SSE recognises and advocates for associative democracy networks to re-embed the economy under social regulation and control.[4] In 2015 the United Nations Research Institute for Social Development (UNRISD) officially recognised the emergence and power of the SSE as an integrated movement (Utting, 2015).

Precarious work and precarious housing are widespread issues across Europe. Solidarity economy solutions for precarious workers have been developed since the 1990s in Belgium and France for freelancers. The public policy innovation is known as Business and Employment Cooperatives and is supported through public sector social security partnerships.

Smart in Belgium is a good example. It was set up in 1997 as a mutual society for artists to provide advice, education, invoice management, debt collection and other services including managed workspace (Conaty et al, 2016). The strategy was successful and they steadily expanded the services for any freelance worker. Today Smart is a growing, solidarity cooperative and for a small fee, freelancers pass their invoices to the co-op which reimburses them and in turn collects its repayment from the contractor. If co-op members fall ill, sickness and social security benefits can be claimed through Smart from the state. Deliveroo and Uber drivers have joined Smart to secure these worker rights through the co-op. Smart has over 85,000 members in Belgium and another 20,000 members in Germany, France, the Netherlands and other countries where it has set up affiliated cooperatives with local partners.

Since 2010 two in three new jobs in the UK have been created through self-employment. By the end of 2018 there will be more self-employed than public sector workers (Conaty et al, 2017). Indycube is a cooperative in Wales and England providing managed workspaces in over 30 locations. It has formed a partnership with Community Union to provide a joint package of trade union and cooperative services for freelance workers to help them secure worker rights. Both are working with Smart to introduce their more comprehensive model to the UK.

---

[4]   The Global Social Economy Forum is a growing international network of cities and associative democracy networks working to develop SSE solutions. See www.gsef-net.org/

Moving forward

Public-cooperative partnerships offer a wide range of new and important opportunities for citizens to help advance the public good in a democratic manner without expanding the size of the state. Mayor Blasio in New York has established a growing programme to support and invest in worker cooperatives. The United Steelworkers have co-developed with the Mondragon Cooperative Corporation a Union Co-op model. The Evergreen Cooperatives in Cleveland, Ohio have developed a municipal partnership for Mondragon-type solutions and a $200 million investment fund. This has funded worker cooperatives in green construction and solar power installation on public buildings, for local food growing on a CLT site and an industrial-scale laundry for the city's hospitals (Democracy Collaborative, 2018). Preston in Lancashire has been working to replicate the Evergreen model through a public-cooperative partnership (Chakrabortty, 2018).

Barcelona's mayor Ada Colau and her party, Barcelona en Comu, are developing a 'commons collaborative economy' with 1,300 cooperative, commons and neighbourhood projects that account for 10% of the local economy (Bollier, 2016). Som Energia Co-op in the city is Catalonia's first green energy co-op. Public-cooperative deliberation and policy is being co-developed through procommuns.net and Decim.Barcelona ('Decide Barcelona').

Similarly, Bologna has developed a local bylaw, the Bologna Regulation for the Care and Regeneration of Urban Commons. This provides a means to foster participatory budgeting and joint public-cooperative investment. A good example is the Campi Aperti co-op in Bologna, a food commons network with five fair-trade markets in partnership with the city and organic food cultivation on the equivalent of 300 premier league football pitches (De Angelis, 2017). Reviving the practice of municipal bylaws for the commons is also being developed in Ghent.

In 2015 Co-operatives UK completed a two-year study of cooperative and solidarity economy innovation both internationally and across 15 sectors of the UK economy (Mayo, 2015). The research identified 55 innovations including community buyouts of village shops, community-owned pubs, community land trusts for affordable housing (from East London to Leeds), community supported agriculture, GP cooperatives and community-owned health centres, an expanding range of community development finance organisations, the 850 cooperative schools in secondary education supported by trade unions and local authorities, supporter-owned football clubs, community-owned media, city farms, community-owned gardens, technology co-ops and employment/resettlement co-ops.

Following the 2014 report of the Welsh Co-operative and Mutuals Commission, the Welsh Government has been lending support to public-cooperative partnerships (Conaty, 2015). The creative work in Wales highlights what can be done in other regions of the UK. A joint partnership between the Welsh Government, housing associations, the Wales Co-operative Centre and the Confederation of Co-operative Housing has led to an expanding programme to develop a broad range of cooperative and Community Land Trust housing. A CLT in West Rhyl has been developed along with new co-op housing schemes in Cardiff, Newport, Torfaen, Merthyr Tydfil and Carmarthenshire.

Additionally, social cooperation forums have been established first in Wales and more recently in England. The Welsh social cooperation forum has succeeded in securing an amendment to the Social Services and Wellbeing (Wales Act) 2014 that places a statutory obligation on local authorities to consider as a priority community-led and cooperative solutions for the provision of care services.

In 2016 the Welsh Government established a Care to Co-operate Fund with the Wales Co-operative Centre to provide advice and guidance to new social cooperatives and for existing social enterprises willing to give votes and voice to their workers, volunteers and service users by converting to a social cooperative. Cartrefi Cymru is a social enterprise for adults with learning disabilities. It has 1,200 staff across Wales and converted to a social cooperative in 2017. Community Lives Consortium (CLC) is a similar organisation working in Swansea and Neath/Port Talbot that has become a social cooperative (Conaty et al, 2017). CLC has developed a commons system for multi-stakeholder decision making for its disabled and carer members.

A successful 'Building a Co-operative Country' conference in Cardiff in 2017 brought together community-based co-op developers in the fields of housing, social care, renewable energy and finance. This has led to the emergence of a Mutuals Alliance for Wales to coordinate the development work and to raise the profile of public-cooperative partnerships.

The fundamental argument made by Tawney (1921), Cole (1920) and Polanyi (1944) for socially re-embedding the economy by taking people, land and money out of the market is crucial for guiding new public policy. The innovations to develop cooperative finance solutions in Spain and Italy, common ownership solutions for land in the UK and USA, and multi-stakeholder governance in Italy and Quebec are fundamental elements for public-cooperative partnerships to succeed.

The debacle of PFI underscores the need to make markets our servant and no longer an unaccountable master. This does not mean that the state should retreat into itself, but it should explore new ways to work with cooperative partners. A common challenge for smaller cooperative enterprises for housing, renewable energy and residential care homes is that they cannot easily secure patient low-cost capital and a co-operative ecosystem of support is needed (Lawrence et al, 2018).[5] Fortunately, work is underway to develop new public and cooperative financial institutions to help address this issue (Johnson, 2017), and more will undoubtedly be done when public policies fully catch up with what we have learnt about the potential of public-cooperative partnerships.

References

Alperovitz, G. (2013) *What Then Must We Do? Straight talk about the next American revolution*, Harford, VT: Chelsea Green Publishing.

Birchall, J. (1988) *Building communities - The co-operative way*, London: Routledge.

Birchall, J. (1997) *The International Co-operative Movement*, Manchester: Manchester University Press.

Blewitt, J. (2017) *Claims for a Decent Life and a True Democracy*, Green House.

Bollier, D. (2016) 'Barcelona's brave struggle to advance the Commons', *Counter Solutions*, 30 November.

Bollier, D. (2017) 'The Future is a "pluriverse" – an interview with David Bollier on the potential of the commons', *Transnational Institute of Social Ecology*, 30 April.

Burns, D., Cowie, L., Earle, J., Folkman, P., Froud, J., Hyde, P., Johal, S., Rees Jones, I., Killett, A. and Williams, K. (2016) *Where does the money go? Financialised chains and the crisis in adult residential care*, Manchester: CRESC (Centre for Research on Socio-Cultural Change).

Chakrabortty, A. (2018) 'In 2011 Preston hit rock bottom. Then it good back control', *The Guardian*, 31 January.

Claeys, G. (1987) *Machinery, Money and the Millennium – from moral economy to socialism 1815–1860*, Polity Press.

Cockerton, P. and Whyatt, A. (1984) *The Workers Co-operative Handbook*, ICOM.

---

[5]   The returns on capital secured on PFI typically range from 12% to 14% – more than double the average 5% returns on pension funds (Burns et al, 2016).

Cole, G. D. H. (1920) *Guild Socialism: a plan for economic democracy*, Bibliolife.

Conaty, P. (2011) *A Co-operative Green Economy: new solutions for energy and sustainable social justice*, Co-operatives UK.

Conaty, P. and Large, M. (2013) *Commons Sense: co-operative place making and the capturing of land value for 21st century Garden Cities*, Co-operatives UK.

Conaty, P. (2014) *Social Co-operatives: a democratic co-production agenda for care services in the UK*, Co-operatives UK.

Conaty, P. (2015) *A Collaborative Economy for the Common Good*, The Wales Co-operative Centre.

Conaty, P., Bird, A. and Ross, P. (2016) *Not Alone: trade union and co-operative solutions for self-employed workers*, Manchester: Co-operatives UK and the Wales Co-operative Centre.

Conaty, P., Bird, A. and Ross, C. (2017) *Organising Precarious Workers: Trade union and co-operative strategies*, TUC report by Co-operatives UK and the Co-operative College.

Cooley, M. (1982) *Architect or Bee? The human/technology relationship*, Boston: South End Press.

Co-operatives Europe (2015) *The Power of Co-operation: Co-operatives Europe key figures 2015*, Brussels: Cooperatives Europe.

De Angelis, M. (2017) *Omnia sunt Communia: on the commons and the transformation to post capitalism*, London: Zed Books.

Democracy Collaborative (2018) 'The Democracy Collaborative joins Jeremy Corbyn's new Community Wealth Building Unit as advisors', 8 February [Press release] https://democracycollaborative.org/content/democracy-collaborative-joins-jeremy-corbyns-new-community-wealth-building-unit-advisors

Greater London Council (GLC) (1985) *The London Industrial Strategy*, July 1985, London: Greater London Council.

Hall, P. and Ward, C. (2014) *Sociable Cities: the 21st-century reinvention of the Garden City*, Routledge.

Hirst, P. (1994) *Associative Democracy: new forms of economic and social governance*, Polity Press.

Hopkins, E. (1995) *Working-class Self-help in Nineteenth Century England*, UCL Press.

International Co-operative Alliance (ICA) (2014) *Co-operatives and Employment: a Global Report*, Brussels: International Cooperative Alliance.

Johnson. C. (2017) *Time for a Public Bank for Wales?*, Public Policy Institute for Wales.

King, M. (2013) *Heat Services: towards a mutual future in Haringey*, District Energy Development Ltd., January.

Lawrence, M., Pendleton, A. and Mahmoud, M. (2018) *Co-operatives Unleashed – Doubling the size of the UK's Co-operative sector*, London: New Economics Foundation.

Mayo, E. (editor) (2015) *The Co-operative Advantage - Innovation, co-operation and why sharing business ownership is good for Britain*, Co-operatives UK and New Internationalist.

Monbiot, G. (2018) 'The PFI bosses fleeced us all. Now watch them walk away', *The Guardian*, 16 January.

Merrick, R. (2018) 'John McDonnell to pledge "irreversible shift to worker-run public services after Tories" "failed privatisation model"', *The Independent*, 10 February.

National Audit Office (NAO) (2018) *PFI and PF2: the report of the Comptroller and the Auditor General*, HM Treasury, January.

Office for Civil Society (OCS) (2017) *Introduction to Public Service Mutuals,* 21 August.

Ostergaard, G. (1997) *The Tradition of Workers' Control*, Freedom Press.

Polanyi, K. (1944) *The Great Transformation: the political and economic origins of our time,* Reinhart & Company.

Pratley, N. (2017) 'A shocking way to fund UK care homes', *The Guardian*, 12 December.

The Press Association (2017) 'Carillion: government to back loans to firm's struggling contractors', *The Guardian*, 3 February.

Restakis, J. (2010) *Humanizing the Economy: co-operatives in the age of capital*, New Society Publishers.

Tawney, R. H. (1918) 'The Conditions of Economic Liberty', paper on 'Industrial Democracy' republished as a chapter in Tawney, R. H. (1966) *The Radical Tradition*, London: Pelican Books.

Tawney, R.H. (1921) *The acquisitive society*, London: G. Bell and Sons.

Toynbee, P. (2018) 'It is not just Carillion. The whole privatisation myth has been exposed', *The Guardian*, 22 January.

Utting, P. (2015) *Social and Solidarity Economy: beyond the fringe*, London: Zed Books.

Conclusion

15

The Renewal of State–Citizen Cooperation

Henry Tam

When the gap widens between those who have the power to rule and the people they are meant to serve, it becomes ever more likely that the errors of the former will persist, while their prejudices will remain unchallenged. And their abuse of power will seldom, if ever, be overturned. Even those with benign intentions may end up pushing misconceived policies as no one is in a position to secure a change of direction. As for those who have primarily taken power to advance their private gains, the less the population at large can hold them to account, the more they will treat them with disdain.

Democracy is the endeavour to close this gap until the state and its citizens can share the power and responsibility of governing in a spirit of cooperation. Different people may have the best or worst of motives in seeking political power, but if what they actually plan to do is not to go against the public interest, there has to be effective means for that interest to manifest itself and shape the design of government policies (Derber, 2017; Tam, 2018a).

As the contributors to this book have shown, attempts to rely on periodic elections, quasi-market mechanisms, or leaving communities to deal with problems while radically cutting state support have failed to halt the expanding gulf between government institutions and the public. Distrust has soared. Discord has intensified. The political ambitions of a few have managed to sow seeds of confusion that undermine economic stability and threaten community relations. The polarisation between a wealthy elite who can buy control of most things in life, and an insecure majority of the population is also damaging for people's physical and mental wellbeing (Wilkinson and Pickett, 2018).

But there is an alternative. If we put aside abstract assumptions about how human beings must be inherently self-centred, or could not be motivated to work with others to steer collective mechanisms for their common good, we would see in reality that there are plenty of examples of people cooperating to devise and deploy better public solutions. No one is claiming that such cooperation can always be brought forth with ease, or that it can be sustained without having to reconcile strong emotions and overcome the resistance of those who seek to divide and rule. The empirical fact remains that it can be done even where the challenges seem formidable – for example, in deprived areas where communities are already under stress, or in cases involving complex policy issues.

As for the argument that it is all very well for people in academic ivory towers to talk about the value of state-citizen cooperation, but politicians cannot afford such luxury, the fact is that many politicians in local and central government, in different countries, dealing with a wide range of public problems, make it a key objective because they recognise it as indispensable. They realise that policies are more likely to succeed in serving the public if citizens themselves have an informed and meaningful input into the development of those policies. Whereas going it alone not only weakens their chance of getting support from people without a sense of shared ownership of what they seek to implement, but leaves it open for those with a manipulative agenda to deceive people into backing options that would ultimately just benefit the powerful few at the expense of others.

To help politicians, community activists and public officials who want to build better state-citizen cooperation through effective engagement, we need to turn our attention to the approaches that can genuinely give citizens greater understanding and control of the public decisions that affect them. From general civic dialogues and focused deliberative events, to community development and participatory prioritisation, there are proven ways of empowering people to have a meaningful role to play in shaping their own governance.

To recognise that such approaches could be misapplied if one does not grasp how they are meant to be deployed, or that it may take considerable astuteness and determination to bring them forward against resistance from those who prefer to stick with the status quo, is not to concede that they are not worth advancing. On the contrary, there is greater urgency than ever to translate the lessons of how they achieve their impact, to practical plans and policies on a much wider scale to renew state-citizen cooperation.

Some who have never in reality looked into how these approaches unfold in practice may ironically insist that from a 'realist' point of view they will never work. But for anyone willing to learn from the accumulative initiatives and experiments that have taken place, the key question is not if, but how, we should go about promoting more effective and widespread application of approaches that can reconnect citizens with their government institutions at every level.

The UK Government's Together We Can programme was an example of how the lessons from diverse practical initiatives could inform improvements across the country through being systematically collated and disseminated through peer learning (Chapter Five in this book; see also Tam, 2018b, chs 5–7). But it also taught us that a government-led programme was vulnerable to shifts in electoral fortune, and could not be relied on as the sole driver for long-term civic transformation. In addition to assessing what may help or hinder the pursuit of effective engagement, we must also aim to embed the development of our civic capability into the learning culture of our society.

Schools must teach their students to appreciate the implications of political power, unpack ideological and demagogic rhetoric, and apply cooperative techniques in resolving conflicts and finding feasible ways to attain shared objectives among themselves and the wider community. Political parties and state bodies should devote more time to ensuring those who stand for and attain public office have a good understanding of why and how they should engage with their constituents, and what they ought to do to facilitate wider public participation in co-designing policy outcomes that reflect public concerns. Universities, lifelong learning providers, and community groups ought to collaborate more to widen access to lessons about active citizenship, so that the promotion of life skills is not limited to employment-related competence or management of one's personal health and finance, but incorporates as a core element the know-how and confidence in building alliances with one's fellow citizens in articulating the common good and navigating towards its realisation. Community leaders and cooperative entrepreneurs should be ready to provide more routine opportunities for people from all backgrounds to work in new forms of public-cooperative partnership where social, economic and environmental goals can be integrated through the joint deliberations of all those involved, and the benefits generated are shared equitably among all stakeholders.

Looking back on the instructive findings and critical analyses by the contributors to this book, one can only conclude that there is considerable scope and value to improving state–citizen cooperation. For all those interested in taking on the challenge to bring about such improvements, we would encourage them to bear in mind five key recommendations that should guide their efforts:

- Focus on making engagement a lever for change.
- Identify and publicise the value of democratic cooperation.
- Select appropriate and feasible involvement approaches.
- Cultivate inclusive community relations.
- Invest in the development of civic leadership.

Focus on making engagement a lever for change

Although some people will always assume that there is neither the interest nor the energy among the public to engage with government institutions, evidence-based research has consistently found that most people would participate *if* they were confident that it would make a real difference (Power Inquiry, 2006; Ilott and Norris, 2015). Apathy is engendered by the perception that for all the consultation, discussion and reviews, those in power would do whatever they wanted to do anyway.

Before setting up any engagement arrangements, it is therefore vital to have a clear focus on what real options are going to be on the agenda. It may affect a small group of people in one locality or many communities across the entire country. What is critical is that the decision in the end will matter to the people to be engaged in considering that decision. It is not unknown among senior figures in the public sector to think that civic engagement can be attained simply by encouraging members of the public to take part in some activities – regardless of whether those activities connect with any kind of policy option assessment and selection. At one extreme, some even consider urging citizens to volunteer their time to do good work for charities or in their local communities as exemplary attempts to promote civic engagement. In the UK, for example, even though the country has one of the best track records for volunteering in Europe, while lagging behind most other European countries in democratic engagement (Delwit, 2013), it is the promotion of volunteering, rather than democratic engagement, that gets far more political attention and public funding.

When civic engagement is connected to a real policy issue, it must be backed by wider organisational arrangements so that at the outset there is a transparent and shared understanding of what possible options can be considered. There will be constraints that set the basic parameters, and it is not unreasonable for these to be stated, as they may include core commitments to values of equal respect, safety standards, the available budget and the time available for a decision to be reached. It is far better to explain what these are and what scope there is for formulating or choosing different options before one embarks on the engagement exercise. To involve people in detailed deliberations only to reveal some way into the process that various doors are actually closed will only aggravate disillusionment.

Another factor to pin down is the willingness to change among those who have the formal decision-making power. We have seen how effective a tool participatory budgeting can be when it is deployed to promote deliberations that go on to shape decisions about what options to choose. But the worst misapplication of participatory budgeting is undoubtedly when the process has been completed, and the results are known from the participants' choices, some person with the relevant authority steps in to declare, without any further explanation, that those results will not be acted on.[1]

The last component to put in place *before* one launches into an engagement initiative is a plan for implementation. It does not have to cover all the possible details, but the feasibility of any option to be considered cannot be properly assessed without some thinking going into how it may be carried out. At one end of the spectrum, there are projects to rethink public transport for young people that cannot actually go very far, because the contracts for many of the routes in question have been handed to private companies that have no intention of taking on the task of implementing any alternative proposed by young people. At the other end, we have the monumental blunder of staging a referendum on the UK leaving the European Union without any stocktake of implementation issues, so that citizens are asked to back one option or another without any inkling about the risks, lack of feasibility and unmanageable disruption associated with a certain course of action.

---

[1]   Exceptions may of course have to be made in cases where the demands go against the stated parameters, are reached through violation of the inclusive procedures laid down, or cannot be reconciled with the discovery of previously unknown facts that render the demands inappropriate.

Identify and publicise the value of democratic cooperation

There is a common perception that when politicians and public officials meet with a gathering of members of the public, it is either some kind of polite public relations exercise, or a confrontational crisis event dominated by rage and frustration. Processes designed for democratic cooperation are far from being well known or understood. The benefits from such engagement are generally overlooked. Indeed, when it comes to local government accounting, for example, there is the standard reference to 'the cost of democracy' relating to any expenditure associated with elections and subsequent activities of councillors, but nothing corresponding to the benefit of democracy.

Instead of insisting that sceptics should appreciate civic engagement is important in its own right (which it is), more should be done to make the case for its deployment, especially in terms that will strike a chord with those holding government positions. Significantly, there is growing support for identifying benefits beyond conventional financial transactions (Savitz and Weber, 2006; Retolazza et al, 2016), and the receptiveness to these considerations is rising in public institutions at all levels.

The European Commission has produced guidance on assessing the value of citizen engagement (Davies and Simon, 2012). The World Bank Group has issued a strategic framework for mainstreaming citizen engagement to achieve improved results (Manroth et al, 2014). And Caroline Antsey, one of its former managing directors, was unequivocal in stating that 'citizen engagement is essential for open government and effective development, strengthening the quality of policymaking and the "science" of service delivery with improved social accountability' (Antsey, 2013).

In the UK, as a result of the Together We Can programme and other related initiatives to review and disseminate findings about civic engagement and empowerment, there is much to draw on in terms of case studies and accumulated expertise in capturing the difference effective approaches can make (Rogers and Robinson, 2004; Gaffney, 2005; McCabe et al, 2007). Positive impact was found in all policy areas: drop in reoffending rates, reduction in use of hospital emergency services, consensus building through collective deliberations, higher education attainment, improved local economic development, raised tenant satisfaction with housing management, and increased trust and confidence in public bodies.

Far from treating cooperation with citizens as some nice-to-have side activity, its proponents should be ready to cite examples of how well-executed engagement processes have led to greater benefits. According to a review by the Department of Communities and Local Government (Blears, 2009), there is a wide range of examples of improved outcomes. Birmingham City Council's community involvement initiative for safer neighbourhoods led to a reduction of 14% in all crime in the project areas compared with a 7% drop in other comparator areas in the city; with youth crime reducing by 29% compared with a 12% drop elsewhere; and achieved a saving of £6,406,000 for an investment of £600,000 after just one year of operation. In the East of England, 231 communities developed plans in partnership with public bodies, setting out over 9,000 individual actions to improve their locality; 47% of these actions were taken forward by the communities themselves and 34% carried out by public service providers. Portsmouth City Council conducted an ongoing engagement exercise with local communities in its £9 million Copnor Bridge project, and was able to complete it one month early, minimise traffic disruption and achieve a 10% saving on the budget.

What is consistently found in these and numerous other examples is that where people are given genuine opportunities to reflect and contribute their views on the development of public actions, there is a good chance it will lead to more satisfactory and cost-efficient outcomes. In an extensive evaluation study carried out by SQW Consulting for the UK government, it was found that the spread of neighbourhood management practices,[2] particularly in deprived areas, led over a three-year period to more residents feeling they can influence local decisions, and to higher levels of satisfaction with the police, street cleaning and their local area as a place to live[3] (SQW, 2008).

Select appropriate and feasible involvement approaches

While academic research has found different types of approach to engage state and citizens in closer cooperation (Involve, 2005; Smith, 2010), many people holding government positions still either believe

---

[2]   One of the innovative features of neighbourhood management was the introduction of a locally based, easily accessible manager who is there to discuss with local residents issues of concern to them, across conventional public service boundaries, and who is given the support to resolve them with the different agencies involved.

[3]   On all the measures, the scores for residents in the neighbourhood management areas were higher than the comparator areas.

that none of these methods really works or assume there is one standard technique to adopt for every occasion. In reality, a wide range of practices have been developed and refined for different circumstances, but they only work effectively if they are chosen sensibly and applied with the necessary know-how. To make the right selection, a number of factors should be considered.

First of all, there is the question of who ought to be involved. If it is a large group, can it be organised through a number of smaller groups so that everyone has a realistic chance to engage with discussions? If the group concerned has a representative structure, are we confident that its members will be content to leave the engagement to those who are currently holding the representative positions? In other cases, would a random sampling procedure help to bring together a manageable group to discuss the issues? The logistics such as locations and duration need to be planned carefully so that people invited to attend do not find they have to travel too far or make themselves available at the most inconvenient time.[4]

With some issues, such as disputes over local planning proposals, an approach such as Planning for Real[5] may suffice in combining intracommunity familiarisation with the moderate level of conflict resolution that is required. But where lack of interactions has created an atmosphere of suspicion, informal community events may be desirable to help strangers get to know one another first. In cases where intimidation and violence has divided communities, more extensive outreach and reconciliation may well be necessary before any engagement in joint deliberations is possible (Chapman and Van Der Merwe, 2008).

It is critical to ensure that the approach to be adopted can manage the interactions of the people who will be involved. This involves setting out and enforcing the ground rules on, for example, mutual respect, civil discourse and the adjudication and exclusion of lies and misinformation; handling emotional tensions and resolving them with due empathy; fair facilitating of discussions in reviewing pros and cons,

---

[4]   Compensatory payment for time taken out and travel costs may also need to be considered in some cases.

[5]   Planning for Real involves local people visiting a local venue where a 3-D model of the area with the contested proposals have been put together by local people themselves, and differences in opinions are aired and revised through facilitated exchange over mutual give-and-take.

questioning experts, formulating suggestions and weighing options; and overseeing the resolution process.[6]

The approach will also need to be competent in communicating the outcome to others who are not at the discussions, and keep everyone informed of how the agreed decision is being taken forward. It is one of the most common causes of disillusionment with civic engagement that there is no follow-through or feedback so that the impression is given that nothing happens after all that has been discussed at length. And feedback is not only vital to maintain trust and belief in the responsiveness of the state body in question, it is also necessary to provide the opportunity to track and assess progress and, where appropriate, revise details and adjust direction so that citizens can learn from the implementation process, and those carrying out the decisions can learn to adapt them in the light of public feedback.

Cultivate inclusive community relations

Those holding government positions (or seeking public office) should recognise that a genuinely cooperative relationship with their fellow citizens needs a long-term foundation. The electoral routine of politicians asking once every few years for one's vote and making no contact thereafter[7] is not going to be much improved by holding the odd engagement event now and then. Between specific engagement exercises there should be communications to cover not just how the outcomes of those exercises are being followed up on, but also what other policy explorations may be in the pipeline, and any other day-to-day or strategic issues people may want to discuss.

We have seen the difference neighbourhood management schemes could make when the public knew there was someone they could turn to on a regular basis. This requires reasonable continuity of personnel and ethos to underpin the sustainability of supportive interactions. Some politicians cannot resist the temptation when they take over – even when it is from someone of the same party – to change as many things as possible. Some public managers think it is good to keep moving staff around so they are constantly refreshed in what they do. But in either case, what benefits there are from such changes should be judged in relation to the unhelpful disruptions that can cause to

---

[6]   Which may have as its objective consensus-building, prioritisation of proposals or majority selection of one option.

[7]   Or in a safe seat, one may not get even that one call – from any of the parties.

people who will no longer know who they are supposed to speak with in the public organisation in question, or what they can expect.

In addition to government bodies having regular and constructive communications with the public, the communities being engaged must themselves be not so divided that it would render shared deliberations impossible. It has been rightly pointed out that if engagement is just offered to those who are swiftest in putting themselves forward, it can easily lead to a participation gap between the better-off and the marginalised (Dalton, 2017). The targeting of neighbourhood management and other initiatives in the more deprived areas, as we have seen, can help to redress some of the potential imbalance across the country. But within any given area, suitable forms of community development should be promoted to ensure people from all socioeconomic backgrounds are kept in touch and given realistic opportunities to share their views.

Other differences arising from age, gender, health, ethnic or other factors may also mean that some people face exclusionary barriers in having their say as citizens (Crick and Lockyer, 2010). Equality does not mean that everyone should be given the same treatment, but that those hampered by prejudices, disabilities or other disadvantages can be treated in a manner that will help them overcome the specific barriers. Instead of assuming that people who are really concerned will always find a way to get their voices heard, networks of community-based support should be sustained with funding and in-kind aid so that they can enable those who are most in need of help to make their concerns known.[8]

Support for greater local autonomy ought to be calibrated in line with the principle of subsidiarity, so citizens' call for collective action can be taken up by organisations with sufficient capability to respond effectively (Evans and Zimmerman, 2014). Not all solutions, especially those requiring substantial resource and collective capacity, can be carried out effectively by individuals or groups in their own neighbourhood. It is vital to have a framework for assessing what can be left to community groups operating on their own, what can be entrusted to local authorities and local people working in partnership, and what has to be the shared responsibility of central and local

---

[8]   One of the most devastating effects of the post-2010 UK government's austerity drive is the termination of countless community organisations that had previously provided much needed support to people who could not otherwise get their perspectives taken into account by those in power locally or nationally.

government,[9] and the communities they both serve. Attempts to pass endless social and economic burdens to individuals who cannot cope without collective political support are nothing more than an abdication of democratic responsibility (Wills, 2016).

Invest in the development of civic leadership

It is not paradoxical to recognise that in order to engender more citizen involvement, we need strong civic leadership. Effective leaders depend on having mutual trust and understanding with those who rely on their judgement, and that mutuality takes root to the extent it is nourished through deliberative interactions. When people can see that their views and concerns are thoughtfully taken into account by those who are there to act on their behalf, they are more likely to engage in finding and backing suitable solutions.

In the absence of someone providing the requisite leadership, however, people can share ideas continuously without anyone having the authority or confidence to take on the task of converting the discussions into tangible action. A group can become organisationally paralysed because its members are under the misunderstanding that it would be arrogant for anyone to take charge (Tam, 2014). Of course, there is no guarantee that those who do by whatever route come to take charge will not ignore what everyone else may think, unless there are training, guidance and accountability procedures to ensure they engage others as partners in their civic missions.

The value and techniques of citizen engagement should feature prominently in the advice and training provided to those holding or seeking public office (Pitchford et al, 2009; Gardiner, 2010). It is one of the oddest assumptions that while people applying for positions in almost any organisation – especially those with substantial power, resources and responsibility – should not only possess the suitable aptitudes, but also be tested for them through assessment and interviews, all that is somehow unnecessary when people are standing for government positions.

The system for developing and selecting political leaders must start to take on board the more structured and critical approaches adopted in virtually all other fields of recruitment. One aspect that should receive particular attention is that of empathy. Those who want to have the opportunity to exercise power on behalf of other people must have

---

9   Not to mention, where appropriate, transnational organisations such as the EU or the UN.

sufficient sensitivity and ability to reach out to understand the feelings and reasoning of others, to respond to and reconcile differences, and explain what can or cannot be done under the circumstances. Those who come up short but are willing to learn to improve should be given the appropriate support. While leaders can call on technical experts to help them deal with financial or policy details, they cannot delegate the function of forming a democratic relation with the citizens they serve.[10] If improvement proves beyond their reach, the selection criteria should rule them out as possible candidates.

Apart from investing in improving formal training provisions and selection arrangements, the development of civic leadership can also benefit from the informal sharing of expertise and experience through learning networks. We have looked at how facilitated exchange through the likes of the Civic Pioneers, the National Empowerment Partnership or the Guide Neighbourhoods can increase knowledge among participants, and build confidence through mutual support (Chapter Five in this book). Academics and policy experts can also contribute more by committing to long-term sharing of their ideas and findings on state–citizen cooperation with public leaders.[11]

Conclusion

By empowering communities to be partners in tackling the challenges they face, engaging citizens in shaping public policies and facilitating participation in deliberative decision making, state–citizen cooperation enables societies to pursue the democratic goal of living under regimes that will truly govern with the people.

In Part One of our book, we have seen that far from being an unrealistic aspiration, it is not only a practical endeavour, but a vital ingredient for our physical and mental health, as well as for our social and political wellbeing. It can be sought where emotions run high, inequalities are widespread, and the issues are highly complex. Indeed,

---

[10] To bring the issue of empathy into sharp relief, it was reported that Trump was given a cue card to remind him to say 'I hear you' in case his indifference showed through when he was talking at the White House to survivors of the mass shooting at the Marjory Stoneman Douglas High School in Parkland, Florida (Belam, 2018).

[11] For example, among the contributors to (Crick, 2001; Brennan et al, 2007; Mayo and Annette, 2010), are academics and policy experts in the UK who have been engaged as active citizens in the ongoing promotion of democratic empowerment. Internationally, there is the important work facilitated by the Ash Institute of Democratic Governance and Innovation, the University of Harvard (See Borins, 2008).

it is because all these aforementioned factors are often unavoidable that we need more effective cooperation between state institutions and citizens to work out public policies and actions that will serve the people satisfactorily. And contrary to assumptions that people with political power would not want to go down this route, it is in fact the case that politicians with high office have learnt that they cannot do their job without it.

There are of course a wide range of approaches that can be taken. In Part Two, we considered examples from different countries, in diverse contexts, and discovered what should be prioritised in varying circumstances. There are important differences between participants voting to determine which out of a list of proposals will be selected, and members deliberating to see if they may reach a consensus. There are different ways to make use of community development in response to the actual state–citizen relations in any given situation. Community action in itself may promote or undermine the common good, depending on the extent inclusive civic dialogues have played a part in guiding the action in question. And the distinctive backgrounds and characteristics of diverse citizens should always be factored into the design of engagement approaches, so that common pitfalls can be avoided, and the chance of a real sense of efficacy being attained is maximised.

In Part Three, we turned our attention to how we can expand our civic capability. We learnt that citizenship education's significant potential can only be realised if teachers get more robust guidance and better training in meeting the developmental objectives. We found out what those elected to public office could do to give ordinary citizens more opportunities to enhance their readiness and confidence in participating, or even a helping hand in gaining experience in seeking and holding public office themselves. We discovered how the Take Part approach can help to bring learning institutions and democratic activists together to enable more people to be able and prepared to get involved with tackling public problems. Last but not least, we were introduced to the development of public-cooperative partnerships as an alternative form of collaboration that can boost democratic control without handing more power to the state or the market.

We conclude with this final chapter and the five recommendations on how to take forward the advice set out in this book. In the end, no government can ever function well if it cuts itself off from the public it exists to serve. And the prospects of achieving and sustaining effective state–citizen cooperation will depend on how far the lessons we have considered are learnt and applied.

References

Antsey, C. (2013) 'Citizen engagement in development projects: what we know, what we need to do and learn', *Voices: perspectives on development*, Washington, DC: World Bank: http://blogs.worldbank.org/voices/citizen-engagement-in-development-projects

Belam, M. (2018) '"I hear you" – Trump uses cue card to remind him to listen to shooting survivors', *The Guardian*. www.theguardian.com/us-news/2018/feb/22/i-hear-you-trump-uses-cue-cards-to-remind-him-to-listen-to-shooting-survivors

Blears, H. (2009) 'Empowerment delivers more efficient outcomes', in the annex to *Community Spirit in a Cold Climate* (the CSV Edith Kahn Lecture), London: DCLG.

Borins, S. (ed) (2008) *Innovations in Government: research, recognition and replication*, Washington, DC: Brookings Institution Press.

Brennan, T., John, P. and Stoker, G. (eds) (2007) *Re-energising Citizenship: strategies for civil renewal*, Basingstoke: Palgrave Macmillan.

Chapman, A. R. and Van Der Merwe, H. (2008) *Truth and Reconciliation in South Africa*, Philadelphia: University of Pennsylvania Press.

Crick, B. (ed) (2001) *Citizens: towards a citizenship culture*, London: Wiley-Blackwell.

Crick, B. and Lockyer, A. (eds) (2010) *Active Citizenship: what could it achieve and how?*, Edinburgh: Edinburgh University Press.

Dalton, R. J. (2017) *The Participation Gap: social status and political inequality*, Oxford: Oxford University Press.

Davies, A. and Simon, J. (2012) *The Value and Role of Citizen Engagement in Social Innovation* (a deliverable of the project: 'The theoretical, empirical and policy foundations for building social innovation in Europe'– TEPSIE), Brussels: European Commission, DG Research.

Delwit, P. (2013) 'The end of voters in Europe? Electoral turnout in Europe since WWII', *The Open Journal of Political Science* 3 (1): Table 3.

Derber, C. (2017) *Welcome to the Revolution: universalizing resistance for social justice and democracy in perilous times*, London: Routledge.

Evans, M. and Zimmerman, A. (eds) (2014) *Global Perspectives on Subsidiarity*, New York: Springer.

Gaffney, M. (2005) *Civic Pioneers: local people, local government, working together to make life better*, London: Home Office. http://webarchive.nationalarchives.gov.uk/20120920061439/http://www.communities.gov.uk/documents/communities/pdf/152002.pdf

Gardiner, T. (2010) *Community Engagement and Empowerment: a guide for councillors*, London: IDeA (Improvement & Development Agency).

Ilott, O. and Norris, E. (2015) *Smarter Engagement: harnessing public voice in policy challenges*, London: Institute for Government.

Involve (2005) *People and Participation: how to put citizens at the heart of decision-making* (a Civil Renewal Unit *Together We* Can research report), London: Involve.

Manroth, A., Hernandez, Z., Masud, H., Zakhour, J., Rebolledo, M. and Mahmood S. A. (2014) *Strategic Framework for Mainstreaming Citizen Engagement in World Bank Group Operations: engaging with citizens for improved results*, Washington, DC: World Bank Group.

Mayo, M. and Annette, J. (eds) (2010) *Taking Part: active learning for active citizenship, and beyond*, Leicester: National Institute of Adult Continuing Education.

McCabe, A., Purdue, D. and Wilson, M. (2007) *Learning to Change Neighbourhoods: Lessons from the Guide Neighbourhoods Programme*, London: DCLG. http://webarchive.nationalarchives.gov. uk/20120920045010/http://www.communities.gov.uk/documents/ communities/pdf/changeneighbourhoodsreport.pdf

Pitchford, M., Archer, T. and Ramsden, S. (2009) *The Duty to Involve: making it work*, London: Community Development Foundation.

Power Inquiry (2006) *Power to the People: an independent inquiry into Britain's democracy*, York: Joseph Rowntree Reform Trust.

Retolaza, J. L., Leire, S.-J., and Maite, R.-R. (2016) *Social Accounting for Sustainability: monetizing the social value*, New York: Springer.

Rogers, B. and Robinson, E. (2004) *The Benefits of Community Engagement: a review of the evidence*, London: Home Office (Active Citizenship Centre).

Savitz, A. with Weber, K. (2006) *The Triple Bottom Line: how today's best-run companies are achieving economic, social and environmental success*, Hoboken, NJ: Jossey-Bass.

Smith, G. (2010) *Democratic Innovations: designing institutions for citizen participation*, Cambridge: Cambridge University Press.

SQW (2008) *Neighbourhood Management Pathfinders: final evaluation report people, places, public services: making the connections*, London: DCLG (Department for Communities & Local Government).

Tam, H. (2014) 'The meekest link', *Question the Powerful*. https:// henry-tam.blogspot.co.uk/2014/11/the-meekest-link.html

Tam, H. (2018a) *Time to Save Democracy: how to govern ourselves in the age of anti-politics*, Bristol: Policy Press.

Tam, H. (2018b) *What Should Citizens Believe? Exploring the issues of truth, reason and society*, Sheffield: Citizen Network.

Wilkinson, R. and Pickett, K. (2018) *The Inner Level: how more equal societies reduce stress, restore sanity and improve everyone's wellbeing*, London: Penguin.

Wills, J. (2016) *Locating Localism*, Bristol: Policy Press.

261

Index